"Ron Leaf, Mitch Taubman and John McEachin provide the necessary action to substantiate the expectation that quality programming in schools leads to meaningful progress for students. *It's Time For School! Building Quality ABA Educational Programs* focuses on the essential values of creating and sustaining a school based ABA program for children with Autism. Every element of a comprehensive program is considered and can be implemented with the expectation of the best possible results for students. All stakeholders must first share the common belief that every child can make progress and that progress for some of our students may often depend on a quality ABA program. It is the district's responsibility to provide the focus, remove barriers and expect the best outcomes for our students."

Charlene Green
Deputy Superintendent, Student Support Services
Clark County School District
Las Vegas, Nevada

"In my special education law practice, I have worked extensively with school districts nationwide, in conjunction with the top experts in the field, on a variety of issues involving educational programming for students with Autism Spectrum Disorder. As a result, I find *It's Time For School! Building Quality ABA Educational Programs* to be an incredibly comprehensive resource that will assist educators in developing highly appropriate programming for children with autism. Additionally, this work is an outstanding guide to assist legal practitioners in understanding the principles of Applied Behavior Analysis (ABA) and how those principles can be utilized in the development of IDEA-compliant school-based programs. This manual is superbly researched and written and provides invaluable guidance to educators, legal practitioners, and parents of children with autism that should serve to foster a better understanding of educational programming for this very unique population of children."

Charles Weatherly, J.D.
Weatherly Law Firm

It's Time for School!
Building Quality ABA Educational Programs for Students with Autism Spectrum Disorders

Autism Partnership

Ron Leaf, Ph.D.

Mitchell Taubman, Ph.D.

John McEachin, Ph.D.

with chapters co-written by:

Marlena Driscoll, M.A., LMFT

Alicia Ellis, M. Ed., M.S.

Craig Kennedy, Ph.D.

Toby Mountjoy

Tracee Parker, Ph.D.

Leticia Palos-Rafuse, M.S.

Jon Rafuse, M.A.

Rick Schroeder

Jennifer Styzens, M.S.

Andrea Waks, J.D.D.

Tammy White, M. Ed.

DRL Books Inc.

It's Time for School! Building Quality ABA Educational Programs for Students with Autism Spectrum Disorders

Copyright © 2008 Autism Partnership

Published by: DRL Books Inc.
37 East 18th Street, 10th Floor
New York, NY 10003
Phone: 212 604 9637
Fax: 212 206 9329

Book Layout: John Eng
Editorial Technician: Sue Lee
Cover Art: Ramon Gil

Library of Congress Control Number: 2008920855
ISBN: 978-0-9755859-3-1

To the most inspirational, influential and important teachers in my life!

Dad, Mom, Justin, Jeremy, Cole and Jamie

– Ron

To Mont Wolf,

The most brilliant, decent, and inspiring person I have had the honor of knowing

And to Tiffany and Whitney

You are my life

– Mitch

To Andrew, Nick and Shawn,

the students who make me proud

– John

About the Authors

Marlene Driscoll, M.A., LMFT

Marlene Driscoll is a Licensed Marriage and Family Therapist specializing in work with families of children with autism. She is currently the Site Director for the Autism Partnership Seal Beach office and her duties include clinical supervision, counseling, program development and interventionist training and development. Ms. Driscoll began working with Drs. Leaf and McEachin in 1992 as a consultant for the Behavior Therapy and Learning Center, a center focusing on parent training for families with developmentally disabled children. She earned her Master's degree in counseling from Loyola Marymount University in 1996. She has extensive experience in the use of Applied Behavioral Analysis and early intervention with children with autism. She has consulted with families and school districts throughout the United States and internationally.

Alicia M. Ellis, M.Ed., M. S.

Alicia Ellis worked for over 20 years in the field of Special Education as a Speech-Language Pathologist and as a Special Education Administrator in the sixth largest school district in the United States. Ms. Ellis received her Master of Education degree from the University of Nevada, Las Vegas and a Master of Science degree in Speech Pathology from San Jose State University. Ms. Ellis served as an adjunct professor teaching both graduate and undergraduate university courses in language disorders at San Jose State University as well as at the University of Nevada, Las Vegas. Until her death in 2002, Ms. Ellis was sought after to present nationally and internationally in the areas of Autism and Language Disorders and worked tirelessly as an administrator supporting teachers and speech pathologists in developing effective programming for students with Autism.

Craig H. Kennedy, Ph.D.

Craig Kennedy is Chair of the Special Education Department, Professor of special education and pediatrics and Director of the Vanderbilt Kennedy Center Behavior Analysis Clinic. His research focuses on the environmental, genetic, and neurobiological causes of problem behavior in people with developmental disabilities. He is a board certified behavior analyst and a member of the board of directors of the Society for the Experimental Analysis of Behavior. He is a member of the American Association on Mental Retardation, Association for Behavior Analysis, American College of Neuropsychopharmacology, Society for Neuroscience, and TASH. He is a former associate editor for the *Journal of Applied Behavior Analysis*, *Journal of Behavioral Education*, and *Journal of The Association for Persons with Severe Handicaps*.

Ronald Leaf, Ph.D.

Ronald Leaf is a licensed psychologist who has over 35 years of experience in the field of Autism Spectrum Disorder. Dr. Leaf began his career working with Ivar Lovaas while receiving his undergraduate degree at UCLA. Subsequently he received his doctorate under the direction of Dr. Lovaas. During his years at UCLA, he served as Clinic Supervisor, Research Psychologist, Interim Director of the Autism Project and Lecturer. He was extensively involved in several research investigations, contributed to the *Me Book* and is a co-author of the *Me Book Videotapes*, a series of instructional tapes for teaching autistic children. Dr. Leaf has provided consultation to families, schools, day programs and residential facilities on a national and international basis. Ron is the Executive Director of Behavior Therapy and Learning Center, a mental health agency that consults with parents, care providers and school personnel. Dr. Leaf is a Co-Director of Autism Partnership. Ron is the co-author of "*A Work in Progress*", a published book on Behavioral Treatment.

John McEachin, Ph.D.

John McEachin is a clinical psychologist who has been providing behavioral intervention to children with autism as well as adolescents and adults with a wide range of developmental disabilities for more than 30 years. He received his graduate training under Professor Ivar Lovaas at UCLA on the Young Autism Project. During his 11 years at UCLA, Dr. McEachin served in various roles including Clinic Supervisor, Research and Teaching Assistant, Visiting Professor and Acting Director. His research has included the long-term follow-up study of young autistic children who received intensive behavioral treatment, which was published in 1993. In 1994 he joined with Ron Leaf in forming Autism Partnership, which they co-direct and they have co-authored a widely used treatment manual, A Work in Progress. Dr. McEachin has lectured throughout the world and has helped establish treatment centers and classrooms for children with autism in North America, Australia, Asia and Europe.

Toby Mountjoy

Toby Mountjoy is the Associate Director of Autism Partnership. Mr. Mountjoy is responsible for overseeing over 100 full-time staff in the Hong Kong, Singapore and Tokyo offices. Mr. Mountjoy has been working with individuals with autism for over 12 years in a multitude of ways. He has provided direct therapy, parent training and has supervised home and clinic based ABA programs in the Asian offices. Mr. Mountjoy has also opened and overseen ABA based kindergarten programs in both Singapore and Hong Kong. In January 2007, Mr. Mountjoy established the first fully registered primary school for children with autism in Hong Kong, which has a capacity of up to 64 children. In addition, Mr. Mountjoy has also regularly consulted to agencies, school districts and families in other countries including the Phillipines, Columbia, Indonesia, Malaysia, USA, China and Vietnam.

Leticia Palos-Rafuse, M.S.

Leticia Palos-Rafuse has been a staff member of Autism Partnership since 1996. Her experience implementing intensive Applied Behavior Analysis programs for autistic children spans eleven years. She earned her Bachelor's degree in Psychology from Loyola Marymount University, Los Angeles in 1996. She received her Master's degree in Behavior Analysis from St. Cloud University, Minnesota in 2005. She has presented at conferences on Applied Behavior Analysis and has provided consultation to school districts, families and other related agencies both nationally and internationally. Leticia has worked within the Maui school district teaching and providing on-site continuous management of a pre-school model classroom program while training district employees. Formerly, she co-taught an elementary school model classroom providing ongoing mentoring and training to Autism Partnership personnel. Currently, Mrs. Palos-Rafuse provides consultation and training to families and school districts.

Tracee Parker, Ph.D.

Tracee Parker has over 25 years of treatment and research experience in the field of Autism and Developmental Disabilities and earned a Doctoral degree in Psychology from UCLA in 1990. Her training experience included five years working on the UCLA Young Autism Project directed by Dr. Ivar Lovaas. During this time, she served in the capacities of teaching and research assistant as well as Clinic Supervisor. As a research assistant, Dr. Parker was closely involved in a number of studies including the long term treatment follow-up of young autistic children and changes in self-stimulatory behavior during treatment. Dr. Parker worked 12 years at Straight Talk Clinic, Inc., a residential and day behavioral treatment program, serving adults with developmental disabilities. She served as Associate Director until 1997. Dr. Parker is currently a Clinical Associate with Autism Partnership and Associate Director for Behavior Therapy and Learning Center. Dr. Parker has presented at national and international conferences in the areas of behavioral treatment, autism and social/sexual issues and intervention. Over the past 20 years, she has provided consultation to residential and day programs, school districts, families, and other related agencies.

Jonathan Rafuse, M.A.

Jon Rafuse graduated from UCLA in 1988 with a Bachelor's Degree in Psychology and then went on to receive a Master's degree in Clinical Psychology from Antioch University in 1991. In 1992, he began working for the May Institute in Chatham, Massachusetts, eventually running one of the off-campus group homes housing students dramatically impaired with Autism Spectrum Disorder. In 1995, he joined the Autism Partnership staff, providing intensive Applied Behavior Analysis services to the families of children diagnosed with Autism. His experience in this specific area of Behavioral Psychology spans 15 years. Currently, Mr. Rafuse is a consultant providing advanced training, mentoring and supervision to service providers and teachers within school districts across the United States. He has presented both nationally and internationally at conferences on Applied Behavior Analysis, and has consulted and trained families, program staff and school districts throughout the United States, England, Saudi Arabia, Australia and New Zealand.

Richard Schroder

Rick Schroder has been a staff member of Autism Partnership since 1995. His experience implementing intensive Applied Behavior Analysis programs for children with Autism Spectrum Disorder spans ten years. He was a therapist and senior therapist at the UCLA Autism Project directed by Ivar Lovaas. He earned his Bachelor's degree in Psychology from UCLA. He provides consultations and training to families and school districts throughout the United States. He is a Special Education Teacher for a middle school model classroom and has presented at international conferences on the treatment and education for students with Autism Spectrum Disorder.

Jennifer Styzens, M.S.

Jennifer Styzens has over 20 years of experience in the field of developmental disabilities and autism and received her Master's at St. Cloud State Univerisity. Formerly, she served as the Director of Client Services for Straight Talk Clinic, which provided residential and day treatment services to adults with developmental disabilities, and worked as a parent trainer for the Behavior Therapy and Learning Center, which provides training to parents of children with developmental disabilities. She has been a staff member of Autism Partnership since 1997 and has presented at national and international conferences in the areas of behavioral treatment, autism and social/sexual issues and intervention. Over the past 20 years, she has provided consultation to residential and day programs, school districts, families and other related agencies and is a special education teacher for a middle school model classroom.

Mitchell Taubman, Ph.D.

Mitch Taubman worked with Dr. Ivar Lovaas as an undergraduate at UCLA in the early 1970s, providing treatment to children with autism, ADHD, and other disorders. Subsequently, he attended the University of Kansas and studied with such founders of Applied Behavior Analysis as Dr. Donald Baer, Dr. Todd Risely, Dr. James Sherman, and his Doctoral Advisor, Montrose Wolf. Upon completing his Ph.D. at the University of Kansas, He returned to UCLA post-doctorally, where he brought Teaching Interactions, from the Kansas model, to autism treatment. At UCLA, he served as an Adjunct Assistant Professor of Psychology and as Co-Principal Investigator with Dr. Lovaas on a Federal Grant directed at autism treatment. After this post-doctoral work, he obtained his License as a Clinical Psychologist and also served as Clinical Director of Straight Talk, a program providing residential and day treatment services to adults with autism and other developmental disabilities. Dr. Taubman is currently the Associate Director of Autism Partnership, where he provides treatment oversight, training, and consultation both nationally and internationally.

Andrea Waks, J.D.D.

Andrea Waks is the Director of Client Services at Autism Partnership. She began working with children with autism in the late 1970s at UCLA on the Young Autism Project, where she served as a Senior Therapist, Research Assistant, and Teaching Assistant. Andi has worked with Dr. Leaf and Dr. McEachin on the Young Autism Project, the Behavior Therapy and Learning Center, Straight Talk, and Autism Partnership. She earned her Master's degree in General Psychology at Pepperdine University in 1983 and returned to school in 1993 to pursue a law degree. She practiced special education law, representing families of children with autism, before returning to Autism Partnership full-time. Her current duties include conducting behavioral assessments, IEP preparation, policy review, and classroom consultations. She consults with families and school districts both locally and nationally.

Tammy White, M. Ed.

Tammy White has over 20 years of teaching experience in the field of Special Education and received her Master of Education degree from the University of Nevada, Las Vegas. In addition, Ms. White has served as an Adjunct Professor at the University of Nevada, Las Vegas in the Special Education department. Her work for nearly 10 years has focused on collaborating with schools and with school districts to develop and enhance effective programs for students with Autism. She has presented at national conferences on topics related to educational programming for students with autism, inclusive programming for students with disabilities, and positive behavioral supports for students with emotional disturbance. Ms. White currently works as a Behavioral Consultant for Autism Partnership where she teaches in an Autism Training Classroom, providing hands-on training to mentor teachers and staff, as well as consults with families and school districts locally and nationally.

Preface

At last a book that establishes the advantages of a quality setting for the ASD student. The book covers how to establish an ABA Classroom, comprehensive training, consultations, evaluations, and one-to-one and group instruction. It also addresses the quality of service from a school district level, from the supervisor, to the teachers, to the bus driver, making sure that there is a strong link to the structure of each child's school experience.

The book relates how to determine the best placement and how to optimize that placement. It raises increasing the receptiveness to ABA in the classroom setting and addresses the need for evaluation, consultation and ongoing training for all staffing. The book defines the relationships between school staff and consultation with checklists and a how-to primer. There is also an emphasis on keeping data and measurement and the importance of the functionality of a behavioral assessment.

This is a book that impacts and enhances every classroom for the child diagnosed with Autism Spectrum Disorder and is recommended reading for parents, teachers and professionals.

Ron, Mitch & John

Table of Contents

Introduction

The authors have captured the essence and the detail for developing an appropriate educational program for children with autism. They provide not only the skeletal foundation for beginning the phases of understanding and implementing an autism program. Autism is one of the hardest areas for special education directors to provide programs to children that are truly designed and also effectively provide a free and appropriate educational program. Dr. Leaf et al. takes the special education director, superintendent, classroom teacher, paraprofessional, direct service personnel, supplementary service personnel and parents to an understanding of the disorder.

The book is a must read for educators as well as parents. Following the path in the book will allow a school district to build and to maintain a philosophical and effective program. The importance of continued training and building capacity is of utmost importance for funding bodies to understand. If a district follows the blueprint in the book, it will be able to address the required "peer reviewed to the extent practicable" requirement in the reauthorization of IDEIA 2004 for all special education programs, related and supplementary services in providing children's IEPs.

As the past director of Pupil Personnel for Knox County Schools in Knoxville, Tennessee, a school district of 55,000 students, I had the privilege of working with Dr. Leaf and his organization in developing our program for autistic children. We continue to have Dr. Leaf and his staff to provide ongoing training to our staff three to four times per year. We developed our program following the blueprint stated in the book and have been successful not just in providing a legally defensible program but as Dr. Leaf states, an appropriate educational program for children.

Autism is a difficult area for educators to address. One of the reasons is the wide range of severity of the disorder through the broad definition. A second area of difficulty for educators is the parental adherence to the many different approaches to education the child. A third area of difficulty is the expense and intensity of educationally services that range across the varied services from a totally inclusive program to a one on one program. A fourth area of difficulty is the rapid increase in the identification of children. The growth at times seems geometric. In our district we grew from identifying 32 children with autism in 1996 to over 475 students in 2007.

With the plethora of difficulties for the educator, it becomes easy for us to try a shot gun or eclectic approach hoping to please as many parents and educators as we can. A district must identify its philosophical basis for providing the educational program and not succumb to the easy approach of trying to be all things to all people. It is critical for a district to develop its program, not in isolation of the general education program. The district must address generalization and developing the functional independence of the student as he progresses from a child to an adult.

I strongly recommend that the text be a working text for all school districts and be one that is used to guide, develop, implement and maintain the district's educational program for children with autism. Following the text will allow a district to develop its capacity to provide with fidelity a program that has a high degree of efficacy for children. I know I will use the information from the text and what I have learned from Dr. Leaf and his staff in my work consulting with school districts.

Dr. John McCook
Director of Pupil Personnel
Knox County Schools
Knoxville, Tennessee

Chapter 1

ADVANTAGES OF SCHOOL SETTINGS

By Ron Leaf & Toby Mountjoy

Applied Behavior Analysis (ABA) zealots often reject schools as a learning environment for children with Autism Spectrum Disorder (ASD). A common misperception is that children with ASD can only learn effectively in one-to-one settings and therefore school is not appropriate. However, there are many advantages to having a child in a school setting where systematic programs are being implemented throughout the day by trained teachers. During the research project at the UCLA Young Autism Project (YAP), school was conceptualized as providing an opportunity for children to learn in a more natural way. Participation in circle time, art centers and on the playground was regarded as a critical component of treatment. Although we certainly knew that one-to-one intervention was essential, we also viewed group learning as an important component of treatment. This chapter will discuss some of the potential benefits to a child attending school.

NATURAL LEARNING ENVIRONMENT

In our culture, it is considered a natural step for children to move into a more formal learning environment starting around age five if not earlier. This is an age where most children are able to benefit from group instruction leading to growth in many important areas. School is a place where children are introduced to academic skills along with social, language and play skills. For younger children, preschool provides a more formal environment for learning which gives children a head start on the school experience. The school setting, like the home setting, is simply another environment for learning but affords certain additional opportunities that do not exist at home. These experiences can be critical in development of learning readiness skills, such as how to learn in groups, interacting with other children, playing and working cooperatively, and understanding school rules and routines.

The children who achieved "best outcome" through treatment provided by the YAP did so, at least in part, because of the kind of school placement in which they were able to learn. Being able to learn effectively in a "typical classroom" requires many skills that cannot be taught in a one-to-one session. Having systematic programming in a school setting can help to teach those skills which will be critical later on if the child is to benefit from a mainstream classroom environment which would be considered the most natural learning environment for a child.

SOCIAL OPPORTUNITIES

School provides a wonderful opportunity to work on social skills and develop friendships (Kamps, Leonard, Vernon, Dugan, et.al., 1992; Kamps, Walker, Maher, & Rotholz, 1992; Kalyva & Avarmidis, 2005). There is an immediately available group of children. We do not have to recruit them, they are already there! From this group, we can identify students who are eager to interact with our children, as well as assess the type of peer that our child is drawn toward (Jones & Schwartz, 2004). Additionally, if the interaction "sours" there are plenty of others from which to choose (Leaf, Taubman, Bloomfield, Palos-Rafuse, McEachin, Leaf, 2005). School can also provide parents an opportunity to meet other parents which can make setting up additional play dates with other children outside schooltime easier. We should not pass up this opportunity.

We must capture all of the social opportunities though out the day. Obviously, recess, play and lunch are ideal times to work on socialization skills. However, teachable moments occur from the time a child gets off the bus until they board the bus to go home. If a child is working on a craft activity and needs glue that another child is using, he will need to practice social communication in order to have his need met. Circle time, toileting and snack provide other opportunities to work on socialization, as well as other critical areas such as communication and behavior control.

School provides exactly the kind of forum that is needed to work on skills like sharing, cooperation, compromising and negotiating. At school, we can set up individual, small or large group teaching situations to work on socialization programs. Depending on our child's skill level and needs, we can work on parallel, joint or cooperative play. Programs designed to work on increasing tolerance, participating, or even initiating interactions can occur throughout the day. As an example, a child may be given points or stickers every time he or she initiates a comment to another peer or perhaps receives reinforcement for responding to peers' requests (Barrish, Saunders, & Wolf, 1969). More advanced social skills that can be systematically developed in school include increasing awareness of others, understanding others' likes and dislikes, turn taking, and eventually understanding of the premise that if I go along with what a peer would like to do, they will be more willing to join in something that I would like to do.

OBSERVATIONAL LEARNING

Perhaps one of the biggest skill deficits in children with ASD is their ability to learn observationally (Varni, Lovaas, Koegel, Everett, 1979) . That is, they often do not acquire information in casual ways (e.g., observing others, watching television, listening to conversations, etc.). This is most likely a result of a number of factors. First and foremost it is one of the defining characteristics of autism. Children on the spectrum typically are not very aware and do not interact with the world around them when compared to their typical peers. Often they lack interest in what is going on in their environment and are not naturally drawn to engage with others. Additionally, a majority of children do not possess the attentional skills that are necessary to learn observationally. Therefore, acquiring information through casual observation is highly unlikely.

It is this inability to learn indirectly that makes one-to-one intervention so successful. Providing direct instruction squarely in front of the child makes it more difficult to ignore. But continuing to do one-to-one instruction indefinitely is not a great solution. It is a very inefficient way to learn, and we do not mean this just in the economic sense. Because children with ASD have difficulty picking up large amounts of salient information from the natural environment, there are thousands of concepts that they would need to be taught! There simply is not enough time to teach them everything they need to learn through direct instruction. The majority of information that typically developing children learn is acquired indirectly through observational learning. Children are constantly learning new skills simply from becoming keen observers and they are learning all day long, regardless of whether there is a teacher in front of them. It is critical that children with ASD are also learning from the time they wake up until the time they go to sleep. To accomplish this, it is not sufficient to be able to learn from direct instruction; they must also be able to learn observationally.

For the children in YAP who achieved "best outcome," the therapists did not have to teach every concept, word or play skill. Through treatment, the children were taught how to become better observational learners and how to learn independently. It would have been impossible to teach them everything. To reach best outcome, children have to begin to learn from what is going on around them instead of requiring direct instruction to learn every new word or to acquire any of the multitude of concepts and skills that are needed to close the gap with their peers.

Unfortunately, there is not enough emphasis placed on teaching observational learning skills. Moreover, professionals and parents often are led to believe that children with ASD are incapable of learning observationally. Consequently, only direct instruction is provided. With systematic teaching, children with ASD can become observational learners. We feel observational learning is one of the most critical skills a child can acquire. Therefore, we place tremendous emphasis on teaching observational learning and do so very early in intervention. We should not hope that merely placing a child with ASD in a classroom will automatically develop observational learning. It is a skill that will only develop from careful planning.

Teaching a child to learn observationally can begin very early in the therapy process. Whereas in the past, we often waited until a child had acquired intermediate language skills (e.g., beginning conversational skills) before introducing an observational learning curriculum, we now begin observational learning as part of the earliest stages of intervention (e.g., nonverbal imitation). Once a child is able to imitate a therapist's action (e.g., throwing a ball, waving a flag, rolling a car) it is time to being teaching observational learning skills. For example, we will arrange to have another child participating in the session. Instead of asking the child to follow our actions, we will ask them to copy the actions of the peer. Therefore, instead of looking directly at the teacher, the child must learn to attend to the other child. We then systematically increase the number of children as well as the complexity of the imitation. In this way, the child has begun to learn through the observation of others.

As intervention proceeds, observational learning becomes more complex. For example, when we begin receptive labeling, we will ask other children to label objects and then ask our child to give us those things which have been previously labeled by their peer. Eventually, we will expect our children to be able to attend and obtain information presented in an indirect manner, such as answering questions involving information they have heard after listening to a brief conversation. It is critical that children with ASD acquire the ability to attend to and learn from salient information in their environment.

Once a child has become an observational learner, then acquisition of information can be tremendously accelerated. School provides an ideal forum to continuously work on observational learning.

GROUP INSTRUCTION

It is essential that children be able to learn in social environments. The majority of the instruction that occurs in school happens in group situations. Although it may be difficult for children with ASD to learn in a group setting, it is a skill they can develop and it is vital. Learning in groups is an extension of observational learning. When an observational learning program has two or more peers, the child is learning in a "group" instructional format. To facilitate skill generalization, it will be important that the structure of intervention systematically approach a larger group format. The jump from doing observational learning with one other peer or adult to a classroom with 20 children can be huge. Many children may require a stepping stone to get there. This can often be achieved by doing smaller group formats with fewer children and a curriculum directed towards developing attending, observational learning and other group readiness skills. We have found that many children can benefit greatly from a group early on in intervention if the curriculum highlights development in the right skill areas.

The advantages of learning from group instruction are many. Besides the efficiency of acquiring information and the naturalness of the instructional format, the group offers other advantages (Taubman, Brierley, Wishner, Baker, McEachin, & Leaf, 2001; Polloway, Cronin, Patton, 1986). Group instruction allows for the use of "vicarious contingencies." That is, the child does not have to experience consequences directly. From observing another student who receives reinforcement for paying attention, our child can learn the benefits of staying tuned in. Similarly, when another child loses reinforcement for engaging in disruptive behaviors such as yelling, we can expect that our child will learn as well, without having to directly experience the consequence.

Children with ASD may have difficulties paying attention when faced with less direct teaching. As a group size increases so do distractions, noise, and length of time between opportunities to interact directly with the teacher or to actively respond. Teachers are also less able to provide as much attention per child. Children may be required to attend for longer periods of time without performing skills or being required to do anything (i.e., story time) which might contrast greatly with a one-to-one session where the child has the constant attention of the teacher and may be asked to perform skills much more frequently. As the one-to-one session is totally directed toward the child, it is somewhat easier to pay attention. Group teaching can provide the opportunity to teach better direct and indirect attending skills in terms of duration and quality as well as develop tolerance to noise and distractions.

There are many other skills that can be learned in a group setting that are more based on instructional format. Often in a group there are many different kinds of instructions provided, including individual instructions within the group (i.e., sequential instructions); instructions that require participation by the whole group (i.e., choral instructions); and conditional instructions (i.e., overlapping instructions). A group provides a great opportunity to learn how to effectively discriminate and follow the different kinds of instructions that would be provided in a typical classroom environment. Children can also be taught other very useful skills such as waiting their turn to answer questions or to perform other tasks.

Research conducted at Autism Partnership (Taubman, et.al., 2001) demonstrated that essential elements of Discrete Trial Teaching could be incorporated into group instruction for children with ASD. The students were able to acquire multiple skills through participation in group and it was possible to bring disruptive behavior under instructional control within the group format. An interesting benefit of group instruction was highlighted in another study (Taubman, Papovich, Palos & Styzens, 2001) which showed that students acquired skills which were targeted for a fellow group member, but which was not taught directly to any other student.

Group instruction is clearly an advantage of learning in the school setting, which cannot be readily obtained if home is the exclusive setting for intervention. School provides a continuous opportunity for group learning. The size and nature of the group can be adjusted as needed and the proportion of time spent in group learning can tailored to meet the needs of each student.

GENERALIZATION

One final reason why we think children with ASD need to attend school as early as possible is that it affords a fantastic opportunity to tackle the problem of generalization. Although failure to generalize skills is often viewed as a shortcoming of ABA, it is actually a manifestation of the learning style of children with autism (Lovaas, 1993; Jones, Simmons, Frankel, 1974). Parents are often frustrated by this phenomenon. Although they know their child can label objects, they are horrified when they are unable to perform this task during an evaluation. Consequently, they believe that their child's performance does not accurately reflect his or her skill level. This variance in performance may be a result of multiple factors. Being in a new setting, unfamiliarity with the tester, different materials or a tester not using familiar phrases may all account for the child's performance. These are all problems associated with generalization that must be addressed and school is the perfect place to do so.

Stokes and Baer's (1977) seminal article on how to overcome generalization difficulties included many recommendations. Many of their recommended procedures for promoting generalization can be accomplished in school. For example, they recommend that intervention should be extended into settings that were not initially targeted (i.e., "Sequential Modification"). They also suggest that teaching should occur in multiple settings with multiple teachers (i.e., "Train Sufficient Exemplars"). Again, this is easy to do in the school setting. Another recommendation to facilitate transfer of skills was to use procedures that occur in natural settings (i.e., "Program Common Stimuli"). Being in school affords the opportunity to sample the kinds of language used, the way activities are conducted, the kinds of materials used there, etc., and make sure that they are being exposed extensively in the home and/or clinic therapy sessions. In other words you want to make sure that you are evolving in the therapy sessions in the direction of how things are done at school rather than trying to make school become a clone of Discrete Trial Teaching.

REFERENCES

Barrish, H.H., Saunder, M., & Wolf, M.M. (1969). Good behavior game: Effects of Individual contingencies for group consequences on disruptive behavior in a Classroom. *Journal of Applied Behavior Analysis,* 2(2), 119-124.

Jones, C.D., & Schwartz, I.S. (2004). Siblings, peers, and adults: Differential effects of Models for children with autism. *Topics in Early Childhood Special Education, 24(2),* 187-198

Jones, F.H., Simmons, & JQ., Frankel, F. (1974). An extinction procedure for eliminating Self-destructive behavior in a 9 year old autistic girl. *Journal of Autism & Childhood Schizophrenia,* 4(3), 241-250.

Kamps, D.M., Lenoard, B.R., Vernon, S., & Dugan, E.P. (1992). Teaching social skills To students with autism to increase peer interactions in an integrated first-grade classroom. *Journal of Applied Behavior Analysis, 25(2), 281-288.*

Kamps, D., Walker, D., Maher, J., & Rotholz, D. (1992). Academic and environmental effects of small group arrangements in classroom for students with autism and other developmental disabilities. *Journal of Autism and Developmental Disorders,* 22(2), 277-293.

Leaf, R.B., & McEachin, J.J. (1999). <u>A Work in Progress: Behavior Management Strategies</u> and a Curriculum for <u>Intensive Behavioral Treatment of Autism</u>. New York, NY: Different Roads to Learning.

Leaf, R.B., McEachin, J.J. & Taubman, M. (2008). <u>Sense and Nonsense: It Has To Be Said</u>. New York, NY: Different Roads to Learning.

Lovaas, I.O. (1993). The development of a treatment-research project for developmentally disabled and autistic children. *Journal of Applied Behavior Analysis,* 26(4), 617-630.

Polloway, E.A., Cronin, M.E., & Patton, J.R. (1986). The efficacy of a group versus one-to-one instruction: A review. *RASE: Remedial & Special Education,* 7(1), 22-30.

Taubman, M., Brierley, S., Wishner, J., Baker, D., McEachin, J., & Leaf, R.B. (2001). The effectiveness of a group discrete trial instructional approach for preschoolers with developmental disabilities. *Research in Developmental Disabilities,* 22(3), 205-219.

Taubman, M., Papovich, S., Palos, L., & Styzens, J. The Impact of a Brief School Relevant ABA Program for Students with Autism. Paper presented at the meeting of the Association for Behavior Analysis, 2001 Annual Convention, New Orleans, LA, 2001.

Varni, J.W., Lovaas, I.O., Koegel, R.L., & Everett, N.L. (1979). An analysis of observational learning in autistic and normal children. *Journal of Abnormal Child Psychology,* 7(1), 31-43.

Chapter 2

ESTABLISHING ABA CLASSROOMS
For Students With Autism

By Mitch Taubman, Ron Leaf, Marlena Driscoll, Tammy White & Alicia Ellis

With the substantial educational need that is presented by students with autism and the increased demand experienced by educational entities, the requirement for quality, efficient, and effective educational services for students with autism has grown significantly. What follows is a framework for establishing Applied Behavior Analysis (ABA) classrooms for students with autism, training personnel who staff such classrooms, and for overseeing and assessing the ongoing operation. The design provides a model for others to not only understand but actually see ABA instruction effectively implemented in the classroom. More importantly, it provides a means through which to develop in-house professionals capable of providing training and ongoing supervision for the district in the years to come.

In the past, educational interventions for students with autism may have been concerned with single children, specific problem areas, and particular techniques. Such efforts now involve systemwide impacts. Changes are made in whole school communities as complex approaches and comprehensive programs are developed. In order to address needs of students with ASD sufficiently, school districts and other educational entities must provide a broad range of educational services. These services make up an autism program and need to be supported by a uniform, underlying philosophy and vision in order to enable its success. Programs need to have substance, continuity and be well integrated into the system as a whole. Mechanisms must be built into the program to evaluate the progress of the students and the program's progress toward pursuing its vision.

The ABA Classroom Model description and the Training Protocol that follow should serve as a framework for establishing ABA classrooms for students with autism. It is meant as a guide to assist educational entities in efforts to set up comprehensive, evaluation supported, systemwide efforts intended to address the needs of students with autism. It includes information on a model for developing classrooms and training staff, as well as on necessary training curriculum content.

PART I: A MODEL FOR DEVELOPING STAFF SKILLS

In order to most effectively establish ABA classrooms for students with autism, it is important to impact systems. This not only means campus communities, but also for there to be sustaining changes district-wide. We have found that when districts commit to growing in specific ways, then not only do ABA classrooms flourish, but constituents are supported, litigation goes down, and most importantly, students improve.

Commitments must be made that involve the following factors:

- A district-wide philosophy regarding autism education and programming

- All personnel including district and site administrator "buy-in" and support of the philosophy (e.g., understanding that Applied Behavior Analysis based instruction is best practice for educating students with autism)

- The development of educational continua from pre-school to high school

- An integration of efforts and consistency within that continuum

- A commitment to extensive staff training

- The establishment of district specialists necessary to provide in-house program development, training, and ongoing consultation for the long term

Many variations of training and consultation models exist for establishing ABA classrooms for students with autism. While each education entities will have specific needs, the following training model is illustrative of one variation. It represents a comprehensive, district-wide format, with essential elements for establishing ABA classrooms for students with autism and for the professional development of their staff.

WORKSHOPS

Initial/Didactic Workshop. This is typically a two or three day workshop presented in lecture format. It is intended to be an initial orientation to autism spectrum disorders, ABA theory and philosophy, basic procedure and technique, and other introductory considerations (see Appendix A). It also can serve as an opportunity to assess and classify participants in terms of their interest in and potential fit for the ABA approach.

Hands-On Workshop. This is typically a five day, experiential workshop. Although containing lecture elements, it is intended primarily to furnish opportunities for supervised hands-on practice in applying ABA instruction techniques to students with autism (see Appendix A). The workshop also allows for the further assessment of the participants interest, motivation and ability to apply the ABA teaching approach.

Advanced Workshops. These may typically be one or two day workshops and can include lecture and experiential elements. They traditionally serve as follow up workshops and can be on sophisticated topics for advanced staff or on thematic areas that relate to issues needing attention on a reccurring basis.

DEMONSTRATION/TRAINING CLASSROOM

As part of systemwide change, a school site and classroom are selected to serve as the district's demonstration and training site. Staffed by highly trained, highly proficient personnel, this class is designed to serve several purposes. First, it functions to provide high quality educational and interventional services to its students with autism. Second, it serves as a representative version of a comprehensive ABA classroom. And third, it is designed to operate as a training site.

Once the classroom has been established, teachers from the district are selected to participate in the training sequence. As part of the process, the district instructor in training, or Trainee, can observe classroom operation and ABA application and then practice the application of these skills with the students of the model classroom. The instructor will receive ongoing training, feedback, discussions and supervision in a range of areas (see Appendix A) before returning to their own classrooms.

COMPREHENSIVE TRAINING AND INTERN TRAINER

Based on a number of factors, including desire and capability, Trainees (teachers selected to replicate the model) are identified for participation in extensive training. After attending the initial and hands-on workshops, the Intern Trainer (an experienced ABA classroom instructor) typically spends one week in the Trainee's classroom, providing information, preparing the Trainee for the remainder of the training, assisting in the assessment and determination of needs, connecting with relevant personnel and parties, and initiating the collaborative classroom set-up process. After this, the Trainee (and, potentially, an instructional assistant from the Trainee's classroom) spends time (typically one to four weeks) in the Demonstration/Training classroom, receiving intensive and extensive training (see Appendix A). Simultaneous to this, the Intern Trainer works in the Trainee's classroom as the instructor in the Trainee's absence. They provide on-site training to remaining personnel, continue the collaborative classroom setup, develop and implement programs, and coordinate with the Trainee regarding all efforts. When the Trainee and other staff return to the Trainee's classroom, the Intern Trainer continues to spend time there, typically one week, providing orientation and additional training. This continues the classroom establishment process, assisting with program development and instruction as necessary, and providing feedback and supervision. Trainees receive follow-up consultation (see below) and attend advanced workshops as indicated. In some cases, Trainees may become workshop trainers and consultants for the district (see below). In some circumstances, the Trainee's classrooms become additional Demonstration Classroom sites for further new Trainee rotations.

ONGOING CONSULTATION

Follow-up Consultation. Full day, follow-up consultations are provided on a regular basis, typically two to four times a month, to the Trainee/Intern classroom subsequent to the departure of the Intern Trainer. Initially, several professionals will provide support to the Trainee and this may include consultation from the Intern Trainer, Demonstration Classroom Instructor or Behavior Specialists. Consultation includes additional training, feedback, and supervision, provision of resource information and materials, and assistance in such areas as behavior program and curriculum development, program implementation and instructional effort, schedule, classroom environment, data, and other areas of instruction and classroom operation (see Appendix A). Over time, Follow-Up Consultation is decreased in the length and frequency of visits, and with the transfer of support from outside to within district personnel (see below).

General Consultation. Additional outside consultations are provided on a periodic basis to classrooms for students with autism other than the Trainee/Intern sites. Staff within such classrooms have attended the Initial and Hands-On Workshops. Coordination with within district personnel regarding such efforts is essential, given the more limited nature of such consultations. Frequently, those individuals that have been selected to become in-house or district consultants will typically overlap during these consultations to gain greater experience and to follow up on recommendations made to the classroom personnel.

Specific Student Consultations. Periodically and as indicated, limited consultations may be provided on an individual student basis for specific issues and circumstances. Such consultations are recognized as having specified, narrowed, and limited impacts and typically indicate the need for more generalized efforts.

TRANSFER OF EFFORTS–BUILDING CAPACITY

An objective of the Training Model is the fading of training and supervision from an outside source and the development of district personnel to assume the role of in-house consultants. We refer to this process as "Building to capacity" and it is the core of our efforts to create long lasting, sustainable change within the system. In order to build internal capacity training and consultation, efforts are directed not only at autism classroom staff, but also to program development, supervisory, training, and mentoring personnel who are to operate in support and oversight capacities. Such personnel not only attend workshops and consultations, but also receive direct instruction, support, and supervision on training, program establishment, and consultation skills. Gradually over time, these staff take on greater responsibility and increasingly function independently within the district or as educational entity Specialists, Trainers, and Consultants.

EVALUATION

In order to assess needs, a formal evaluation protocol is recommended. Such evaluation should not only test students and measure their progress over time, but assess classrooms and the Training Model as well. Measures should include objective classroom data collection (see Chapter 9), standardized testing, fidelity and quality control measures such as classroom checklists (see Appendix B), and, as appropriate, staff skill acquisition and performance inventories. Assessment should occur within and between classroom, in order to evaluate the impacts of training and replication efforts. With such evaluations, the impact and effectiveness of training efforts can be established, and informed decisions on continuation, adjustments, or discontinuation of educational programs for students with autism can be made.

PART II: A MODEL FOR ESTABLISHING ABA CLASSROOMS

THE RESEARCH

Much research exists demonstrating the importance and effects of Applied Behavior Analysis (ABA) interventions in educational settings for students with autism (Fenske, Zalenski, Krantz, & McClannnahan, 1985; Handleman, Harris, Kristoff, Fuentes, & Alessandri,1991; Kamps, Walker, Dugan, Leonard, Thibadeau, Marshall, Grossnickle, & Boland, 1991; Strain & Hoysen, 2000). Overall program evaluation type research as well as procedural investigations have shown that ABA services in educational settings is critical to the treatment of persons with autism. Rationales include the suitability of the venue for teaching as well as the opportunities furnished for instruction in academic, setting relevant, leisure, recreational and social skills, and facilitating generalization to regular education settings. Extensive research has demonstrated a wide variety of behavior analytic procedures and instructional strategies to be effective for students with Autistic Disorder. Such procedures include discrete trial teaching (Lovaas, 1987; Handleman, & Harris, 1983; Polloway, Cronin, & Patton, 1986; Taubman, Brierly, Wishner, Baker, McEachin, & Leaf, 2001), time delay prompting (Farmer, Gast, Wolery, & Winterling, 1991), group instruction (Kamps, Dugan, Leonard,& Daoust, 1994; Kamps, Walker, Maher, & Rotholz, 1992), peer mediation (Kamps, Kravits, Lopez, Kemmerer, Potucek, Harrell, 1998; Kamps, Barbetta, Leonard, & Delquadri, 1994), imbedded instruction (Chiara, Schuster, Bell, & Wolery, 1995), behavioral momentum, (Ray, Skinner, & Watson, 1999), activity schedules (Hall, McClannahan, & Krantz, 1995) and inclusion (Kamps, Leonard, Potucek, Garrison-Harrell, 1995; Harris, Handleman, Kristoff, Bass, & Gordon, 1990). Positive benefits have been shown to endure over the long term within comprehensive school based programs (Harris and Handleman, 2000; Fenske, et. al., 1985; Strain & Hoysen, 2001). Within these comprehensive analyses, the need for assessment of overall, as well as specific, impacts has been addressed.

ABA interventions for students with autism in school settings have illustrated that several benefits can be accrued from treatment in such settings. Intervention in schools has provided the opportunity to address behaviors and skills specific to the educational setting. Such skills can include following school routines, rules, and structures as well as succeeding in semi-structured group play, recreational, or social situations (Dugan, Kamps, Beonard, Watkins, Reinberger, & Stachaus, 1995; Kohler, Strain, Hoyson, Davis, Donina, Rapp, 1995; McEvoy, Nordquist, Twardosz, Heckaman, Wehby, & Kenny, 1988). Another advantage of intervention in schools is the social and recreational opportunities afforded. Research effort has been devoted to the establishment of play skills in children with autism (Wulf, 1985; Rettig, 1994)

Interventions in school also provide the opportunity to work on specific instructional modalities such as responding to group instruction (Taubman, et. al, 2001), and vicarious and observational learning (Browder, Schoen, & Lentz, 1987). Some studies on observational learning with children who have learning disabilities as well as autism and other developmental disabilities have demonstrated the use of such a process to teach specific skills in schools (Keel & Gast, 1992; Schoen, & Ogden,1995; Shipley- Benamou, Lutzker, and Taubman, 2002; Wolery, Ault, Gast, Doyle, Griffen, 1991).

In sum, there is extensive empirical support at procedural and programmatic levels for the effectiveness and benefit of ABA educational interventions for persons with autism. Along with behavioral services in homes, centers, and communities, school-based interventions add unique and necessary components to full and extensive ABA treatment for individuals with autism.

THE ABA CLASSROOM MODEL

The description which follows contains the major programmatic elements of a comprehensive model for ABA intervention in the classroom. Although each classroom will be uniquely designed based on the distinct needs and nature of students, staff, districts and other factors, the following components are most typically present in individually tailored forms. Much of the components of the Training Protocol are designed to provide the staff training necessary for quality implementation of these programmatic elements.

STRUCTURE AND ORGANIZATION

Typically, the ABA classroom is a special education class (e.g. special day classes) on a regular education campus. It may be designated as an autism class or may be a mixed category class. In some cases, as in pre-school versions, it may be a class with regular education students with various proportions of special education students and ABA program and structure. We have worked with ABA preschool classes that were in fact regular education early childhood education classes with a small proportion of high functioning children with autism. However, such classes, in order to address the needs of the special education students, contain subtle, imbedded (see below) ABA programming and have the capacity for pull-out concentrated (see below) teaching and programming as necessary. Components of the model discussed below have also been incorporated into resource and included settings.

Much of the discussion to follow in this section pertains to the typical ABA classroom. Within the model we are describing, the classrooms are structured and organized to approximate regular education classrooms in order to facilitate generalization. From pre-school to high school, the decor and environment reflect this objective and create a positive atmosphere conducive to instruction. Schedules and arrangements are included to approximate general education as much as possible. In general, the classroom set-up allows for the application of instructional formats (individual and group teaching), assignment of staff and students (often including the grouping of students based upon facilitation of instruction), attention to instructional subject matter and curricula, ease of movement and transition through the environment, and approximation to typical classrooms.

At the pre-school level, the daily schedule includes circle time, center-based instruction, and recreational/social opportunities. All this approximates typical early childhood educational arrangements. As noted, a center-based instructional format is utilized, whereby the students rotate through centers that emphasize various instructional areas (e.g., Language Arts and Art; see Instructional Targets and Curricula, below), whether in group or individual format.

At the elementary level, seating arrangements and instructional formats (e.g., teaching from a distance) are utilized which approximate those of regular education classrooms to whatever extent possible. Subject areas (e.g., reading, math, etc.) are also included, and students rotate through these areas in approximation of regular education elementary programs. Daily schedules attempt to parallel regular elementary education experiences as well.

At the secondary level, again seating arrangements, and instructional formats approximate regular education as much as possible. Students also move through periods (in addition to whatever periods are spent included in the regular education campus–see below) through the day, so that schedules and subject areas approach general education as closely as possible.

Each classroom schedule contains the typical instructional and programmatic routine, as well as daily variations (for example, periodic Community-Based Instruction). Instruction and programming are scheduled throughout the entire day. Even recess and nutritional breaks are viewed as times for programming and learning. In fact, given the nature of autism and its effect on social interaction, these time periods are often of increased importance with regard to instruction, planning and support. Each schedule contains the instructional subjects to be addressed, the instructional formats to be utilized (e.g., individual instruction, large group), and routine activities (e.g., recess and lunch). Sample schedules are provided in the addendum to the "Structure and Organization" section of the Training Protocol.

BEHAVIORAL PROGRAMMING

The procedural approach to dealing with disruptive and problematic behavior, and the philosophy behind the procedures, utilized in the ABA classroom model is discussed at length in "A Work in Progress." What follows, however is a brief overview of the programmatic approach to problematic behavior in the ABA classroom.

Initially, Tier 1 and 2 (Kennedy) functional behavior assessments are conducted to ascertain information on the nature, topography, and functions of problem behavior. Such assessment is conducted throughout the behavior programming efforts. Following initial functional assessment, positively oriented behavior management procedures are employed as a means for decreasing interfering or disruptive behavior and building positive replacement skills. These strategies included both reactive and proactive elements. The central focus of reactive procedures is on abundant differential reinforcement for shaping de-escalations of disruptive behavior as well as for the rewarding of spontaneous occurrences of desirable behavior and the absence of disruptive behavior. Proactive procedures included wide-reaching contingency management systems, (e.g., token economies, contingency contracts, self management systems, etc.) as well as the teaching and differential reinforcement of specific, functional alternative behaviors. In this way, the teaching of skills and the motivation to use skills are connected and supported.

While some behavior programming may be class-wide (e.g., a token system for the entire class), much programming is individualized in relationship to the students' behavior problems, needs, and capabilities. Emphasis is on practicality as well. For the students, this translates into a strong focus on the teaching of functional alternatives. For the teaching team, this involves the design of programs that can be reasonably implemented in a classroom setting. Plans that take into consideration implementation constraints tend to result in increased effectiveness.

BEHAVIORAL INSTRUCTION

Discrete Trial Instruction. Described in detail elsewhere (Leaf & McEachin, 1999), the highly positive Discrete Trial Teaching approach utilized in the model includes several essential elements. In its basic form, this teaching procedure involves an instruction, prompting and prompt fading as necessary, opportunities for participant's response, and differential reinforcement along with a brief interval between each trial. Emphasis is always on abundant and meaningful positive reinforcement and individualization of the instruction based on the student's needs. No aversive or punishing contingencies or techniques are used, outside the loss of potential reinforcement (e.g., loss of privileges, etc.). Discrete trial teaching occurred in individual, small group, and large group arrangements. The components and effectiveness of one-on-one discrete trial instruction has been described in numerous studies and descriptive books and articles (see the research of Ivar Lovaas and colleagues, the "Me Book", and "A Work in Progress").

Group Instruction. Group discrete trial instruction has been shown to be an effective adjunct to individual discrete trial instruction (Taubman et al, 2001). Group discrete trial teaching incorporates the sequential and choral presentation of discrete trials but also includes components in which trials between students overlapped and occur concurrently.

In the sequential group instruction, discrete trial instruction is provided to each participant on a random rotating basis. A trial for one participant is closed before another trial is initiated for another participant, and each trial between participants is independent from and unconnected to the other. During choral group instruction, every trial is presented concurrently for all participants in the group, and all are expected to provide the same response, chorus like, in unison.

Overlapping group instruction involves the opening of trials for some participants before the closing of trials already initiated for others. The trials are overlapping, and in such a manner, the learning, behaviors or responses of one participant is interconnected with those of another. This approach may take many forms. As an example, a student may be provided an instruction. While he or she is performing the desired response, another student is provided an instruction which requires attention and then a response to the teacher with regard to the first participant's activities or performance. Both students are then provided feedback, and both trials are closed in close temporal proximity. In another example, when a student refuses to respond to an instruction, no direct feedback is immediately given but a second student is given an instruction. That second student then successfully responds and receives enthusiastic praise, which serves as the consequence for the first student which then closes the initial trial. As a third example, after an instruction is provided chorally to some members of the group, a similar but individualized instruction is immediately provided to a single student. This unique instruction conforms to the developmental level and curriculum needs of that one student. By timing the individual instruction to occur so that the student is responding with the rest of the group, this procedure can help the student understand what is required of them during choral or group instruction. All students are then provided feedback concurrently and the imbedded instruction is gradually faded for our target student. Also included are instructions which required interactive, cooperative, or dependent responding on the part of two or more students (for example a task within which effort on the part of both students is necessary for completion) during which students' trials are overlapped. Instruction also included the differential reinforcement of one or several students for appropriate group responding (e.g. attending, patient sitting, or helping) in the middle of another student's trial.

Since trials are presented on an individual basis, curricula, behavior programming, and within session teaching adjustments (e.g. the fading of prompts) can be individualized. Additionally, since learning is overlapping and often interconnected, programmed and incidental opportunities for observational learning (acquisition through the learning or responding of another) are abundant. Also chances are increased for the promotion of joint attention (social orienting and referencing), social interest, and social skill development.

The overlapping group model challenges certain tenets of discrete trial technique proposed as critical to success with students with autism, namely the need for trials between students to be distinct and the necessity of at least some requisite individual teaching (Lovaas, 1996; Handleman, et. al., 1991; Kamps, et. al., 1992; Kamps, et. al., 1991; Lovaas, 1981). However, its demonstrated effectiveness and the rationales for its incorporation into ABA classroom instruction adequately address these earlier concerns.

Within the group model, overlapping, sequential, and choral teaching methods are well integrated. For example, for a language goal that included the teaching of an expressive label, instruction may involve choral imitative trials with the label imbedded in a sing along, sequential direct teaching of the label receptively with students holding relevant items, and overlapping trials teaching the label expressively with the inclusion of modeling and observational learning. Rather than only adhering to a rigid, overly scheduled protocol, these elements are flexibly provided so that instruction is responsive to a number of within session factors. Examples of such factors include students' need (e.g. a unique occurrence indicates that a task previously taught chorally needs to be addressed sequentially), opportunity (e.g. a student unexpectedly provides an observational model), within session progress (e.g. a student takes an unanticipated leap in availability to choral instruction), and behavior difficulties (e.g. an increase in disruptive behavior suddenly indicates a need for overlapping instruction). With this flexible application, discrete trial guidelines and group teaching approaches are specified, structured and systematic. This interventional approach represents a combined responsiveness to procedural rule governance and within situation shaping (Jahr, 1998). We call this structured flexibility.

The teacher's role in the group instruction consists of providing instruction, prompts and consequences. The teacher is also responsible for the integration of the various group approaches, individualization of instruction, within session adjustments in teaching, and coordination with instructional assistants. The overlapping, concurrent element of the group instruction was conducive to the integration of efforts between the teacher and instructional assistants. Aides were placed behind the members of the group and coordinated with the teacher, who provided the majority of instruction and was positioned in front. In this arrangement, aides assisted in prompting as well as with the opening and/or closing of trials which, for some students, overlapped with trials directed at other students by the teacher. Aides were guided in their participation by the prompts, requests, and directions of the teacher. Since the teacher is the primary instructor in typical educational settings, efforts are directed at approximating that kind of arrangement as much as possible. The goal is for the aides, and the assistance they provide, to be faded as much and as quickly as possible, so that, to the greatest extent possible, independent learning can occur in a typical group setting.

A number of benefits can be accrued with group discrete trial teaching. For example, behavior management advantages can be offered by group instruction. Abundant opportunities exist for the use of vicarious reinforcement, that is the opportunity for one person to observe the positive pay-off another person receives for their behavior. For example, trials containing disruptive behavior can be overlapped with trials containing other students' appropriate behavior and contingent reinforcement. Other features can further positively impact behavior. Opportunities are offered for students to provide instructions, prompts, and feedback to each other in response to other students' mildly disruptive behavior and to provide positive consequences for others' appropriate responses. The positive effects of these peer mediated efforts have been witnessed. Additionally afforded by the group approach are opportunities for the directing of attention, in an extremely naturalistic manner not available in one to one instruction, away from attentionally motivated acting out behavior and toward other students in the group. Finally, chances for the reduction of demand-provoked acting out is provided, since in group teaching, instructional requirements are rotated and divided across the entire group, as opposed to being concentrated on one student.

Within group instruction, a benefit of the overlapping model is the opportunity presented for individualization of instruction. We have found that, even with a range of targets and functioning levels of students, overlapping and concurrent yet individualized instruction in group is not only viable, but is, in many cases, co-facilitative. For example, we have noted situations in which trials for a student who was learning an object label expressively were imbedded in the learning of another that was being taught to expressively combine attributes with labels. The end result was the enhancement of the acquisition of both students.

Another benefit of the group discrete trial model is the opportunity afforded for social interaction and observational learning. As opposed to individual teaching, overlapping teaching provides not only exposure to other students and their learning, but chances to teach generalized observational learning skills. Such an approach allows for systematic and directed observational instruction ("Do what that student is doing" for example) is accomplished through the purposeful imbedding of students' discrete trial instruction within each other's teaching. Within group discrete trial teaching we have witnessed numerous incidents in which children have acquired goals targeted for other students, additional to and often more advanced than their own.

Further benefits of group discrete trial teaching include the efficiency and naturalistic quality of the instruction. Say for example, that a group instructional session, for eight students lasts 20 minutes. During that time, the high volume of effective, group instruction affords simultaneous yet individualized discrete trial teaching to the students who are present. This is roughly equivalent to the teacher conducting two and a half hours of individual discrete trial instruction. Such efficiency offers one way schools and school districts can provide access to practical yet effective discrete trial instruction, supplemental to one to one discrete trial teaching, when such instruction is indicated.

The group instruction with its sequential, choral, and overlapping elements presents in a very naturalistic manner. Much instruction in regular education settings at most grade levels occurs in groups and involves interactive and overlapping engagement between students and teachers. This naturalistic aspect group discrete trial teaching not only enhances the overall appeal of such behavioral instruction, but potentially facilitates the generalization of instruction to included settings.

Group discrete trial teaching represents a complicated instructional methodology. In addition to the inclusion of the guidelines essential to competent discrete trial instruction, it involves the integration of the imbedding process (see below), individualization of targets, and within session, across trials adjustments, along with precise orchestration between teachers and instructional assistants. And while it is challenging to conduct group discrete trial teaching, it is even harder to be systematic in such instruction. While it is sometimes difficult in one on one teaching to be systematic, it is exponentially more challenging to do so in group discrete trial teaching. Identification of goals and progressive, structured movement (e.g. fading of prompts, expansion of the task, etc.) to those objectives in group teaching is critical to students' acquisition and success.

Imbedded and Concentrated Teaching. Behavioral instruction is conducted in a concentrated as well as in an imbedded fashion. Imbedded instruction is teaching which occurs in its natural context. It occurs during the typical situations in which targeted skills would customarily be required such as during transitions, group instruction, lunch, assemblies, art lessons, recess and the like. In concentrated or isolated teaching, instruction occurs in pull-out fashion, in a situation contrived to focus on a specific targeted behavior or skill. Concentrated teaching may be one-to-one, but also can occur in a group. It is just instruction occurring in concentrated fashion outside of the natural context.

We have found (Taubman et al, 2002) that students' acquisition of skills is facilitated when there is integration of all teaching efforts. That is, when there is coordination between imbedded and concentrated instruction. As further integration of efforts, both imbedded and concentrated teaching could occur in individual or group formats.

An illustration of the coordination of imbedded and concentrated teaching would be a situation in which progress is slow or hampered during imbedded teaching. Efforts would then be directed at teaching the skill in concentrated fashion to hasten acquisition, with instructional efforts then being transitioned back to imbedded instruction. As an example, if a child was having a difficult time learning from the instruction imbedded during recess to respond to the "freeze bell", additional instruction would be provided outside of recess and in concentrated fashion on stopping all action in response to a signal. The imbedded and concentrated effort would be coordinated to promote generalization of the learned response to independent performance during recess.

Teaching Interactions. For students who have the language and cognitive capability, ABA instructional methods in addition to discrete trial teaching are used. This primarily includes Teaching Interactions (TIs), an elaborated modeling-practice-feedback type instructional technique developed as part of the Teaching Family Model for delinquent youth (TF ref). Such a technique has several benefits for individuals with autism as it allows for structured training of more complex, often nuanced skills in a highly natural, interpersonal, conversational format. A host of target areas including social, learning to learn, communication, recreation/leisure, school routine, and academic skills can be addressed using the TI.

Although described in detail elsewhere (Teaching Family Handbook, 1980), the primary components of the TI are:

1. Initiation and Labeling

2. Rationale

3. Demonstration/Description

4. Practice

5. Feedback

6. Behavior Management Program Consequence

These components may be present or absent in a specific TI session depending upon the needs, capabilities, and progress of a student. TI sessions may look like formal instructional sessions with the teaching nature of the interaction and the presence of the steps formally delineated, or it may appear more like a "buddy chat" with the necessary steps present but presented in a discussion format that seems more informal. In either case, the teaching is always structured and systematic, given the needs of students with autism.

The instructional session part of the TI is accompanied by two other components. They are: Discrimination Training and Generalization Programming.

Discrimination training involves sessions in which students learn differences between forms of responding. This is typically between undesirable and desirable responding. It could include identifying the difference between the old inappropriate behavior and the new, to be learned, appropriate alternative. It could also include differentiating between different social cues or could also include noticing the different outcomes that occur based on different behavioral alternatives (to strengthen rationales). Discrimination training may often proceed actual instruction in necessary skills, but at times can be concurrent to the TI instructional sessions.

As initial TI sessions often occur in role play settings, Generalization Programming is necessary to ensure that the student uses the skills learned in naturally occurring situations. Limitations in generalization found commonly in autism underscore the importance of programming in this area. Typically, using the technology of generalization outlined by Stokes and Baer (1977), efforts are directed fading the use of newly learned behavior into natural situations. This is often done by identifying several dimensions which separate the simulations or role-plays from natural circumstances. These might include the following:

- People

- Setting

- Time

- Predictability

- Authenticity

- Provocativeness

Hierarchies are created for each relevant dimension and the student is moved along hierarchies, at whatever pace indicated, until necessary responding is occurring independently in natural situations. For example, if a student is learning to not interrupt when peers are discussing information that is of interest to the student, initial sessions will be structured with a teacher in concentrated fashion around material that is not highly compelling. Over time, sessions will be altered so that the structure is less obvious, the occurrence of situations that require the skill appear more natural and occur unpredictably, happen with peers, and involve discussions with highly enticing information.

It has been our experience that all components of the teaching interaction, discrimination training, TI teaching sessions, and generalization programming are necessary for successful implementation of skills. As with discrete trial teaching, teaching interactions can be conducted in individual and group formats, and in imbedded and concentrated fashion.

Other Instructional Formats. In addition to discrete trial teaching and teaching interactions, other teaching methods are utilized in the ABA classroom. In fact, efforts are made to move toward the use of typical teaching styles whenever possible for generalization purposes. This includes group instruction, teaching at a distance, lecture styles, incidental teaching and even typical instructional teaching strategies such as teaching at abstract level down (customary in regular education) rather than specific content up (typical in ABA curricula). Efforts are directed therefore not only on specific material, but on learning to learn. That is, teaching students with autism, to the extent possible, to learn within different and typical learning modalities.

Instructional Balance. Although instruction and programming occur throughout the day, in the end the ABA instruction in the ABA classroom is about balance. Several areas of balance are involved. These include balance between the following:

- group and individual instruction

- imbedded and concentrated teaching

- planned systematic teaching and capture of teachable moments

- actual teaching and activity related assistance (guidance and facilitation of behavior that produces the behavior [e.g. child gets their backpack] or a product [e.g., a mother's day card], but doesn't involve actual teaching)

- direct teaching and the construction and guidance of natural situations (e.g., games with typical peers) that allow for learning to occur

- pacing and intensity of programming and instruction

How elements of instructional balance are distributed is based upon many considerations. These include staff, schedule demands, and the unexpected, but most specifically student needs. These needs are defined by the students' IEPs and by the daily, ever-changing dynamic of their performance and progress.

Instructional Targets and Curricula. We have come to learn that, in the field of education, the term "curriculum" has several meanings, many of which may be at odds with a traditional ABA definition. For the sake of discussion, when "curriculum" is utilized, we are referring to instructional content.

The ABA classroom model we are discussing utilizes, to the extent possible given students' capabilities, a layering of curriculum format. Layers can include the following:

- Thematic content (Integrating all subject areas—used pervasively in regular education)

- Academic Subject Area (Art, Math, Reading, Social Studies, etc.)

- Instructional Activity (Art project, Reading Assignment, etc.)

- Behavioral Targets (Including Replacement Skills)

- ABA Curriculum (e.g., Curriculum from "A Work in Progress")

ABA curriculum includes targets in language, social skills, play, recreation/leisure areas, school-related skills (e.g., lining up, cafeteria routines, assembly requirements, etc.), activities of daily living, community based instruction, cognitive (including academic) targets, and learning to learn skills. In the traditional, in-home one-to-one ABA instructional format, the ABA curriculum (along with behavior programming) is the entire focus. At certain times, for example within some concentrated teaching, this may also be the case in the ABA classroom model. However, in classroom settings, ABA curriculum is often included within and along with the other instructional content areas listed above.

This layering approach is similar to the concept of scaffolding in education. The layers taken together constitute the daily lesson plan for each student. All layers, especially the last two, are tied to students' IEP goals and objectives.

The rationales for this stratification of curriculum have to do with the location of the instruction: These are classroom settings. This is the manner in which instructional content is provided in typical educational settings. By layering curriculum in this manner, generalization is promoted and students become more independent. We have also found (Taubman et. al.) that such instruction that includes layering of curriculum can result in successful acquisition of targeted ABA curricular targets. However, it has also been found that in such an arrangement, content in other layers (e.g., in the thematic areas) not directly instructed can be learned by the student as well. Such incidental acquisition certainly argues for the layered curriculum format.

The layering of curriculum approach integrates well with other components of the ABA classroom model discussed above, including the combination of imbedded and concentrated teaching, as well as group and individual instructional formats.

INCLUSION AND TYPICAL PEERS

The topic of inclusion and surrounding issues is discussed at length in the chapter "Illusion of Inclusion in *Sense and Nonsense: It Has To Be Said* (Leaf, McEachin & Taubman, 2008). However, it should be mentioned that the ABA classroom model incorporates ample opportunities for learning in included settings and with typically developing peers. Integration into regular education classrooms and reverse mainstreaming opportunities are often abundant and designed specifically toward meeting the individual needs of students. Under LRE guidelines, the goal is to provide the maximum in effective functional learning in inclusion, balanced with instruction and programming that must occur in special education settings. All inclusion however, includes imbedded instruction and programming involving the elements described above.

Work involving typical peers is clearly necessary not only for inclusion but for specific instructional content in such areas as social, play, and learning to learn skills (e.g., observational learning). However, the ABA classroom model tends to avoid using typical peers as props for the purposes of educating special needs students. Such a usage is not only unfair to the regular education students, it is unfair to the special needs students as well because they typically do not lead to reciprocal friendships.

We try hard therefore to make sure that educational arrangements and specific ABA work that involves typical peers also include benefits for those children. And while those peers may serve to mediate the intervention at times, care is taken to not consistently put them in the therapist role. They all need to be just kids and students that act as junior therapists do not make equal friends.

REFERENCES

Aman, M.G., Singh, N. N., Stewart, A.W., & Field, C. J. (1985). The Aberrant Behavior Checklist: A behavior rating scale for the assessment of treatment effects. <u>American Journal of Mental Deficiency, 89</u>, 485-491.

Browder, D. M., Schoen, S. F., & Lentz, F. E. (1987). Learning to learn through observation. <u>The Journal of Special Education, 20</u>, 447-46.

Chiara, L., Schuster, J. W., Bell, J. K., & Wolery, M. (1995). Small-group massed-trial and individually-distributed-trial instruction with preschoolers. <u>Journal of Early Intervention, 19</u>, 203-217.

Cornelius, P. L. & Semmel, M. I. (1982). Effects of summer instruction on reading achievement regression of learning disabled students. <u>Journal of Learning Disabilities, 15</u>, 409-413.

Crowell, D. C. & Klein, T. W. (1981). Preventing summer loss of reading skills among primary children. <u>The Reading Teacher,35</u>, 561-564

Dugan, E., Kamps, D., Leonard, B., Watkins, N., Reinberger, A.,& Stackhaus, J. (1995). Effects of cooperative learning groups during social studies for students with autism and fourth-grade peers. <u>Journal of Applied Behavior Analysis, 28</u>, 175-188.

Edgar, E., Spence, W. M., & Denowitz, L. A. (1977). Extended school year for the handicapped: Is it working? <u>The Journal of Special Education, 11</u>, 441-447.

Elliott, S.N., Gresham, F.M., Freeman, T., & McCloskey, G. (1988). Teachers' and observers' ratings of children's social skills: Validation of the Social Skills Rating Scales. <u>Journal of Psychoeducational Assessment</u>, 6, 152-161.

Farmer, J. A., Gast, D. L., Wolery, M., & Winterling, V. (1991). Small group instruction for students with severe handicaps: A study of observational learning. <u>Education and Training in Mental Retardation, 26</u>, 190-201.

Fenske, E. C., Zalenski, S., Krantz, P.J. & McClannahan, L. E. (1985). Age at intervention and treatment outcome for autistic children in a comprehensive intervention program. <u>Analysis and Intervention in Developmental Disabilities, 5</u>, 49-58.

Gilliam, J. & McConnell, K. (1997). <u>Scales for Predicting Successful Inclusion</u>. Austin, TX: Pro-Ed.

Hall, L. H., McClannahan, L. E., & Krantz, P. J. (1995). Promoting independence in integrated classrooms by teaching aides to use activity schedules and decreased prompts. <u>Education and Training in Mental Retardation and Developmental Disabilities, 30</u>, 208-217.

Handleman, J.S. & Harris, S.L. (1983). A comparison of one-to-one versus couplet instruction with autistic children. <u>Behavioral Disorders, 9</u>, 22-26.

Handleman, J. S., Harris, S. L., Kristoff, B, Fuentes F., & Alessandri, M. (1991). A specialized program for preschool children with autism. <u>Language, Speech, and Hearing Services in Schools, 22,</u> 107-110.

Harris, S. L. & Handleman, J.S. Age and IQ at intake as predictors of placement for young children with autism: A four-to six-year follow-up. <u>Journal of Autism and Developmental Disorders, 30</u>, 137-142.

Harris, S.L., Handleman, J.S., Kristoff, B., Bass, L., & Gordon, R. (1990). Changes in language development among autistic and peer children in segregated and integrated preschool settings. <u>Journal of Autism and Developmental Disorders, 20</u>, 23-31.

Kamps, D. M., Barbetta, P. M., Leonard, B. R., & Delquadri, J. (1994). Class wide peer tutoring: An integration strategy to improve reading skills and promote peer interactions among students with autism and general education peers. <u>Journal of Applied Behavior Analysis, 27</u>, 49-61.

Kamps, D. M., Dugan, E. P., Leonard, B. R., & Daoust, P. M. (1994). Enhanced small group instruction using choral responding and student interaction for children with autism and developmental disabilities. <u>American Journal on Mental Retardation, 99,</u> 60-73.

Kamps, D. M., Kravits, T., Lopez, A. G., Kemmerer, K., Potucek, J., Harrell, L. G. (1998). What do the Peers think? Social validity of peer-mediated programs. <u>Education and Treatment of Children, 21,</u> 107-134.

Kamps, D. M., Leonard, B., Potucek, J., Garrison-Harrell, L (1995). Cooperative learning groups in reading: An integration strategy for students with autism and general classroom peers. <u>Behavioral Disorders, 21,</u> 89-109.

Kamps, D. M., Walker, D., Dugan, E. P., Leonard, B. R., Thibadeau, S. F., Marshall, K., Grossnickle, L., & Boland, B. (1991). Small group instruction for school-aged students with autism and developmental disabilities. <u>Focus on Autistic Behavior, 6,</u> 1-18.

Kamps, D. M., Walker, D., Maher, J., & Rotholz, D. (1992). Academic and environmental effects of small group arrangements in classrooms for students with autism and other developmental disabilities. <u>Journal of Autism and Developmental Disorders, 22,</u> 277-293.

Keel, M.C. & Gast, D. L. (1992). Small-group instruction for students with learning disabilities: Observational and incidental learning. <u>Exceptional Children, 58,</u> 357-368.

Kohler, F. W., Strain, P. S. , Hoyson, M. Davis, L., Donina, W. M., & Rapp, N. (1995). Using a group-oriented contingency to increase social interactions between children with autism and their peers. <u>Behavior Modification, 19,</u> 10-32.

Larsen, L., Goodman, L, & Glean, R. (1981). Issues in the implementation of extended school year programs for handicapped students. Exceptional Children, 47, 256-253.

Leaf, R., & McEachin, J. (1999). <u>A work in progress. Behavior management strategies and curriculum for intensive behavioral treatment of autism.</u> New York, NY: DRL Books.

Leaf, R., & McEachin, J, & Taubman, M.T. (2008). <u>Sense and Nonsense: It Has To Be Said.</u> New York, NY: DRL Books.

Lovaas, O.I. (1987). Behavioral treatment and normal educational and intellectual functioning in young autistic children. <u>Journal of Consulting and Clinical Psychology, 55,</u> 3-9.

McEvoy, M. A., Nordquist, V. M., Twardosz, S., Heckaman, K. A., Wehby, J. H., & Denny, R. K. (1988). Promoting autistic children's peer interaction in an integrated early childhood setting using affection activities. <u>Journal of Applied Behavior Analysis, 21,</u> 193-200.

Papovich, S., Rafuse, J., Siembieda, M., Williams, M., Sharpe, A., McEachin, J., Leaf, R., & Taubman, M. (2002). <u>An Analytic Comparison of Data Collection Techniques Used with Discrete Trial Teaching in an Applied Setting for Persons with Autism.</u> Paper presented at the meeting of the Association for Behavior Analysis, 20021 Annual Convention, Toronto, Canada.

Polloway, E. A., Cronin, M. E., & Patton, J. R. (1986). The efficacy of group versus one-to-one instruction: A review. <u>Remedial and Special Education,</u> 7, 22-30.

Ray, K. P., Skinner, C. H., & Watson, T. S. (1999). Transferring stimulus control via momentum to increase compliance in a student with autism: A demonstration of collaborative consultation. <u>School Psychology Review,</u> 28, 622-628.

Rettig, M. A. (1994). Play behaviors of young children with autism: Characteristics and intervention. <u>Focus on Autistic Behavior, 9,</u> 1-6.

Schoen, S. F., & Ogden, S. (1995). Impact of time delay, observational learning, and attentional cuing upon word recognition during integrated small-group instruction. <u>Journal of Autism and Developmental Disorders, 25,</u> 503-519.

Shipley-Benamou, R., Lutzker, J. R., & Taubman, M. (2002). Teaching daily living skills to children with autism through instructional video modeling. Journal of Positive Behavior Interventions, 4, 165-175.

Sparrow, S., Balla, D., & Cicchetti, D. (1984). Vineland Adaptive Behavior Scales. Circle Pines, MN: American Guidance Service.

Strain, P. S., & Hoyson, M. (2000). The need for longitudinal, intensive social skill intervention: LEAP follow-up outcomes for children with autism. Topics in Early Childhood Special Education, 20, 116-122.

Stokes, T.F.,& Baer, D.M. (1977). An implicit technology of generalization. Journal of Applied Behavior Analysis, 10, 349-367.

Taubman, M., Brierley, S., Wishner, J., Baker, D., McEachin, J., & Leaf, R.B. (2001). The effectiveness of a group discrete trial instructional approach for preschoolers with developmental disabilities. Research in Developmental Disabilities, 22, 205-219.

Taubman, M., Palos, P., Soluaga, D., Papovich, S., Leaf, R., & McEachin, J. (2002). Examination of the Effects of Components of an ABA Education Program for Students With Autism. Paper presented at the meeting of the Association for Behavior Analysis, 20021 Annual Convention, Toronto, Canada.

Taubman, M., Papovich, S., Palos, L., & Styzens, J. (2001). The Impact of a Brief School Relevant ABA Program for Students with Autism. Paper presented at the meeting of the Association for Behavior Analysis, 2001 Annual Convention, New Orleans, LA.

Wolery, M., Ault, M. J., Gast, D. L., Doyle, P. M, & Griffen, A. K. (1991). Teaching chained tasks in dyads: Acquisition of target and observational behaviors. The Journal of Special Education, 24, 198-220

Wulf, S. B. (1985). The symbolic and object play of children with autism: A review. Journal of Autism and Developmental Disorders, 15, 139-148.

Chapter 3

WHAT MAKES A GOOD SCHOOL DISTRICT?

By Ron Leaf and John McEachin

We are often asked to evaluate the quality of services provided by school districts. Typically, the impetus for the request is litigation. Before they pursue litigation or decide to settle, they want to know our opinion on whether we feel they are educationally "defensible."

What makes a District "defensible"? At a minimum it is necessary to conduct a proper IEP, collect data, and dot your I's and cross your T's (Enright, Azelrod, 1995). But, being defensible is not only a matter of being procedurally sound. In our opinion "defensibility" boils down to providing quality education. When quality education is provided, districts will prevail in due process hearings. When quality education is provided, parents will be satisfied. When quality education is provided, teachers and aides will be happy in their jobs. **And when quality education is provided, children will make meaningful progress!**

Sense THE BEST WAY TO BUILD "DEFENSIBLE PROGRAMS" IS TO PROVIDE QUALITY EDUCATION THEN LITIGATION WOULD BE A DISTANT MEMORY!

Our opinion as to whether a District is "defensible" is based upon our analysis of whether quality education services are being provided. We have found the following dimensions to be indicative of quality education.

ADOPTING ONE THEORETICAL ORIENTATION

School Districts are often proud to announce that they have an "eclectic" philosophy. Eclectic models of education have become very fashionable and unfortunately the field of education has historically been driven by philosophizing rather than empirical analysis of outcomes. This makes the field vulnerable to fads where ideas catch on and become popular because they are intuitively or emotionally appealing regardless of their scientific validity. In the case of eclecticism it has the additional allure that comes from the belief that "more is better". Districts believe is that by doing a little bit of everything they can capture the varied benefits of multiple approaches while at the same time avoiding the disadvantages that each entails just by itself.

In an effort to avoid the pitfall of a one-size-fits-all mentality they try to become all things to all students. This can lead to a revolving door of consultants and trainings and smorgasbord plates of educational programming that includes a taste of ABA, a generous portion of TEACCH, a pinch of Verbal Behavior, a dash of Sensory Integration (SI), accompanied by PECS, Floor Time and a savory sauce of "traditional" educational programs. They have been led to believe that they are following "Best Practice." This belief comes as much from the fact that everyone else thinks it is a good idea than from careful analysis of whether and how it might work. All too often what is actually being provided is a disconnected hodgepodge of services!

There are other reasons why school districts favor an "eclectic" education besides its seductive intuitive appeal. Attorneys seem to be big fans of this model and recommend it as a way to become more defensible. This stems partly from a desire to avoid not offering something that might turn out to be the magic bullet. It is true that if the services the district currently offers are inadequate, then providing a wider range of approaches does increase the chance that some part of what they are doing would lead to more positive outcomes. But expanding services based on speculation about what may be helpful and without critical evaluation for the claims that are made is a big mistake. Methodologies must have scientific evidence as to their effectiveness and should not be implemented merely because of custom or a willingness to accommodate parental preference. And there needs to be consideration of how the different elements of a program fit together.

Another reason for widespread adoption of an eclectic model and reluctance to commit to a single cohesive approach is that so many parents want different things for their children. Parental requests are important and need to be considered carefully, but should only be adopted when they make sense. In an attempt to be more conciliatory and hopefully avoid litigation, some IEP teams will approve a battery of services even when they recognize that the strategies have a questionable foundation. But ultimately it does not at all ensure the best education for students and in the long run it may actually lead to more litigation! Districts are perplexed because they gave the parents what they were requesting, so why would they litigate? Although they may have asked for an array of services or perhaps that one "cure" they saw on television, all they really want is for their child to make meaningful progress. If progress does not occur because the district failed to uphold its responsibility to identify appropriate methodology based on scientific research, they are legally vulnerable despite having provided what the parents were asking for. Appeasement is a certain formula for litigation (Freeman, Green, Leaf, Sperry, Waks & Weatherly, 2002).

Finally, there are districts who offer a disconnected array of approaches in a mistaken effort to assure that the IEP is individualized. The belief is that not every student's program can have the same underlying foundation. An approach like ABA is not recognized as appropriate for many children, because it is not viewed as being comprehensive, and therefore, other options must be provided. ABA is an all-encompassing methodology that is systematic, individualized, designed to enable students to learn, and is scientifically proven. The empirically derived principles of learning apply to all children, adolescents and adults. ABA is appropriate for students who are cognitively impaired, as well as those who are gifted. There are numerous journals devoted to utilizing ABA with all types of individuals as well as thousands upon thousands of research publications documenting the effective application of ABA to every conceivable skill.

What student does not need this at the core of his education program? How can a district get in trouble for recognizing that this is exactly the unified model that provides the means to comprehensively meet the needs of each individual student?

People need to be willing to stand up and advocate for what makes sense and resist the fads that are being embraced all around us. Again, this is not to say that school districts should not have knowledge and training in multiple areas. School districts need to receive training in approaches that have been shown to be effective through solid experimental research. However, it is essential that a district become grounded in one theoretical orientation. A comprehensive discussion regarding the need to adopt a cohesive theoretical model is included in *Sense and Nonsense: It Has to Be Said!* (Leaf, McEachin and Taubman, 2008).

TRAINING AND SUPERVISION: EARLY AND ONGOING

The quality of education will be directly related to the training, support, and ongoing supervision that staff receives (Greenwood, Carta, Hart, & Kamps, 1992; Hundert, Hopkins, 1992; Kamps, 1997; Leblanc, Ricciardis, & Luiselli, 2005; Petscher, & Bailey, 2006). Naturally, one could not be considered as trained simply because one attended a workshop (Smith, Parker, Taubmann, & Lovaas, 1992). Even participating in a year of training and supervision often is not sufficient. We have found, that on average, districts require at least three years of ongoing training and supervision before they are able to become more independent. Even then, they need occasional consultations. It is a lengthy process and we understand it is costly. However, it is what helps school districts provide quality education and therefore become "defensible."

All too often, district administrators just do not understand that extensive training is required in order for their staff to become proficient. The same way you could not learn to fly a jet with one day of training, staff cannot be sufficiently prepared until they receive intensive and ongoing training. They simply do not seem to appreciate just how complicated it is to implement ABA. When administrators are informed that training is such an extensive and ongoing process, they often think they can "save" money by skimping on training. This is extremely short sighted and they end up wasting enormous amounts of money because of litigation. It always comes back to the best way of being defensible is to provide quality education.

BUY IN: BUS DRIVER TO SUPERINTENDENT

The success of programming is based upon programming being implemented as consistently as possible. To borrow a cliché, "a program is only as strong as its weakest link!" All too often we observe principals providing negative attention to students or removing them from non-preferred activities in an attempt to stop crying. Even though they may feel they are providing assistance they may actually be reinforcing disruptive behaviors. Unfortunately, their lack of understanding and knowledge may undermine a good program. Similarly, cafeteria workers, recess monitors and bus drivers can be instrumental in program success or failure! If a child has a poor experience on the bus, the child will be far less receptive at school or home. Similarly, cafeteria workers can help facilitate a positive lunch thereby leading to better socialization, communication and eating.

In order for children to receive quality education it is essential that administrators, as well as all other personnel understand ABA and receive training in its application so that they can be more consistent with teachers and aides in their interaction with students (Gillat & Sulzer, 1994; Martens & Ardoin, 2002). At the very least, if they are not trained they should be willing to defer to those who are trained and not sabotage programming.

We have provided training to ancillary personal such as school nurses, school administrators, cafeteria workers, recess monitors and bus drivers. Although it has been less intensive than the training we have provided to teachers and aides, it has been useful in increasing their understanding of autism and ABA. Most importantly, providing practical strategies such as catching students being good and not providing negative attention has been beneficial for students when they are on the bus, in the cafeteria, and in the hallways. We understand that we cannot expect complete consistency among all school personnel, but the more everyone can all be on the same page, the better the students' success.

Unfortunately, school administrators often reveal that they have no idea regarding special education and therefore how to evaluate the effectiveness of their special education programs. After all, they were not trained in Special Education. By providing training administrators are better equipped to evaluate their staff and more importantly they can provide the necessary support and training. When administrators express their support for training, their staff are more willing to take training seriously and consider following recommendations. Additionally administrators who are supportive of "good ABA" are also more likely to make their staff accountable.

Administrative support is also essential for parents. When parents feel that administration more fully understands their children, they are more trusting and therefore more patient with the process. Most importantly, when administrators more fully understand autism and effective teaching, they will help assure that quality education occurs!

The National Research Council (2001) recognized that buy-in at the top levels was essential. *"Administrative attitudes and support are critical in improving schools"* *(Page 8).*

OUTREACH

Naturally, education does not start and stop in the classroom. It is essential that those who have primary contact with the student, inside and outside of the classroom, are involved. A sign of a good program is when there is the consistent application of programming in all environments. This necessitates ongoing meetings with parents.

We suggest the following:

A. Daily communication, whereby the teacher uses a teacher-friendly communication log to convey meaningful information about how the student did behaviorally and instructionally.

B. A monthly meeting in which the staff meets with the parent and provides a summary of the previous month as well as identifying the continuing goals and objectives. This meeting provides the opportunity to evaluate the programs effectiveness and a means by which to increase consistency of intervention. Inconsistency in the application of interventions will greatly thwart educational effectiveness.

C. Monthly parent-training meetings are invaluable to help increase the skill level of parents. These meetings not only enhance consistent programming, but also give parents the knowledge and skills to be more effective with their children. Additionally through such trainings, children's eating, sleeping and toileting issues can often be resolved, thereby helping students become more receptive learners.

Through such outreach efforts school and parents become far more collaborative thereby reducing hostility that results in a multitude of difficulties. Moreover, when parents receive training, they, just like teachers, become more effective and feel less helpless and hopeless. Charlene Green, the Assistant Superintendent of Clark County Unified School District, likes to remind us: "We don't own the information, we need to share it with everyone!" (Freeman, Green, Leaf, Sperry, Waks & Weatherly, 2002)

COLLABORATION

In a school district, it is virtually impossible for everyone to agree. With multiple disciplines and philosophies, the stage is set for conflict. However, minimizing conflict is essential in order to keep everyone's energy applied in a constructive direction. Adopting a single and cohesive theoretical framework helps get everyone on the same page and working together in a unified manner. Training is an important part of obtaining buy-in and helping staff members understand how they can contribute to the process of educating students. Outreach is an opportunity to accomplish the same with parents and others outside of the district. It is important to establish a sense of teamwork so that individual agendas do not interfere with the goal of providing quality education. Resolution of contention and facilitation of collaboration should primarily be a proactive effort. With conviction for an ideology of teamwork, it will be much easier when conflict does occur to "agree to disagree" on the small stuff, because there is fundamental agreement on the big stuff.

ORGANIZATION

Often the best districts can be ruined by disorganization. When the staff is not able to perform their duties because they are being pulled away from their primary responsibilities, programming will suffer. When the staff is unaware of policies and philosophy, programming will suffer. And when communication between staff is lacking or non existent, programming will suffer!

Too often, it happens that the most talented personnel are stuck attending unproductive IEP meetings and running around from school to school putting out fires. Their talent is absolutely being wasted. They are not able to provide the necessary intervention to children or support and training to staff. How many times have you seen an outstanding teacher saddled with too many students, students who are very challenging and demand tremendous time and emotional energy and not provided with sufficient resources to accomplish her job? They get the hardest jobs because others are not competent enough to do it. Rather than fix the problem, they burn out the most valuable resources that exist within the district. These wonderful teachers were drawn to the field because of their love for children and their enormous talents. But over time, they find themselves spinning their wheels and are far removed from providing a quality education. They retire all too early to pursue another field so that they can feel productive, successful and appreciated. **WHAT A SHAME!!!**

Unfortunately, teachers do not get paid enough for this critical life-changing occupation! Furthermore, they must endure tremendous stress, undeserved criticism and outright character assassination. They are not just responsible for one student and one IEP! They often have to deal with dissatisfied parents and hostile attorneys. Parents should be incredibly appreciative and supportive. Hostility simply does not make teachers better and it will sabotage children's education.

Administration must be equally as supportive. Support means providing staff with extensive training and resources as well as time to prepare all the necessary activities! Perhaps more importantly, administrators must recognize that it is a lengthy process for a teacher to become a star!

ORGANIZATIONAL "DO's"

- Adopt one consistent approach: develop expertise and consistency

- Provide early and ongoing training

- Facilitate buy-in for ALL school personnel

- Provide outreach to parents and the community

- Collaboration among everyone

- The better the organization the better the education

REFERENCES

Block, J. S., Weinstein, J., & Seitz, M. (2005). School and parent partnerships in preschool years. *Autism Spectrum Disorders: Identification, education, and treatment (3rd Ed.)*. D. Zager. Mahwah, NJ, Lawrence Erlbaum Associate Publishers: 229-265.

Bondy, A. (1996). What parents can expect from public school programs. *Behavioral Intervention for young children with autism: A manual for parents and professionals*. C. Maurice, Green, G., & Luce, S.C. Austin, TX, Pro-ed: 323-330.

Cole, C. L., & Bambara, L.M. (1992). "Issues surrounding the use of self-management interventions in the schools." *School Psychology Review* 21(2): 193-201.

Embry, D. D. (2002). "The Good Behavior Game: A Best Practice Candidate as a Universal Behavioral Vaccine." *Clinical Child and Family Psychology Review* 5(4): 273-297.

Enright, S. M., & Azelrod, S. (1995). "Applied Behavior Analysis working in the classroom." *School Psychology Quarterly* 10(1): 29-40.

Etscheidt, S. (2003). "An analysis of legal hearings and case related to individualized education programs for children with autism." *Research and Practice for Persons with Severe Disabilities* 28(2): 51-69.

Etscheidt, S. (2006). "Behavioral Intervention Plan: Pedagogical and Legal Analysis of Issues." *Behavioral Disorders* 31(2): 223-243.

Fox, J., & Davis, C. (2005). "Functional Behavior Assessment in Schools: Current Research Findings and Future Directions." *Journal of Behavioral Education* 14(1): 1-4.

Freeman, B.J., Green, C., Leaf, R., Sperry, L., Waks, A., & Weatherly, C. (2002). Autism Spectrum Disorders: Providing Children with Meaningful Education." Symposium presented at Child and Family Service Conference. Oahu, Hawaii.

Gillat, A., & Sulzer B.A. (1994). "Prompting Principals' managerial involvement in instructional improvement." *Journal of Applied Behavior Analysis* 27(1): 115-129.

Greenwood, C. R., Carta, J.J., Hart, B., Kamps, D., Terry, B., Arreagarmayer, C., Atwater, J., Walker, D., Risley, T., & Delquadrit,J. (1992). "Out of the laboratory and into the community: 26 years of applied behavior analysis at the Juniper Gardens Children's project." *American Psychologist* 47(11): 1464-1474.

Hundert, J., & Hopkins, B. (1992). "Training supervisors in a collaborative team approach to promote peer interaction of children with disabilities in integrated preschools." *Journal of Applied Behavior Analysis* 25(2): 385-400.

Kamps, D. M. (1997). "The Behavior analysts' role in facilitating interventions in general education settings." *Journal of Behavioral Education* 7(1): 81-89.

Kazdin, A. E. (1989). *Behavior Modification in applied settings (4th Ed)*. Belmont, CA, Thomson Brooks/Cole Publishing CO.

Kohler, F. W., & Strain, P.S. (1992). "Applied Behavior Analysis and the movement to restructure schools: Compatibilities and opportunities for collaboration." *Journal of Behavioral Education* 2(4): 367-390.

Lavigna, G. W., Christian, L., & Willis, T.J. (2005). "Developing behavioral services to meet defined standards within a national system of specialist education services." *Pediatric-Rehabilitation* 8(2): 144-155.

Leblanc, M. P., Ricciardi, J.N., Luiselli, J.K. (2005). "Improving Discrete Trial Instruction by Paraprofessional staff through and abbreviated Performance Feedback Intervention." *Education and Treatment of Children* 28(1): 76-82.

Leaf, R.B., & McEachin, J.J. (1999). <u>A Work in Progress: Behavior Management Strategiesand a Curriculum for Intensive Behavioral Treatment of Autism</u>. New York, NY: Different Roads to Learning.

Leaf, R.B., McEachin, J.J. & Taubman, M. (2008). <u>Sense and Nonsense: It Has To Be Said</u>. New York, NY: Different Roads to Learning.

Martens, B. K., & Ardoin, S.P. (2002). "Training School Psychologist in behavior support consultation." *Child and Family Behavior Therapy* 24(1-2): 147-163.

Moxley, R. A. (2004). "Advance Behavioral Application in Schools: A Review of R. Douglas Greer's Designing Teaching Strategies: An Applied Behavior Analysis Systems Approach." *Analysis of Verbal Behavior* 20: 135-140.

Mulick, J. A., & Butter, E.M. (2002). "Educational advocacy for children with autism." *Behavioral Interventions* 17(2): 57-74.

National Research Council (2001). <u>Educating Children with Autism</u>. Washington, D.C.: National Academy Press.

Neef, N. A., Mace, F.C., Shea, M.C., & Shade, D. (1992). "Effects of reinforcer rate and reinforcer quality on time allocation: Extensions of matching theory to educational settings." *Journal of Applied Behavior Analysis* 25(3): 691-699.

Olley, J. G., Rosenthal, S.L. (1985). "Current Issues in school services for students with autism." *School Psychology Review* 14(2): 223-243.

Petscher, E. S., & Bailey, J.S. (2006). "Effects of training, prompting, and self monitoring on staff behavior in a classroom for students with disabilities." *Journal of Applied Behavior Analysis* 39(2): 215-226.

Roscoe, E. M., Fisher, W.W. Glover, A.C., Vokert, V.M. (2006). "Evaluating the relative effects of feedback and contingent money for staff training of stimulus preference assessments." *Journal of Applied Behavior Analysis* 39(1): 63-77.

Simpson, R. L. (1995). "Individualized education programs for students with autism: Including parents in the process." *Focus on Autistic Behavior* 10 (4): 11-15.

Skinner, M. E., & Hales, M.R. (1992). "Classroom teachers "explanations" of student behavior: One possible barrier to the acceptance and use of applied behavior analysis procedures in the schools." *Journal of Educational and Psychological Consultation* 3(4): 219-232.

Smith, T., Parker, T., Taubmann, M., & Lovaas, I.O. (1992). Transfer of staff training from workshop to group homes: A failure to generalize across settings. *Research in Developmental Disabilities,* 13(1) 57-71.

Spann, S. J., Kohler, F.W., & Soenksen, D. (2003). "Examining Parents Involvement in and Perceptions of Special Education Services: An Interview with Families in a Parent Support Group." *Focus on Autism and Other Developmental Disabilities* 18(4): 228-237.

Sugai, G., & Horner, R.H. (2002). "Introduction to the special series on positive behavior supports in school." *Journal of Emotional and Behavioral Disorders* 10(3): 130-135.

Zhang, C., & Bennert, T. (2003). "Facilitation in meaningful participation of culturally and linguistically diverse families in the IFSP and IEP process." *Focus on Autism and Other Developmental Disabilities* 18(1): 51-59.

Chapter 4

WHAT MAKES A GOOD CLASSROOM?

By Ron Leaf, Rick Schroeder & Leticia Palos-Rafuse

There are numerous factors that contribute to a good classroom. First and foremost, the teacher and the aides are essential to the quality of the class. As discussed previously, the support of Administration, from the Superintendent to the Principal, is critical. When one observes a classroom, there are several factors that are telling about the quality of that classroom.

USE OF REINFORCEMENT

Perhaps one of the most important ingredients of success in students and teachers alike is the quality of the reinforcers that are available. "Good" classes have extensive and high-quality reinforcers (Lerman, Kelley, Vorndran, Kuhn, & LaRue, 2002; McKerchar & Thompson, 2004). It is not surprising since reinforcement will serve as motivation for change. Naturally, it is a poor sign when staff is resistant to the use of reinforcement.

Staff resistance is often based on observing reinforcement being used poorly as well as their misunderstanding of reinforcement. Often, they comment that students should behave and learn without reinforcement. First, if a student can learn without reinforcement, then it is unlikely that they will require special services. Furthermore, reinforcement is a natural part of daily life whether one is aware of it or not. Everyone needs reinforcement. The question is how much and what kind. For individuals with special needs, we cannot take reinforcement for granted. It is something that has to be given special consideration, just like a person who has diabetes needs to be on a special diet.

In fact, potential reinforcers exist throughout a typical class routine. However, they tend to be non-contingent and therefore are not being utilized in the most effective way. Things like being the line leader, going for a drink of water, running errands for the teacher, getting extra recess time, or having free time, are all things that can be employed as reinforcers with very little additional effort. In fact, most classrooms have some kind of contingency management system in place. Often, they tend to be *response cost systems* that involve the potential loss of privileges, warnings, and other negative consequences. There tends to be less emphasis on positive motivational systems. What is needed is a more systematic approach, more reliance on positive reinforcement, and generally a higher rate of reinforcement. It is important not to become judgmental about how much reinforcement a student receives. Some people simply need more reinforcement.

Initially, and possibly for a long time, students will need a very high rate of reinforcement. Students may also need more tangible and artificial reinforcers (e.g., small toys, stickers, or even food) to start. Over time, it will be possible to fade out this kind of reinforcement as the student becomes more fluent in the desired skills and therefore less effort is required to accomplish the work. The goal is for reinforcement to eventually be provided as naturally as possible and hopefully identical to how it is utilized in classrooms for typically developing students. It may, however, take some time to get there.

Good classrooms not only have extensive reinforcement available but they utilize them correctly. Effective use of reinforcement requires systematic application. The following are perhaps some of the most important factors in the use of reinforcement (Leaf & McEachin, 1999):

1. "REINFORCERS" SHOULD BE REINFORCING

Have you ever heard someone say, "Oh, that student doesn't like reinforcers"? What this really means is that the teacher has not correctly identified what to use as reinforcement. By definition, whether it is a toy, an activity, or engagement with another person, in order for it to be a reinforcer, it has to be motivating enough to produce behavior change. Reinforcers are determined by the student, not the teacher. If a student does not show a high level of interest, does not show some positive emotional response, and does not seek out what you are using as a reinforcer, then most likely it is not actually a reinforcer.

2. REINFORCEMENT SHOULD BE CONTINGENT

Contingency is the essence of the proper use of reinforcement. This means that the child only gains access to the reinforcer when the targeted behavior is displayed. Contingency also means that the student does not experience reinforcement when inappropriate or disruptive behaviors occur.

It should be absolutely clear to the child what needs to be done to earn the reinforcer. As a consultant observing a classroom, when we can easily discern what a student has to do in order to earn a reinforcer, even without asking any of the staff, we know reinforcement is being used contingently. It should be obvious to anyone who observes in the room (e.g., cafeteria worker, parent, principle) what the contingency is. If we cannot figure it out, it is unlikely that the student understands what he needs to do to earn the reinforcer and most probably, the reinforcer is not being used consistently.

3. USE A VARIETY OF REINFORCERS

An ironic fact of using reinforcement is that each time a reinforcer is used it becomes less reinforcing. This is termed reinforcer satiation. Consider when you first listen to a new music CD. You are excited about hearing it and you want to listen to it again and again. However, after each time you hear it, you become a little less interested in hearing it again. After a while, you may even become totally disinterested and it goes on the shelf. If classrooms are only using a small selection of reinforcers throughout the day, then those reinforcers will soon become obsolete. To help slow this satiation, a wide variety of reinforcers should be utilized so that the presentation of each reinforcer is spread throughout the day.

4. CONTINUALLY DEVELOP NEW REINFORCERS

Identification of new reinforcers should be a continuous process throughout the school year since reinforcers will inevitably satiate at some point. Do not give up quickly when you find that a student does not respond to some new item. You have to sell it!! Help him discover how fun it can be by projecting your own enthusiasm and excitement into the activity. Pair new items with existing reinforcers until the student becomes familiar enough with the new items to actually enjoy them. Many of the best reinforcers require some exposure and learning how to utilize the item before it becomes something that the individual begins to seek out.

Do not allow the student to become overly dependent on just a few favorite things. You will have to ensure that other items are sampled consistently in between times of having access to the most preferred items. The more they become focused on a certain item, the less often it should be made available in order to prevent them from becoming too narrow in their choices.

Beware of arbitrariness in making choices. Often times a student will immediately reject something without really giving the item a chance to see that it can be fun. Even if they reject the item, take a minute to stay with it and try to sell it by letting them see you having fun with it, and also for them to realize that you will not immediately replace it with some other item. If you too quickly honor the arbitrary rejection of items, you are actually reinforcing them for being hasty and picky.

5. PAIR SOCIAL REINFORCERS WITH TANGIBLE ITEMS

Some children do not find praise or social contact sufficiently motivating to learn appropriate behavior. But it is important for all students to discover the value and enjoyment of social engagement. This is a critical process in moving students toward more natural reinforcers. One way we can build this is to pair the presentation of tangible reinforcers (e.g., toys, activities, privileges, treats, etc.) with social reinforcers (e.g., praise, tickles, high-fives, thumbs-up, etc.). The more these are paired together, the more reinforcing social engagement becomes.

6. USE AGE APPROPRIATE REINFORCERS

When choosing reinforcers, we should look for items that are appropriate for the child's age. Some older children find toddler toys, videos, music, books, or movies very engaging and exciting. However, to use these reinforcers is very stigmatizing and undignified. Continuing these interests will most likely reduce a child's attractiveness to potential friends and acquaintances. Furthermore, if they are not exposed to more age appropriate reinforcers they will most likely be uninterested in engaging with peers their age who are playing with age appropriate toys. Finally, by using age inappropriate reinforcers (as well as materials, dress, etc.) one tends to view the child as being very young and unconsciously treat them in a more childish manner with lower expectations. This can not only become a self fulfilling prophecy, but is ultimately unfair and disrespectful to the child.

7. INITIALLY, REINFORCEMENT SHOULD OCCUR IMMEDIATELY

In order to establish a strong contingency of reinforcement for engagement in appropriate behavior, the delivery of reinforcement should occur immediately upon the display of the appropriate behavior each time it occurs. This maximizes the child's ability to learn the contingency between displaying appropriate behavior and earning reinforcement. Research clearly demonstrates that immediate reinforcement produces the highest rate of behavior change. (Grindle & Remmington, 2002). Once the student understands more complex contingencies, then the process of fading reinforcement can begin.

8. DO NOT WAIT TOO LONG TO FADE REINFORCEMENT

Even though it is important to use high levels of reinforcement initially, we do want to move quickly towards more natural levels of reinforcement. Early in the fading process this may mean earning a reinforcer every other time, or every third time an appropriate behavior is displayed. Later, it may mean developing a token economy system. Fading reinforcement also means moving toward more natural reinforcers as quickly as possible. Some students move very quickly due to their interest in more natural reinforcers such as praise and social activities and, yes, even the love of learning. Yet some students need more time being exposed to pairings of primary and social reinforcement to move toward natural levels. Additionally, some students may always need some level of artificial reinforcement in order to continue to make progress, but the goal is always to attempt to fade reinforcement.

9. INITIALLY, LABEL THE BEHAVIOR BEING REINFORCED

When teaching new behavior, it is important that children learn to identify the behavior that is being reinforced. We can do this by labeling the behavior when we reinforce (e.g., "Good sitting," "Nice calm," "Great looking," etc.). The more clearly we label behavior, the easier it is for the child to understand the connection between their behavior and the reinforcement. Additionally, when we provide corrective feedback, the child will understand more quickly what specifically is being done incorrectly (e.g., "That's not good sitting," "You need to look," etc.). Research shows that stating the contingency speeds the discrimination between desired and undesired behavior.

10. UTILIZE DIFFERENTIAL REINFORCEMENT

We can differentiate the level of reinforcement we give according to the quality of the behavior. Responses the student makes and the type of behavior being exhibited are not merely "right" or "wrong". Sometimes it is fantastic, sometimes it is pretty good, sometimes it is rather mediocre. Superior performance should result either in a higher amount of the reinforcer (e.g., more of it or longer to play) or better quality reinforcement (e.g., a more preferred item). When a variety of reinforcers has been developed, these reinforcers can be categorized into varying levels of motivational power. In general, we distinguish between: A=highest interest; B=moderate interest; C=lower interest (but still reinforcing). Great responding and behavior get an A-level reinforcer. Lesser quality responding and behavior get a B or even a C reinforcer. Lastly, poor responding and poor behavior get corrective feedback and no reinforcement.

SYSTEMATIC BEHAVIOR PROGRAMS

In order to remediate behavior problems and thereby increase students' responsiveness to learning, detailed behavior programs must be developed and implemented. Naturally, staff must be trained so that they can effectively implement the programs. They must know how to react appropriately when disruptive behaviors are exhibited, which we term "reactive programming." More importantly, staff needs to be fully aware of and prepared to implement systematic and comprehensive programs to teach alternative behaviors so that students can appropriately meet their needs, which is termed "proactive programming" (Thompson, Iwata, Hanle, Dozier, & Samaha, 2003).

The need to implement systematic behavior programs might seem obvious. Typically however, educational programs are so focused on academic skills that behavioral needs are overlooked. All too often, behavior programs have not been developed or even discussed. Therefore, staff must "wing it" when disruptive behaviors occur. Without preparation, staff will most likely react in ways that are ineffective or, worse, may actually contribute to an increase in disruptive behaviors. They may react emotionally, thereby providing negative attention which may possibly reinforce the disruptive behavior and is very unlikely to have a deterrent effect. Or they may remove children from tasks, and thereby reinforce avoidance-motivated behaviors. Consequently, the effectiveness of education will be greatly compromised.

Some classrooms focus entirely on providing consequences for disruptive behavior, without any effort in teaching replacement behavior. This often results in children developing new disruptive behaviors in order to replace the ones that have been extinguished. It is unlikely that a child with ASD can figure out on his own what would be the most appropriate way to get his needs met. Proactive programs need to be carefully designed and systematically taught to enable the child to develop appropriate replacement behaviors and skills. Without a strong emphasis on teaching behavior proactively, there is little chance that a child will learn to function independently (Leaf & McEachin, 1999).

Along with having systematic behavior programs in place, the staff must be consistent in implementing the program throughout the school day, as well as at home with parents. Every staff member should know every child's behavior program. Inconsistencies between staff only lead to confusion for the child, blurring the contingency between earning reinforcement and appropriate behavior. Some staff may reinforce behavior that others are working hard to reduce, which most likely only creates confusion on the part of the child and certainly interferes with the goal of eliminating disruptive behavior. In short, consistency is critical in making positive behavioral change!

CONTINUOUS TEACHING

Every second of the day is precious. In order for a student to catch up as much as possible there has to be limited down time. A student has to be engaged in meaningful education from the time they get on the bus until the time they get off the bus. Even the bus driver is part of the educational team! The learning must continue when they get off the bus at home as well.

In the early stages of intervention, children cannot afford long holidays. Not only will they not make the progress that is necessary for them to reach their potential but they will also experience significant regression! Please see *Sense and Nonsense: It Has To Be Said!* (Leaf, McEachin & Taubman, 2008) for a more thorough discussion of regression.

You will often hear that a child needs to have some down time in order to decompress. This is a commonly held belief that does not withstand critical analysis. Research on intensive intervention clearly demonstrates that children can not only tolerate a high level of structure, but they indeed thrive on it. Their downtime is often filled with inappropriate self-stimulation. In the same way that we would not want an alcoholic to use relaxation time as an opportunity to drink, we cannot let a child with ASD have time to self-stimulate. Moreover, there is so much for them to learn and they are so far behind that they cannot afford to waste time.

In order to capture every teaching moment, a teacher must be working continuously. Besides the ongoing instruction, time will be needed to prepare, review data and meet with the team. All too often, teachers are not given sufficient planning time. So they have to squeeze in a few minutes here and there in order to quickly chat with staff. Team planning is so essential that time needs to be built into the schedule so that it is a quality process, not just something done on the fly nor something that forces them to sacrifice precious teaching time.

COMPREHENSIVE PROGRAMMING

We need to educate the whole child! Although language and academics are important, there are other areas that are every bit as critical. Educational plans that address social areas are vital. Students who have good social skills will have a much higher quality of life. By having meaningful friendships, loneliness will be reduced and happiness will increase. We have found that when children have a significant friendship, they are less likely to seek negative attention. They are getting their attentional needs met in an appropriate manner. There are other benefits to developing social skills such as the increase of language skills because of the modeling of natural and more appropriate communication. Additionally, once a child acquires friendships, peer pressure can become an effective tool in controlling behavior problems. We have often found when a student becomes truly concerned about what other students think about him/her, disruptive behaviors come to a screaming halt.

Educational plans also need to address play and recreational skills. Once again, learning play skills will greatly enhance the quality of life. And once again there are multiple other benefits. Play skills are an important part of socialization. Additionally, appropriate play activities become the replacement for stereotypical behavior.

Self-help skills are another domain that good educational programs must address. Children's hygiene, eating and toileting need to be part of the educational curriculum as well. Developing good self-help skills leads to greater levels of independence and strongly enhances the quality of life for many children. At older age levels (but not much older!) we need to focus on daily living skills and community integration. Also, much sooner than people often expect, we need to start developing vocational skills.

NATURAL INTERVENTION

Although systematic programming needs to be part of a good classroom, it is essential that staff use as natural a style as possible. If the teaching is artificial and therefore unnatural, there will be many negative repercussions. The more natural the intervention, the greater the generalization will be. If students are trained in a highly rote manner, they will not be able to respond to the more casual style that they will encounter in most settings. Whenever possible, we want students to participate in less restrictive classrooms. In these classes, it is more likely that teachers will use more natural language and sound less scripted. Therefore, it is critical that students hear similar language so that their performance does not deteriorate when they are being taught by teachers who use a natural style.

Natural intervention is important because it will result in modeling more appropriate language. When the staff uses a more artificial style, students will mimic such language. It becomes clear that they have been exposed to unnatural treatment. We are well aware that we cannot talk to every child with ASD as we might talk to a child with typically developing language. And, of course the implementation of natural language has to be done in a systematic way. But, staff should always be pushing the envelope, just not so much that it becomes frustrating to the student or that they become unable to learn. These thoughts needed to be connected, but feel free to make your own changes.

A balance of individual, small group, and large group instruction also develops skills that will assist students in moving toward less restrictive settings. Least restrictive classrooms rarely provide time for individual instruction, and rely primarily on large group instruction and to a lesser degree on small group instruction. If the goal is for students to meaningfully participate in a less restrictive classroom, they need to be able to maintain appropriate behavior, attend, and respond meaningfully in group settings.

OTHER INDICATORS OF A GOOD CLASSROOM

1. A classroom schedule that is closely followed on a daily basis.

2. Log books for each student that contain objective behavioral data, curricular data, behavioral programs and IEPs.

3. Organized teaching and play materials that are easily available for staff and students. Note: If students are grabbing at materials, then they need to be taught not to do so!

4. Age appropriate teaching materials, including pictures and posters on walls.

5. Clearly and naturally defined areas for play, centers, and groups. Partitions create a sterile and artificial learning environment and do not promote generalization.

REFERENCES

Barry, L. M., & Singer, G.H. (2001). "A family in crisis: Replacing the aggressive behavior of a child with autism toward an infant sibling." *Journal of Positive Behavior Intervention* 3(1): 28-38.

Cuvo, A. J., Lerch, L.J., Leurquin, D.A., Gaffaney, T.J., & Poppen, R.L. (1998). "Response allocation to concurrent fixed-ratio reinforcement schedules with work requirements by adults with mental retardation and typical preschool children." *Journal of Applied Behavior Analysis* 31(2): 43-63.

De-Luca, R. V., & Holborn, S.W. (1992). "Effects of a variable ratio reinforcement schedule with changing criteria on exercise in obese and non obese boys." *Journal of Applied Behavior Analysis* 25(3): 671-679.

DeLeon, I. G., Neidert, P.L., Anders, B.M., & Rodriguez-Catter, V. (2001). "Choices between positive and negative reinforcement during treatment for escape maintained behavior." *Journal of Applied Behavior Analysis* 34(4): 521-525.

Friedman, M. P., & Gelfand, H. (1964). "Transfer effects in discrimination learning." *Journal of Mathematical Psychology* 1(1): 204-214.

Garfinkle, A. N., & Schwartz, I.S. (2002). "Peer Imitation: Increasing social interactions in children with autism and other developmental disabilities in inclusive preschool classrooms." *Topics in Early Childhood Special Education* 22(1): 26-38.

Grindle, C. F., & Remington, B. (2002). "Discrete Trial training for autistic children when reward is delayed: A comparison of conditioned cue value and response making." *Journal of Applied Behavior Analysis* 35(2): 187-190.

Gutierrez, G. R. (1984). "Student preference of sensory reinforcers." *Education and Training of the Mentally Retarded* 19(2): 108-113.

Hagopian, L. P., Toole, L.M., Long, E.S., Bowman, L.G., & Lieving, G.A. (2004). "A comparison of dense to lean arid fixed lean schedules of alternative reinforcement and extinction." *Journal of Applied Behavior Analysis* 37(3): 323-337.

Hanley, G. P., Iwata, B.A., & Thompson, R.H. (2001). "Reinforcement schedule thinning following treatment with functional communication training." *Journal of Applied Behavior Analysis* 34(1): 17-38.

Hoch, H., McComas, J.J., Thompson, A.L., & Paone, D. (2002). "Concurrent reinforcement schedules: Behavior Change and Maintenance without extinction." *Journal of Applied Behavior Analysis* 35(2): 155-169.

Hudson, E., & Demyer, M.K. (1968). "Food as a reinforcer in educational therapy of autistic children." *Behavior Research and Therapy* 6(1): 37-43.

Kamps, D., Dugan, E.P., Leonard, B.R., & Daoust, P.M. (1994). "Enhanced small group instruction using choral responding and student interaction for children with autism and developmental disabilities." *American Journal on Mental Retardation* 99(1): 60-73.

Kamps, D., Walker, D., Locke, P., Delquadri, J., & Hall, R.V. (1990). "A comparison of one-to-one instruction by peers, one-to-one instruction by adults, and small group instruction with children with autism. *Education and Treatment of Children* 12: 197-215.

Kamps, D., Walker, D., Maher, J., & Rotholz, D. (1992). "Academic and Environmental effects of small group arrangements in classrooms for students with autism and other developmental disabilities." *Journal of Autism and Developmental Disorders* 22(2): 277-293.

Kamps, D. M., Walker, D., Dugan, E.P., Leonard, B.R., Thibadeau, S., Marshall, K., Grossnickle, L., & Boland, B. (1991). "Small group instruction for school aged students with autism and developmental disabilities." *Focus on Autistic Behavior* 6(4): 1-18.

Kodak, T., Miltenberger, R.G., Romaniuk, C. (2003). "The effects of differential negative reinforcement of other behavior and non-contingent escape on compliance." *Journal of Applied Behavior Analysis* 36(3): 379-382.

Leaf, R.B., & McEachin, J.J. (1999).   A Work in Progress: Behavior Management Strategiesand a Curriculum for Intensive Behavioral Treatment of Autism.   New York, NY: Different Roads to Learning.

Leaf, R.B., McEachin, J.J. & Taubman, M. (2008).   Sense and Nonsense: It Has To Be Said.   New York, NY: Different Roads to Learning.

Lerman, D. C., Kelley, M.E., Vorndran, C.M., Kuhn, S.A., LaRue, R.H. (2002). "Reinforcement magnitude and responding and responding during treatment with differential reinforcement." *Journal of Applied Behavior Analysis* 35(1): 29-48.

McGinley, H. (1970). "The Development of a conditioned reinforcer through direct and vicarious reinforcement." *Journal of Experimental Social Psychology* 6(3): 364-377.

McKerchar, P. M., & Thompson, R.H. (2004). "A descriptive analysis of potential reinforcement contingencies in the preschool classroom." *Journal of Applied Behavior Analysis* 37(4): 431-444.

Paclawskyj, T. R., & Vollmer, T.R. (1995). "Reinforcer assessment for children with developmental disabilities and visual impairments." *Journal of Applied Behavior Analysis* 28(2): 219-224.

Patel, M. R., Piazza, C.C., Martinez, C.J., Volkert, V.M., & Santana, C.M. (2002). "An evaluation of two differential reinforcement procedures with escape extinction to treat food refusal." *Journal of Applied Behavior Analysis* 35(4): 363-374.

Phillips, D., Fischer, S.C., & Singh, R. (1977). "A children's reinforcement survey schedule." *Journal of Behavior Therapy and Experimental Psychiatry* 8(2): 131-134.

Roane, H. S., Fisher, W.W., Sgro, G.M., Falcomata, T.S., & Pabico, R.R. (2004). "An alternative method of thinning reinforcer delivery during differential reinforcement." *Journal of Applied Behavior Analysis* 37(2): 213-218.

Schoen, S. F., & Ogden, S. (1995). "Impact of time delay, observational learning, and attention cuing upon word recognition during integrated small group instructions." *Journal of Autism and Developmental Disorders* 25(5): 503-519.

Thompson, R. H., & Iwata, B.A. (2005). "A review of Reinforcement Control Procedures." *Journal of Applied Behavior Analysis* 38(2): 257-278.

Thompson, R. H., Iwata, B.A., Hanley, G.P., Dozier, C.L., & Samaha, A.L. (2003). "The effects of extinction, non-contingent reinforcement, and differential reinforcement of other behavior as control procedures." *Journal of Applied Behavior Analysis* 36(2): 221-238.

Van-Houten, R., & Nau, P.A. (1980). "A comparison of the effects of fixed and variable ratio schedules of reinforcement on the behavior of deaf children." *Journal of Applied Behavior Analysis* 13(1): 13-21.

Walls, R. T. (1973). "Delay of reinforcement development." *Child Development* 44(3): 689-692.

Wider, D. A., Normand, M., & Atwell, J. (2005). "Non-contingent reinforcement as treatment for food refusal and associated self injury." *Journal of Applied Behavior Analysis* 38(4): 549-553.

Zarcone, J. R., Crosland, K., Fisher, W.W., Worsdell, A.S., & Herman, K. (1999). "A brief method for conducting a negative reinforcement assessment." *Research in Developmental Disabilities* 20(2): 107-124.

Chapter 5

WHAT MAKES A GOOD TEACHER?

By Ron Leaf, Rick Schroeder & Leticia Palos-Rafuse

Over the years, we have had the opportunity to observe many outstanding teachers. While we would wish for some scientific research which would help us identify the characteristics of highly effective teachers, we are left to draw on our clinical experience. Moreover, it is not black and white. There are many shades in between. Given those qualifiers, the following are seven of the factors that we have found to be associated with effective teachers.

RECEPTIVE

Often it does not really matter if teachers have extensive knowledge about ASD or if they are novices. The more important question is, are they open to change? We will most likely be presenting new information and new ways of looking at old problems. Moreover, we will be making suggestions and asking staff to consider making changes. If they are defensive and unwilling to even consider changing, then it is unlikely that training will be productive. Just as in athletics, those that are most coachable will be the best and most reliable performers.

****IRONY** THOSE WHO HAVE THE MOST EXPERIENCE ARE
OFTEN THE MOST DIFFICULT TO TRAIN!**

This is not to say that we are opposed to staff questioning our recommendations or disagreeing with our philosophy. Questioning and being skeptical, in fact is quite healthy and heavily encouraged. This is the only way to "clear the air," provide clarification, and resolve issues. It is far more productive for a teacher to be forthcoming if there is lack of confidence in the recommendations being made. There may be some confusion that can be clarified or there may be some modifications of the recommendations that may make more sense for the classroom. We are just stressing the need for teachers to be open to change.

SYSTEMATIC

Effective instruction requires a teacher to be extremely systematic! It is critical that each child have sensible objectives and that there be a detailed plan on how to teach those objectives (Fantuzzo & Atkins, 1992). If one attempts to wing it, it is extremely unlikely that the child will meet those objectives rapidly, if at all! Besides a detailed teaching plan, there must also be a comprehensive behavioral plan. Teachers must know what they are going to do when a student exhibits a particular behavior problem and, more importantly, be actively teaching replacement behaviors and skills.

The day must be extremely organized. Every minute has to be productive and well-planned. Recess, snack time and even entering the classroom present important teaching moments. One simply cannot afford to let any of them be wasted. In order to be ready it is necessary to plan in advance ample occasions for working on each objective and know what teaching strategies will be utilized, as well as what consequences are going to be used. Even incidental teaching requires careful planning to maximize the opportunities that will arise throughout the course of the day. Every teaching moment needs to be analyzed on the fly to determine how well the objectives are being met and what adjustments can be made on the spot. Sufficient data must be collected so that longer term trends can be determined, student progress can be documented, and one can determine the effectiveness of teaching strategies. If goals are being met, the teacher knows that instruction is on track and should be anticipating the next steps for the student. If the data reveals that a student is not improving, then changes need to occur.

ADAPTABLE

Although it is important to be systematic, it is also necessary to be flexible. This may seem to be a contradictory concept, but it really isn't. It means that you need to have a plan, but that you are willing to change the plan quickly when necessary. To best meet the needs of the students, teachers cannot become so invested in a program or methodology that they are unwilling to make necessary modifications.

Adaptability will be enhanced by having a thorough knowledge of curriculum. It is essential to be able to quickly modify programs. If a student demonstrates mastery, then a teacher needs to know the next phase. Conversely, if a student is experiencing repeated failures, then a teacher needs to know how to move backward in the program.

A teacher also needs to be able and willing to change teaching strategies. Being able to increase or decrease the complexity of their language, altering reinforcement or increasing or decreasing structure will all be critical. Good teachers simply do not get stuck, they are willing to make changes to best serve their students.

OBJECTIVE

In order to be an effective teacher, one must remain objective. This does not mean being cold or aloof! It means that one must make decisions with one's head and not just one's heart (Fantuzzo, et.al., 1992). It is human nature that if we like someone we are much more willing to see them in the most positive light. However, that may lead us to see progress when it is not really there. Conversely, if it is difficult for us to find the student likeable, then it may be that we are not seeing progress even when there is! Here are three ways to help us remain objective: 1) Collect data; 2) Do not personalize the student behavior or motives; and 3) Do not become dependent on reinforcement from the student.

ENGAGING

Clinical research has shown that the best predictor of a client success in psychotherapy is that the client connects with their therapist. That is, the client must respect and like the therapist in order to be drawn into the therapy process (Emmelkamp, 1988). It is no different for teachers and their students. All of our favorite teachers, and the ones who made the biggest impact in our lives, are the ones to whom we felt most connected. If a student likes a teacher, the student is more likely to exhibit more appropriate behavior and work hard on the lessons. However, if a student does not connect with his teacher then the student most likely will be far less influenced by what the teacher thinks and will not be eager to spend time with the teacher.

One might now ask, how do I as a teacher connect with a student who seems uninterested in connecting with me? The answer lies within the student interests. If a teacher spends time with a student to explore what the student's likes and dislikes are, then a teacher has the opportunity to make connections through these interests. Initially, the teacher should use preferred activities, toys, music, games, etc. to build connections with the students. The mere fact that the teacher is presenting these likes to the students opens the door for building a connection. To take it further, the teacher can make herself part of the fun, interacting in a friendly way while the student is engaging with preferred items, showing interest in what the student is doing, sharing different ways to use the items, and making the whole activity fun together. After doing this many times, the student will be more likely to approach the teacher to play with these items together.

Creativity helps a lot. Even the most reserved student with ASD has somewhere within him a sense of humor. Our mission is to discover where that place is and use humor to draw out the student. Being dramatic and creating suspense helps make a connection with the student. Being silly and playful also helps. Above all, we must not get discouraged nor give up too quickly. Many times we observe teachers heading in the right direction, but simply not going far enough. Perhaps this is because they lack the confidence that their efforts will pay off or because the student is not very responsive. If you lead, the students will follow. Lead bravely!

PROFESSIONAL

A common characteristic of teachers who run a well-organized and productive classroom is their sense and display of professionalism. Punctuality, dress, attitude, and communication are essential characteristics that make the difference between a teacher who runs a pleasant working environment versus an environment that may feel chaotic, stressed, and generally unproductive. Teachers are the captains of their classrooms, and it is essential that they be role models for their staff and students' behavior in the classroom. Teachers set the tone for how each and every day will unfold for the staff, students, and parents. Those who lack the ability to lead their classrooms in a supportive yet directed manner often find that even the daily routine is difficult to implement in a consistent fashion.

Our own punctuality creates and reinforces expectations for staff to be on time and organized, not only when arriving to work, but also when returning from breaks and lunches. Most staff changes occur during natural transition times in the day, and this is when some students may experience behavioral difficulties. Thus, it is essential that the staff consistently be there on time so as not to create any disruptions to the class schedule or routine. Timeliness also applies to the day's schedule of events. The most organized and productive classes are ones that develop a daily schedule that is well suited to meeting the students' needs and follow a consistent schedule. When classes vary too much on most days, the feel is one of disorganization and ineffective programming.

Professional, yet comfortable working dress conveys that this is a serious, but enjoyable working environment. Dress that is too casual may lead to the impression that the classroom is not a place with a serious mission. This may also be misperceived by staff, parents and others as lack of caring. Appearance definitely makes an impression and we want that impression to be one of professionalism and dedication.

Good communication between the staff and teacher, as well as between the teacher and parents builds trust and a sense of leadership (McVay, 1998). A teacher needs to be able to talk to the staff positively and effectively about various issues that may be arising within the classroom. The staff needs to be informed as to any changes in behavioral or curricular programming, and also need to be given feedback about their performance. Communication with the parents is a necessity, since their child may not possess the ability to inform them of what is occurring during their day. It becomes crucial that the parents be informed by the teacher so as to stay current with how their child is performing and so that they may continue consistent programming while their child is at home.

A positive attitude is one of the most important areas of professionalism when taking the role of a teacher in a special education classroom. It is our experience that overall satisfaction in the classroom is heavily weighted on how the teacher presents his or her attitude toward children who might have difficult behavioral issues. Those who take on the challenge with a drive to help students learn new and more productive ways of functioning in their environments, no matter how challenging, frustrating, or overwhelming the situation, have a more satisfying experience within their classrooms. There will always be days when a teacher might be angry with a student's behavior, but the best way to deal with this anger is to remain positive and look for more effective strategies to teach the student an appropriate alternative behavior that will benefit the student and cause others around him to see him in the most positive light.

BALANCED

Even though we are encouraging teachers to incorporate these qualities into their styles of teaching, trying to change too much too quickly could have a negative impact within the class. Even teachers who run excellent classrooms set modest goals for themselves and staff that are not only attainable but can be achieved within a reasonable amount of time, making success much more likely. When more and more successes are achieved, then it becomes easier and easier to make positive changes that benefit the students and staff.

Lastly, we have experienced fabulous and dedicated teachers who run extraordinary classrooms, but find themselves frustrated and unsatisfied with the job they are doing. This is primarily due to overexertion in response to consultant recommendations or parents' suggestions and requests. It is very enticing for a consultant or a parent to make seemingly endless recommendations to a teacher who is open to suggestions and is compelled to implement each one of them meticulously. This has even come to the point where some incredibly talented teachers and staff have left their positions for ones that are less stressful and time consuming. We must not get caught in the trap of overwhelming a good teacher who may already be overwhelmed and who does not want to give the impression that she is not open or receptive to others' advice. We must be reinforcing to the teachers who are making the right commitment to their students and staff and acknowledge the positive changes that they are accomplishing on a daily basis (White, 2004).

REFERENCES

Anderson, D. M., & Ritter, S.A. (1987). Training district personnel as peer consultants and in-service leaders: Implementation and evaluation of a training program. *Special Services in School, 4*(1-2), 77-93.

Babdad, E. (1990). Measuring and changing teachers' differential behavior as perceived by students and teachers. *Journal of Educational Psychology, 82*(4), 683-690.

Barry, A. L. (1994). Easing into inclusion classrooms. *The Inclusive School, December,* 3-6.

Brown, W., Horn, E., Heiser, J., & Odom, S. (1996). Innovative practices project blend: An inclusive model of early intervention services. *Journal of Early Intervention, 20*(4), 364-375.

Davis, B., Smith, T., & Donahoe, P. (2002). Evaluating supervisors in the UCLA treatment model for children with autism: Validation of an assessment procedure. *Behavior Therapy, 33*, 601-614.

Eaves, L. C., & Ho, H.H. (1997). School placement and academic achievement in children with autistic spectrum disorders. *Journal of Developmental and Physical Disabilities, 9*(4), 277-291.

Emmenlkamp, P.M. (1988). Some developments in the research of psychotherapy. Nederlands-Tijdschrift-voor-de-Psychologie-en-haar-Grensgebieden 43 (1), 5-13.

Fantuzzo, J., & Atkins, M. (1992). Applied behavior analysis for educators: Teacher centered and classroom based. *Journal of Applied Behavior Analysis, 23*, 37-42.

Fowler, S., & Baer, D. (1981). Do I have to be good all day? The timing of delayed reinforcement as a factor in generalization. *Journal of Applied Behavior Analysis, 14*(1), 13-24.

Galloway, C., & Chandler, P. (1978). The marriage of special and generic early education services. *In M. Guralnick (Ed.) Early Intervention and the Integration of Handicapped and Nonhandicapped Children,* 261-287.

Gersten, R., & Woodward, J. (1990). Rethinking the regular education initiative. Focus on the classroom teacher. *Remedial and Special Education, 11*(3), 7-16.

Giangreco, M., & Broer, S. (2005). Questionable utilization of paraprofessionals in inclusive schools: Are we addressing symptoms or causes. *Focus on Autism and Other Developmental Disabilities, 20*(1), 10-26.

Kirgin, K., Brukmann, C., Atwater, J., & Wolf, M. (1982). An evaluation of teaching family (achievement place) group homes for juvenile offenders. *Journal of Applied Behavior Analysis, 15*(1-16).

Leaf, R.B., & McEachin, J.J. (1999). A Work in Progress: Behavior Management Strategiesand a Curriculum for Intensive Behavioral Treatment of Autism. New York, NY: Different Roads to Learning.

Leaf, R.B., McEachin, J.J. & Taubman, M. (2008). Sense and Nonsense: It Has To Be Said. New York, NY: Different Roads to Learning.

McVay, P. (1998). Paraprofessionals in the classroom: What role do they play? *Disability Solutions, 3*(1), 2-9.

Myles, B. S., & Simpson, R.L. (1989). Regular educators' modification preferences for mainstreaming mildly handicapped children. *Journal of Special Education, 22*(4), 479-492.

Robertson, K., Chamberlin, B., & Kasar, C. (2003). General education teachers' relationships with included students with autism. *Journal of Autism and Developmental Disorders, 33*(2), 123-130.

White, T. (2004). The ABA classroom: A teacher's perspective. Presented at International Week, Autism Partnership, Seal Beach, California.

Chapter 6

DETERMINING THE BEST PLACEMENT AND MAKING IT WORK

By Ron Leaf & Jon Rafuse

Deciding where a student should be placed is not a simple decision. As discussed earlier, we do not believe all children should be placed in inclusion. Nor do we feel all students should be in segregated placements. Put simply, placement should be based upon which class will provide the child with the best educational opportunity for meeting their needs balanced against the social benefits that may be available through inclusion. However, this is rarely a clear choice. It is a complex decision based on multiple factors.

The student's behaviors, skill levels and learning style should be of primary consideration in placement (Leaf, McEachin & Taubman, 2008). To obtain full educational and social benefit from inclusion, a student needs to have behavioral control (Simpson & Myles, 1996). For example, if a student is being considered for inclusion, the main criterion that teams tend to consider is the absence of outwardly disruptive behaviors, such as loud tantrums, self-injury, and uncooperative behavior. We would agree that control over these behaviors is critical to the success of an educational placement, especially any type of inclusive setting. However, there are more subtle behaviors that might be overlooked because they are not disruptive, but can nevertheless undermine the success of a placement. Such insidious behaviors might not be recognized unless one is observing carefully. These behaviors include internal self-stimulation, inattention and passive non-compliance.

Imagine the student who sits perfectly during circle time, appearing to watch the teacher and the activity being presented. This child seems to have wonderful behavioral control, sitting for as long as is required, appearing to attend to the lesson. However, if that student is tested or questioned about what was just presented and cannot answer appropriately, then there is a problem. Outward appearances can be deceptive. There are many children who appear to have behavioral control, but in truth are not accessing the information being presented and are actually not learning at all. Remember that learning is an active process, not a passive experience. Upon closer examination it may become evident that the student is preoccupied with internal self-stimulation, while his mind is a million miles away. Such children have learned to mask their skill deficit by sitting nicely, being unobtrusive, and staying quiet. These students do not draw much attention to themselves, but in truth, they are the ones needing some of the highest level of intervention and likely a different placement than full inclusion.

Further, a student being considered for inclusion must display many learning, social, and academic skills. Besides having behavioral control, the student must be able to understand the material and assimilate it at a reasonable level. The student must be able to learn from group instruction, understand and utilize environmental cues, and master the material at a sufficiently rapid pace so that he does not fall progressively farther behind in the content of the lessons. This means a moderate amount of accommodation, but not so much that the nature of the learning is completely different from that of the peers.

This decision is certainly not black and white. To complicate the decision process, there are adult factors that must be taken into account. In the ideal world, these factors would not be relevant to placement considerations. But the world is not perfect so the training and skill levels of the teaching team including the teacher and the assistants assigned to the student or the classroom become important practical considerations (Horner, 2000; Kamps, 1997).

TEACHERS

Successful placement requires a teacher who has the necessary skills and is receptive to working with a student who has these types of learning needs. Unfortunately, there can be huge discrepancies among the teaching abilities you will find even within the confines of one grade in a school (Helps, Newsom, & Callias, 1999; McVay, 1998; Olley & Rosenthal, 1985; Reynolds, Martin-Reynolds, & Mark, 1982). If a placement choice must be made between either 1) a classroom designed for the student's behavioral and skill levels but run by a resistive or unskilled teacher, or 2) a classroom with a curriculum and expectations not well suited to the current level of the student but with an eager, willing and talented teacher, then sacrificing appropriateness of curriculum in favor of teacher qualifications may be the better choice. Similarly, if one must choose between a teacher with extensive experience vs. one who is open minded about the teaching process and willing to work collaboratively, we often would choose the latter.

It is not uncommon that the self-contained classroom has the more skilled instructor as well as a more tailored curriculum compared to the inclusion setting. It may be that placement in the environment with the strongest, most receptive teaching team — even though technically the setting is more restrictive — would provide the necessary instruction to propel the student forward at the fastest rate.

An analogy exists in the placement of players in profession baseball. At the beginning of their careers, baseball players benefit more from playing in the minor leagues because they will receive intensive, individualized coaching specific to their skill needs and will only be faced with a level of competition for which they are ready. Even though the minor leagues represent a restrictive setting, this is the place where they develop their skills so that they will be more successful when they reach the majors. Even later in their careers, there may be times when a player goes down to the minors to get his game back on track. Similarly, the special education classroom may provide the type of individualized teaching that will enable a student to successfully transition and benefit more fully from inclusion.

What about the situation where the personnel in special education do not have the best teaching skills? It can happen that the special education teacher has not received appropriate training and her approach may actually hinder a student's progress. Sometimes, special education teachers may be resistant to change and insist on utilizing techniques and strategies that are not effective. In such a case, the teacher in a mainstream class may actually be better equipped to teach a student even if the student does not have all the skills and behavioral characteristics that we would normally like to see.

Then there are the other professionals the student works with in the course of a school day. These staff include the educational assistant assigned either to the student specifically or to a class in general. As with the teachers leading the classrooms, these paraprofessionals need to be trained and educated in the correct implementation of effective teaching strategies (McVay, 1998). Often, the educational assistant has more impact on the student progress in school than does the teacher. Additionally, there are sessions with speech therapists, occupational therapists, resource teachers, and other providers. If even one of these professionals lacks the skills necessary to continue the behavioral and educational goals of the student, progress can be measurably impeded.

There also needs to be a match between an educator's teaching style and the student's needs and personality. There are many dimensions to the personality of a teacher. There are many ways a teacher interacts with students. There are also many teaching styles. Here are some factors that influence how much impact a teacher has on student progress:

- Some students' learning will be enhanced with a more exuberant approach (e.g., passive students), while others may learn better with a more quiet style (e.g., a student that is frequently agitated).

- Some students may need a fairly structured approach, whereas others would benefit more from flexibility.

- How the teacher deals with behavior and control issues is critical. Some teachers are more authoritative and this may be exactly what is necessary. But there are times when being lenient may actually work better!

- The complexity of a teacher's language can be an important factor. Some teachers tend to be verbose. This could either serve as fabulous modeling for language or be totally overwhelming and therefore distracting and ineffective.

- The tone and volume of a teacher's voice can be important in how the student responds within the placement.

- A teacher with outstanding social skills may do better with students that are shy and not very social.

- It would be best to have staff that are not easily intimidated to teach highly aggressive students.

- Some students benefit from a structured routine and a great deal of preparation for lessons. Others benefit from an approach fostering greater independence and self-governance.

It may be impossible to match the style and personality of the teacher with the student. Or it may be difficult to determine the ideal match. Ultimately, however, data on the student's behavior and progress will be a strong indicator of the compatibility and may serve as an indicator to keep or alter the placement.

Teaching ability is only part of the many critical elements in deciding where a student would benefit the most. Attitude also plays a huge factor. Who is excited to be the student teacher? We know that effectiveness is highly correlated with a teacher's connection with the students. Not surprisingly, teachers who do not want a student in their classroom will simply not be a good teacher for that student, no matter what their training or skill level.

A teacher's expectations regarding children with ASD are also essential (Helps, Newsom, & Callias, 1999; McVay, 1998; Olley & Rosenthal, 1985; Reynolds, Martin-Reynolds, & Mark, 1982). Does she believe that a child can progress or does she believe that the child's outcomes cannot be influenced? Those who believe and expect that a student will progress are more likely to see those results! One important basis for forming one's expectations comes from previous experiences. Obviously, if the teacher has had good experiences with inclusion then she will be a far better candidate.

Sometimes, inclusion teachers are very capable and have the necessary knowledge, but they do not want to have a special education student in their classroom. Often you will hear them say, if I wanted to be a special education teacher, that's what I would have become! The reasons for this attitude may have little to do with the student. Perhaps it is not that they themselves have negative experiences, but they have heard horror stories about the extra burdens a special education student brings to their classroom: all the meetings, the disproportionate amount of time needed for one student, and the potential disruption to their other students. They have no doubt heard talk about the incredible pressure inclusion brings. They dread the real possibilities of teaching under a microscope and the threat of litigation. You will hear the comment that they simply do not get paid enough for all this pressure. Even if the teacher could be forced to accept the student, the question still comes down to, would you want your child to be with a teacher who has this type of attitude?

ADMINISTRATION

Placement is also greatly influenced by administrative support and an administration's attitude. If principals and superintendents embrace special education, then they are far more likely to provide the necessary resources and support to make a successful placement.

Perhaps one of the most critical determinants will be the training that school personnel receive. As discussed previously, early and ongoing training is a must. The quality and frequency of training will likely be determined by the administration. Therefore, one must evaluate the site administrator (usually the principal). As with the teacher, if the principal is not enthusiastic about having a special needs student, the placement could be disastrous.

And just like the teacher, an administrator's perspective of ABA or autism can be based on previous bad experience, misconceptions, or poor training. Similar to the staff in the classroom, the administrators need to be inoculated, trained, and, above all, firmly believe in the effectiveness of these techniques. An exemplary principal must have a variety of skills as well as the capacity to manage classrooms, students, parents, teachers, educational assistants, and the entire staff of the school.

Training staff cannot be overemphasized. From the top down, from the superintendents to the bus drivers, cafeteria workers and janitorial staff, everyone must have an understanding of how they can affect a student and the best methods for doing so.

PARENTS

Parents are also an instrumental factor in the success of their child's education. Their degree of support is every bit as important as administrative support. A parent must be as excited to have a teacher as the teacher is to have a student. When a teacher feels supported and appreciated by the parents, she will be far more effective teaching the child. However, if she knows she lacks the parent's confidence, then this will certainly have a negative impact on the child's education.

Although one may want teachers to just teach and therefore not be affected by tension, this is simply not possible. Teachers' jobs are difficult enough. It is critical that parents work collaboratively with their child's teacher. Even when they disagree, there needs to be a high level of respect and appreciation. Hostility does not work. The bottom line is, regardless of the teacher's ability and administration support, look for another placement if tension and hostility exist from the parents.

As we initially discussed, this issue is not black and white. It is a complex decision with a lot of considerations. One must weigh all these factors and also closely consider the alternatives. Sometimes it is a matter of thinking out of the box and coming up with a combination of services that will best meet a student's needs. It is also a process, since the placement will change as the time goes on. What a student needs in September may be quite different from what is needed later in the year. Also, what will work this year may be far different from next year!

REFERENCES

Abelson, A. G., & Weiss, R. (1984). Mainstreaming the handicapped. The views of parents of non-handicapped pupils. *Spectrum, 2,* 27-29.

Autism Society of America (1991). Educational rights: An intro to IDEA, FERPA & section 504 of the rehabilitation act. *UCLA Evaluation Clinic,* 1-26.

Barry, A. L. (1994). Easing into inclusion classrooms. *The Inclusive School, December,* 3-6.

Boutot, A., & Bryant, D. (2005). Social integration of students with autism in inclusive settings. *Education and Training in Mental Retardation and Developmental Disabilities, 40*(1), 14-23.

Brown, W., Horn, E., Heiser, J., & Odom, S. (1996). Innovative practices project blend: An inclusive model of early intervention services. *Journal of Early Intervention, 20*(4), 364-375.

Bruder, M. B., & Staff, I. (1998). A comparison of the effects of type of classroom and service characteristics on toddlers with disabilities. *Topics in Early Childhood Special Education, 18*(1), 26-37.

Buysse, V., Goldman, B.D., & Skinner, M. (2003). Friendship formation in inclusive early childhood classrooms: What is the teacher's role? *Early Childhood Research Quarterly, 18,* 485-501.

Cohen, S. S., & Zigmond N. (1986). The social integration of learning disabled students from self-contained to mainstream elementary school setting. *Journal of Learning Disabilities, 19,* 614-618.

Cole, K. N., Mills, P.D., Dale, P.S., & Jenkins, J.R. (1991). Effect of preschool integration for children with disabilities. *Exceptional Children, 58,* 36-45.

Cooke, T., Ruskus, J., Apolloni, T., & Peck, C. (1981). Handicapped preschool children in the mainstream: Background, outcomes and clinical suggestion. *Topics in Early Childhood Special Education, 1*(1), 73-83.

Crowell, D., & Klein, T. (1981). Preventing summer loss of reading skills among primary children. *The Reading Teacher, February,* 561-564.

Cushing, L., & Kennedy, C. (1997). Academic effects of providing peer support in general education classrooms on students without disabilities. *Journal of Applied Behavior Analysis, 30*(1), 139-151.

Eaves, L. C., & Ho, H.H. (1997). School placement and academic achievement in children with autistic spectrum disorders. *Journal of Developmental and Physical Disabilities, 9*(4), 277-291.

Edgar, E., Spence, W., & Kenowitz, L. (1997). Extended school year for the handicapped: Is it working? *Journal of Special Education, 1*(4), 441-447.

Fantuzzo, J., & Atkins, M. (1992). Applied behavior analysis for educators: Teacher centered and classroom based. *Journal of Applied Behavior Analysis, 23,* 37-42.

Galloway, C., & Chandler, P. (1978). The marriage of special and generic early education services. *In M. Guralnick (Ed.) Early Intervention and the Integration of Handicapped and Nonhandicapped Children,* 261-287.

Gersten, R., & Woodward, J. (1990). Rethinking the regular education initiative. Focus on the classroom teacher. *Remedial and Special Education, 11*(3), 7-16.

Giangreco, M., & Broer, S. (2005). Questionable utilization of paraprofessionals in inclusive schools: Are we addressing symptoms or causes. *Focus on Autism and Other Developmental Disabilities, 20*(1), 10-26.

Handleman, J., Harris, S., Kristoff, B., Fuentes, F., & Alessandri, M. (1991). A specialized program for preschool children with autism. *American Speech-Language-Hearing Association, 22,* 107-110.

Hanline, M. F. (1993). Inclusion of preschoolers with profound disabilities: An analysis of children's interactions. *Journal of the Association for Person with Severe Handicaps, 17*(205-212).

Harrower, J. K. (1999). Educational inclusion of children with severe disabilities. *Journal of Positive Behavioral Intervention, 1*, 215-230.

Harrower, J. K., & Dunlap, G. (2001). Including children with autism in general education classrooms a review of effective strategies. *Behavior Modification, 25*(5), 762-784.

Helps, S., Newsom, D., & Callias, M. (1999). The teacher's view. *Autism, 3*, 287-298.

Horner, R. (2000). Positive behavior supports. *Focus on Autism and Other Developmental Disabilities, 15*(2), 97-105.

Hunt, P., Farron-Davis, F., Beckstead, S., Curtis, D., & Goetz, L. (1997). Evaluating the effects of placement of students with severe disabilities in general education versus special classes. *Journal of the Association for Person with Severe Handicaps, 22*, 127-137.

Kamps, D. (1997). The behavior analyst's role in facilitating interventions in general educational settings. *Journal of Behavioral Education, 7*(1), 81-89.

Kamps, D., Walker, D., Maher, J., & Rotholz, D. (1992). Academic and environmental effects of small group arrangements in classrooms for students with autism and other developmental disabilities. *Journal of Autism and Developmental Disorders, 22*(2), 277-293.

Knoff, H. M. (1985). Attitudes toward mainstreaming: A status report and comparison of regular and special educators in New York and Massachusetts. *Psychology in the Schools, 22*, 410-418.

Koegel, L. K., Koegel, R.L., Frea, W.D., & Fredeen, R.M. (1001). Identifying early Intervention targets for children with autism in inclusive school settings. *Behavior Modification, 25*(5), 745-761.

Ladd, G. W. (1990). Having friends, keeping friends, making friends, and being liked by peers in the classroom: Predictors of children's early school adjustment. *Child Development, 61*, 1081-1100.

Larsen, L., Goodman, L., & Glean, R. (1981). Issues in the implementation of extended school year programs for handicapped students. *Exceptional Children, 47*(4), 256-263.

Lavalle, L., K., Bierman, K.L., & Nix., L.R. (2005). The impact of first-grade friendship group experiences on child social outcomes in the fast track program. *Journal of Abnormal Child Psychology, 33*(3), 307-324.

Leaf, R.B., & McEachin, J.J. (1999). A Work in Progress: Behavior Management Strategies and a Curriculum for Intensive Behavioral Treatment of Autism. New York, NY: Different Roads to Learning.

Leaf, R.B., McEachin, J.J. & Taubman, M. (2008). Sense and Nonsense: It Has To Be Said. New York, NY: Different Roads to Learning.

Martin, E. (1974). Some thoughts on mainstreaming. *Exceptional Children, 41*(150-153).

Matson, J., Leblanc, L., & Weinheimer, B. (1999). Reliability of the Matson evaluation of social skills in individual with severe retardation (messier). *California School of Professional Psychology, 23*(4), 647-661.

McDonnell, J., Thorson, N., & McQuivey, C. (1998). The instructional characteristics of inclusive classes for elementary students with severe disabilities: An exploratory study. *Journal of Behavioral Education, 8*(4), 415-437.

McConnell, S., & Odom, S. (2000). Assessment in early Intervention and early childhood special education. *TECSE, 20*(1), 43-48.

McVay, P. (1998). Paraprofessionals in the classroom: What role do they play? *Disability Solutions, 3*(1), 2-9.

Mesibov, G. B., & Shea, V. (1996). Full inclusion and students with autism. *Journal of Autism and Developmental Disorders, 26,* 337-346.

Mulick, J. A., & Butter, E.M. (2002). Educational advocacy for children with autism. *Behavioral Interventions, 17,* 57-74.

Myles, B. S., & Simpson, R.L. (1989). Regular educators' modification preferences for mainstreaming mildly handicapped children. *Journal of Special Education, 22*(4), 479-492.

Newman, R. K., & Simpson, R.L. (1983). Modifying the least restrictive. *Behavioral Disorders, 8*(2), 103-112.

Ochs, E., Sadlik-T., Solomon, O., & Sirota, K. (2001). Inclusion as social practice: Views of children with autism. *Social Development, 10*(3), 399-419.

Odom, S., & Diamond, K. (1998). Inclusion of young children with special needs in early childhood education: The research base. *Early Childhood Research Quarterly, 13*(1), 3-25.

Olley, J., & Rosenthal, S. (1985). Current issues in school services for students with autism. *School Psychology Review, 14*(2), 166-170.

Oren, T., & Ogletree, B.T. (2000). Classrooms for students with autism: Student outcomes and program processes. *Focus on Autism and Other Developmental Disabilities, 15*(3), 170-175.

Peck, C. A., & Cooke, T.P. (1983). Benefits of mainstreaming at the early childhood level. How much can we expect? *Analysis and Intervention in Developmental Disabilities, 3,* 1-22.

Quill, K. A. (1990). A model for integrating children with autism. *Focus on Autism and Other Developmental Disabilities, 5*(4), 1-19.

Renzaglia, A., Karvonen, M., Drasgow, E., & Stoxen, C.C. (2003). Promoting a lifetime of inclusion. *Focus on Autism and Other Developmental Disabilities, 18*(3), 140-149.

Reynolds, B. J., Martin-Reynolds, J., & Mark, F.D. (1982). Elementary teachers' attitudes toward mainstreaming educable retarded students. *Education and Training of the Mentally Retarded, 17,* 171-176.

Robertson, K., Chamberlin, B., & Kasar, C. (2003). General education teachers' relationship with included students with autism. *Journal of Autism and Developmental Disorders, 33*(2), 123-130.

Sasso, G. M., Simpson, R.L., & Novak, C.G. (1985). Procedures for facilitating integration of autistic children in public school settings. *Analysis and Intervention in Developmental Disabilities, 5,* 233-246.

Schepis, M., Reid, D., Ownbey, J., & Parsons, M. (2001). Training support staff to embed teaching within natural routines of young children with disabilities in an inclusive preschool. *Journal of Applied Behavior Analysis, 34*(3), 313-327.

Simpson, R. L., Boer-Ott, S.R., & Smith-Myles, B. (2003). Inclusion of learners with autism spectrum disorders in general education settings. *Top Language Disorder, 23*(2), 116-133.

Simpson, R. L., & Myles, B.S. (1996). The general education collaboration model: A model for successful mainstreaming. *Focus on Exceptional Children, 23*(4), 1-20.

Stephens, T. M., & Benjamin, L.B. (1981). Measures of general classroom teachers attitudes towards handicapped children. *Exceptional Children, 46,* 292-297.

Strain, P., & Hoyson, M. (2000). The need for longitudinal intensive social skill intervention: Leap follow-up outcomes for children with autism. *Topics in Early Childhood Special Education, 20*(2), 116-124.

Strain, P., & Shores, R. (1977). Social reciprocity: A review of research and educational implications. *Exceptional Children*(May), 527-531.

Wilde, L., Koegel, L., & Koegel, R. Increasing success in school through priming: A training manual. *University of California, Santa Barbara.*

Williams, S., Johnson, C., & Sukhodolsky, D. (2005). The role of the school psychologist in the inclusive education of school-age children with autism spectrum disorder. *Journal of School Psychology, 43,* 117-136.

Chapter 7

CONSULTATION: WHAT IT IS AND WHAT WE DO
Increasing Receptiveness to ABA

By Marlene Driscoll, Ronald Leaf, Jennifer Styzens & Jon Rafuse

As an agency we are asked to consult to existing programs for a variety of reasons. Frequently, the site coordinator or administrator has recognized the need for ongoing staff development and support in the area of behavior assessment, development of classroom intervention plans and/or consultation for the purpose of crisis intervention. Other times, the request comes about as the result of parent initiated litigation.

The motivation for requesting services is an important consideration when approaching a site and its staff since the reasons underlying the request may be different than stated to the consultant. Additionally, the objectives the agency has in mind may be different from the needs that later on become evident. There also exists a discrepancy between what the consultation process is meant to be and how it may actually unfold in common circumstances. For example, Martens (1993) defines behavioral consultation as the application of behavioral assessment and change methods in educational settings. Caplan (1970) further defines consultation as a voluntary, non-hierarchical relationship between two professionals typically initiated by the client for the purpose of solving a work related problem. These definitions imply that the people receiving consultation are the ones asking for assistance. But in fact, when working with school districts, in most situations, this is not the case. Consultation is typically requested by the school administration and the people receiving consultation are not necessarily entering the relationship with the consultant voluntarily.

Because of this significant difference in the mere definition of what constitutes consultation, it would be naive to assume that because a request for behavior consultation services has been made that all the education professionals involved in that consultation will embrace the presence and input of the consultant. In many cases, the professionals that the consultant will be asked to train have either had unpleasant experiences with other consultants (e.g., overly rigid or aloof in approach, recommendations that are not practical, etc.) or they fundamentally disagree with the premise of behavior intervention, such as the need for Discrete Trial Teaching (DTT).

PREVIOUS EXPOSURE TO ABA

Many teachers' first exposure to ABA may have been an undergraduate psychology class. Frequently video clips, intervention examples and required readings have not been updated to reflect the ongoing evolution of ABA. Intervention demonstrations are often somewhat punitive and not very child friendly. It is possible that the professor did not have a very positive view of ABA and readily imparted this perspective. Unfortunately, this trend continues in contemporary undergraduate and graduate teaching programs. This skewed and inaccurate representation of ABA tarnishes the perspective of a prospective teacher, well before having an opportunity to either attempt it on their own or learn more about it.

Once they enter the teaching profession, the indoctrination continues. Sometimes the propaganda includes real world administrative concerns such as: ABA cannot be implemented in classrooms, and ABA results in astronomical expenditure. There are clinical-sounding complaints such as ABA is experimental and ABA is highly restrictive The campaign may become more extreme such as ABA is the enemy or ABA produces horrible results

They may have been warned that because of ABA, they will have to waste countless hours in training and meetings. They may also have heard how much time will be spent creating teaching materials, lesson plans, schedules, and data sheets for daily, monthly and quarterly data collection. Added to this is learning how to take data and applying it to the instructional content as well as individualizing each student program. These comments and fears only heighten concerns about the exorbitant amount of time the teachers may have to spend away from their classrooms, students and assistants.

In addition, teachers are led to believe they will be living in a fish bowl. Consultants, specialists, district trainees and parents will come to observe their class and watch the process of ABA being applied to a school setting. Finally, teachers fear after all the effort they will possibly end up being dissected in court. Unfortunately, there is more than a grain of truth in much of this.

EXPOSURE TO ABA "EXPERTS"

Adding fuel to the fire, some leaders in the field of ABA can be just as extreme in their convictions, apocryphal comments and stories. They have stated that school districts and teachers are the enemy and that creating an ABA program in a classroom is a pipe dream. They believe that it would be an impure, bastardized representation of ABA and propose that teachers are incompetent and have no clue about what they are doing. They claim that operating in schools should be avoided at all costs. Keep your child safe at home! Develop your own program!

Often, a teacher's experience with ABA providers is limited to the intrusion of family tutors or home-based behavioral experts into their classroom. All too often, these visitors are not trained as effective consultants. Thus, they do not have the understanding, experience and training necessary to develop a good working relationship and rapport with the teachers. Instead, they often disrespect the teacher's home field. They devalue the possible contributions and ideas from the teacher and do not respect the knowledge that teachers have.

Think of the educational and professional direction teachers have chosen. They have gone through at least five years of schooling, a substantial time student teaching, received a credential and then decided to devote their lives to children, all the while knowing that they will be greatly underpaid. Although they do not have expertise in ABA, they are experienced and can be an extremely valuable resource.

The classroom visitors often have limited experience, not only in the application of ABA, but more importantly, how ABA can be applied successfully to a group or class setting. They often do not understand the intricacies inherent in the organization of a classroom, a school or a district, let alone what guidelines are passed down to the district from the county, state and national governments. Many times these visitors have little understanding of the individual and systemic dynamics holding a school together.

Frequently, those who are attempting to impose ABA on a teacher are following a model that does not promote generalization and does not emphasize developing group learning skills. There is a rigid view of what constitutes ABA and they attempt to replicate an individual 1:1 program of the type one would implement at home. Consultants attempt to make the teacher adapt to the student and operate like a home therapist. The goal should be to instruct the teacher on how to develop skills in the student so they may maximally benefit from the social and dynamic classroom environment. Unfortunately, there is frequently a failure to recognize the tremendous learning opportunity that is provided by the classroom.

Without such an understanding and empathy from the visitors invading the classroom, it is no wonder ABA is not embraced with open arms but instead only occurs as a result of legal action. People connected with ABA become the outsiders, the spies who are only there to collect incriminating evidence to use against school staff. Unfortunately, this sets up an adversarial relationship. Often these visitors are only interested in one specific child and treat teachers as if they have nothing to contribute. They convey that teachers are ignorant and ineffective when educating children and cannot positively affect their students' lives. They openly attack the teachers.

Another concern teachers deal with is the disproportionate amount of attention, resources and time given to students with ASD. It is a difficult pill for teachers to swallow. They have an obligation to and compassion for all of the students in their classroom. Therefore, they often accurately view that ABA takes away tremendous time and energy from the rest of their children. When ABA consultants come in so exclusively focused on a single student they are likely to encounter a significant lack of enthusiasm when it is anticipated that the process will detract from the education of the other students in the class.

Often teachers are coerced or at least feel forced to use procedures that they do not feel comfortable using. They may be pressured to use language that does not seem natural or asked to teach skills that they feel are not developmentally appropriate or relevant. They may be urged, without understanding the rationales as to why, to ignore behaviors that they feel should not be ignored (e.g., aggression, rudeness, acting silly, etc.). Basically, they are required to adopt and apply techniques that make them uncomfortable. They may attempt to follow the guidelines they were given, having been told that this is best practice but it is really just capitulation to avoid having to go to court. All this can lead to a great deal of resentment towards ABA from school staff.

RECONCILIATION AND RESOLUTION

Although it may be an uphill battle, it is possible to develop a partnership. In order for consultation to be effective, there are many factors that need to be considered. First of all, consultations in general involve some degree of resistance. The role of the consultant is to assess and evaluate the current learning environment and the teaching style in order to teach the team to adapt their approach to better meet the individual student's needs. This assessment process in and of itself is stress inducing for the staff involved. In order to accurately observe the environment and effectively train staff, the consultant must first establish a relationship with the team.

There is a difference between trainers and effective behavior analysts. Having teachers acquire information alone does not necessarily lead to consultation success. Effective behavior analysts will help teachers understand the process of educating children with special needs. Teachers must understand the rationales behind procedures and become able to independently analyze situations and make their own decisions about how to teach a particular lesson.

Next, it is important to develop an understanding of the history of the site, basic philosophy, past staff training experiences and assess their current receptiveness. If a philosophical disagreement exists, the consultant must determine if this is the product of experiences with poorly executed or ill explained behavioral work.

If this is the case, introducing staff to contemporary, effective intervention and rationales about the importance of various techniques is the place to start. The many myths surrounding behavioral work must be uncovered. The staff will need to see demonstration of flexible, child-friendly approaches as well as how methods can be practically applied in the classroom.

If, however, the staff maintain a philosophy that is fundamentally opposed to behavioral teaching (e.g., they do not agree that it is ethical to use reinforcement, believe that children should be allowed to discover the world in their own way without guidance, etc.) and are not open to reconsidering their ideas, a shift in approach will be necessary. Either the staff assigned to receive training will be willing to learn more about the techniques (or allow members of his/her team to learn), or the administration will need to identify other staff to train who do not have such a conflict.

Either way, the only hope of bringing about change is through the establishment of a good working relationship. To assist in that process we would like to share what has proven to be helpful in the past.

BUILDING THE CONSULTATION RELATIONSHIP:
The Ten Commandments

Many of the challenges faced in consultation are outgrowths of a general culture clash between private behavioral services and the public education system. Consultants need to remember that they cannot impose the same expectations they have in the private sector and that resources are often more limited. A classroom in the public school system is part of a larger educational structure. Because districts are designed to meet the educational needs of every variety of student, the philosophy of intervention may be different. Consultants typically have the luxury of addressing only an individual student's needs. Under these circumstances, resources, materials and teaching strategies focus on a specific student. In the classroom environment, the personnel need to address the needs of multiple students simultaneously. The goal of the consultant in the classroom should be to blend what is effective in behavioral work (e.g., assessing behavior, managing contingencies, introducing task analysis and other effective teaching strategies) into the classroom environment, which can provide opportunities that may not be available in an individual learning environment (e.g., observational learning opportunities, generalization opportunities, classroom routines, and group learning). By blending the best elements of both environments, an effective learning experience can be created that benefits the maximum number of students.

The First Commandment: *Thou Shall Create a Behavioral Culture*

The goal in the initial phase of consultation is to assess the receptiveness and flexibility of involved members and to begin the process of developing a behavioral culture within the classroom. A behavioral culture is an environment where teaching personnel are motivated by the knowledge that they are a powerful influence in the student's world. It is one in which staff take responsibility for managing contingencies and understanding the student's behaviors. It is impossible to create a behavioral culture if the main classroom teacher is not in agreement with the consultation. Ideally, people should volunteer for the additional support. However, greater receptiveness can be developed by demonstrating the functional relationship between behavior and whether the student's needs are being met or not met.

To this end, initial training should focus upon helping classroom staff assess the behaviors of their students. By understanding why behaviors occur and what function they serve, it sets the foundation for excitement based upon the possibility of impacting behavior and making long term change. It begins the critical thinking process, which will lead to the teaching team's ability to be increasingly independent when handling behavioral issues as they arise.

You will know you have succeeded in establishing a behavioral culture when situations arise that indicate the classroom staff are addressing behaviors as a team. For example, one of the staff might ask if you have spoken to another member of the team. The exchange could sound like this:

Teaching staff: We are glad you are here. Did you get a chance to talk to Donna yet?

Consultant: No, I was working with Danielle. Do you know where Donna is?

Teaching staff: Yes, she is running a small group. You won't believe what happened yesterday with Alex. He had to transition from the computer to circle and he didn't act out once! He was saying to himself, calm, calm... It was great, but I will let her tell you all about it.

This type of conversation may reveal that not only is the staff targeting the student's behaviors but, they are assessing behavior and discussing with each other successes or perhaps non-success with behavioral intervention plans. This kind of mutual support and excitement makes the teaching and work environment more positive and productive and is contagious. The strength of the culture becomes important, because if it is well-established, it rubs off on newcomers, those who are initially ambivalent and even those who are mildly resistant. It can withstand some degree of sabotage from those who are "alien" to the culture.

Occasionally there are people in the classroom environment who directly or indirectly sabotage the camaraderie of the team. This may be because they disagree with a behavioral approach or it may involve a personal reason (e.g., threat to their role in the classroom, difficultly with change, a need for chaos in the environment, etc.). It is important to address this situation and decide which of three approaches would most help the teaching environment: educate, contain (neutralize), or remove.

The "educate" strategy. The "educate" strategy should be selected if a member of the teaching team needs more support in implementing behavioral principles. Such an individual may have experienced a lack of success, which often creates a learned helplessness response. Using this strategy, the goal may be to identify a student behavior or skill that the individual finds important to change and that the consultant believes would be an achievable goal. This may help the individual to gain greater success and establish behavioral endorsement. This would be done in an effort to bring them into the team and help highlight them as effective members.

The "contain" strategy. If it is clear that the individual is not open to adding to the team positively, or able to implement behavioral intervention strategies consistently, you may need to contain them. In the private sector, when a team member is not working well with the others and is destructive to the momentum of the work, you can decide to remove them completely. This, however, is not always possible in the classroom setting. The idea is to identify areas of the day or classroom daily schedule in which the person could be productive. You may have to decide to let go of certain priorities in order to maintain the forward growth of the culture.

For example, a situation may arise where a member of the teaching team is unable to follow behavioral protocol because of her personality or style. The team member may love to be with the students and very much enjoys the job. However, the team member does not follow through with behavior plans that involve denying students what they desire. The team member may request help because the students do not listen. Based on the consultant assessment, it becomes clear that the team member is unable to resist withholding desires of the student and typically gives in. When the "educate" strategy has been attempted and failed, the "contain" strategy may be necessary to ensure that behavioral plans are not sabotaged due to the overly good nature of the staff person. An example of the "contain" strategy for the situation described above may be to select activities throughout the day in which the staff could participate that would not detract from the overall effectiveness of the classroom (e.g., help facilitate unstructured play activities in the classroom, prepare materials, oversee students self-help needs not identified as teaching targets, etc.). By employing strategies such as these, the staff may be able to participate with the children in a positive way and contribute to the overall effectiveness of the classroom. This example relates to a team member who wants to be a part of the team but is having difficulty carrying out a meaningful role in the classroom.

The "remove" strategy. If the other two strategies do not bring about the needed change, it may be time to remove the team member from the classroom environment. This may be difficult but if school administration understands the need to develop a strong behavioral culture to maximize student progress, then staff change may need to occur. When utilizing the "remove" strategy, it may be advisable to provide a rationale to the teaching team. Even an ineffective team member may have developed relationships with other members of the team that may require helping them buy in to making change.

The Second Commandment: *Thou Shall Listen.*

It is easy to walk into a situation and see areas in need of improvement and change. It is also frequently possible that the teaching team working in that environment is aware of these needs. Initially, in order to demonstrate respect for the professionals within the classroom, a majority of time may be spent listening to the needs expressed by the teaching team. Listening can also assist the consultant in identifying areas of need and perhaps identify areas in which the teaching team may be resistant if targeted early on. If you sense there is resistance, try to find the source.

Asking questions regarding efforts that have been made in the past, challenges within the system (e.g., frequent placement of additional students, feelings regarding adequate support from administration, availability of reinforcers, etc.), and personal or classroom goals they would like the consultant help to achieve may be helpful. Perhaps the most important way to develop collaboration is to help teachers with their battles. Can you assist administratively? Helping them procure much-needed resources (e.g., teaching materials, reinforcers, etc.), obtaining substitutes so the teacher can participate in training, and being allowed more planning time, can be critical. By listening early on, you acknowledge the talents and opinions of the professionals you will be working with and you will avoid making recommendations that mirror previous efforts. At least you will learn what kind of rationales you should provide if you end up advising them to repeat previous efforts.

The Third Commandment: *No Job is Beneath Thou.*

Talking about the creation of a team is all lip service if the consultant is not willing to contribute in very practical ways. Building a team means respecting others as equals and participating meaningfully in the work of that team. This may mean that the consultant puts aside predetermined training targets and pours juice or helps set up snacks so the classroom assistant and teacher can discuss a student. If a student exhibits a behavior problem and the staff asks for assistance, the consultant may decide that this is an immediate priority and be very willing to help. If the teacher has forgotten potential reinforcers or needed materials for an activity, the consultant can assist in finding them.

There are many considerations in determining whether or not help is warranted. It is important to help but for the right reasons. The consultant's responsibility should be to assess why the team is asking for or needs help. If there is a crisis and the team needs assistance, then help. If the teaching team is understaffed for the day, then help. But keep in mind the question of why since there may be reasons not to help. For example, if the teaching team is ALWAYS understaffed, then strategies that are employed using the consultant as an extra hand will not be helpful on most other days. Also, drawing the consultant into the daily routine may be a way for the teaching team to avoid training. And finally, helping may be viewed by the teaching team or administration as a waste of the consultant's time.

Many people receiving consultation ask the consultant to demonstrate the skill being discussed. Often it is a genuine request. However, it may be an invitation to fail: if you are such an expert, you do it. It is appropriate to model occasionally but not always. There are times when demonstrating can enhance credibility with the teaching team. However, there are risks associated with demonstrating that need to be taken into consideration. First of all, many behavioral strategies are based on reinforcement control. It may not be possible for the consultant to engage with a student and demonstrate the needed skill without first establishing themselves as a reinforcing person.

Secondly, if the consultant decides to jump in and demonstrates success with the student, the team member may either feel inadequate (i.e., I can't do what you can do) or become overly dependent on the consultant to solve the problem (i.e., the team member is always asking for help). It is wise for a consultant to pick moments when modeling will produce desired outcomes. It is important not to leave a staff person feeling powerless in the moment. In most situations it may be best for the consultant to walk the staff through the procedure. While seeing a technique in action can be very helpful, personally implementing a strategy and experiencing success is far more valuable. In the long run, the team member will need to be fluent at implementing the strategies, not merely have passive exposure.

Finally, the decision about whether or not to demonstrate is based on whether the current opportunity fits in with the proactive plan for training. If a skill deficit has previously been identified and this is a planned-for training session, then modeling will not have the kind of shortcomings identified above. Reactive or in-the-moment training increases the risks associated with demonstration.

The Fourth Commandment: *Thou Shall Leave Thy Ego at the Door*

It is a frequent complaint that behaviorists come across as cold and aloof. As consultants we do very little to change this perception when we persist in using behavioral jargon and demonstrate inflexibility in our approach to learning. The unwarranted use of behavioral terminology may distance the consultant from the teaching team. Such use is frequently, and mistakenly, designed to convey expert status but only serves to confuse and irritate. When consulting, utilizing terms common to classroom personnel and providing functional relevant examples and rationales as to why a strategy should be employed can assist in maintaining a collaborative relationship with the teaching team. If technical precision requires use of behavioral jargon, it should be used sparingly and explained clearly, including how the concept is different from what is conveyed by more casual language. For example, it is important for staff to understand the difference between negative reinforcement and punishment and to understand that the technical term punishment represents something different than its meaning in everyday usage.

It is important for the consultant to be confident and forthright in stating opinions while remaining open to new information. The consultant recommendations should be taken as predictions, which may or may not prove correct. That is, he is essentially predicting that if the staff does something in a certain way, there will be a specific resulting outcome. It is important that the consultant acknowledge that not all of his ideas are going to work, and be willing to demonstrate humility. If the consultant presents a "know it all" or "he can fix everything" attitude, alienation may result. We have to be right often enough that our recommendations generally prove to be worth the effort that it takes to implement them.

Being approachable begins when you enter the classroom. It is important to display a friendly demeanor and one that demonstrates respect for the classroom environment (e.g., arriving on time, having a plan for your day, dressing appropriately for the setting, asking where to put your belongings so they are out of way, watching the volume of your voice when providing instruction or feedback so you do not disrupt the classroom, etc.). It is important for the consultant to be respectful of her role in the classroom by conferring with the teacher about how training can best occur in the classroom. What time would be best to discuss individual students or the classroom in general? Would it be best to focus on one staff person a day or would rotating better fit the classroom routine? The consultant needs be comfortable letting a working relationship develop and not be too quick to force his own agenda. It takes time to establish the kind of trust needed for the teaching team to be open and for mutual support systems to develop between the teaching team and the consultant.

Also, you should model efficiency, a positive attitude and a willingness to roll up your sleeves and get the work done, no matter what that may entail. You should model good ABA techniques, including confidence, well thought out rationales for your teaching decisions, analyzing functions of behavior, calmness during noisy behaviors, genuine pride when dispensing reinforcement. You should envision yourself under a critical spotlight during the whole visit, with the teaching staff evaluating your every move and decision. These efforts go a long way to developing a partnership built on mutual respect and trust.

The Fifth Commandment: Thou Shall Maintain a Long Term Perspective.

Patience is a virtue. It is easy to derail a successful consultation by attempting to address too many issues too quickly. It is helpful to keep in mind that significant change in a classroom structure can best be planned for as a two to three year project. All the necessary systems must be in place in order for the teaching team to maintain effective teaching strategies and classroom organization that will lead to a reduction of disruptive/acting out behaviors and an increase in the adaptive and academic skills of the students. This long-term perspective can increase the systematic nature of the training plan and reduce the risk of the teaching team becoming overwhelmed. This perspective can also prevent the consultant from veering too far from the proactive training plan to solve acute problems.

Of course, you also need to provide meaningful information. You want the staff to see that you have value. Provide practical suggestions. Although it may not be what you feel is the top priority, making the teacher's job easier results in more willingness to listen to you in the future. This can be difficult, because you may feel urgency in accomplishing your mission and to institute change across the board immediately. But you need to be patient, understand the process, and see the small steps as valuable and progress in the right direction. After a while, the steps build upon themselves and the speed of progress picks up considerably. Developing a relationship is time-consuming. Developing a collaborative, working relationship takes even longer.

Addressing some of the lesser priorities will lead to quicker resolution of the bigger priorities. For example, see if there is a way to reduce the teacher workload. Helping to create and implement a simplified, user-friendly data system can reduce resistance. Reducing resistance will enable you to more quickly move on to the issues requiring greater time, trust and planning. Prioritizing and reducing objectives can also be a huge relief to the teaching team. They will feel better able to accomplish their jobs if they initially have fewer targets to address. As the skill level increases and the students are responding appropriately, the objectives can be increased and made more challenging. Focusing on decreasing behavior problems should be a top priority and will earn you respect.

Develop a training plan. It is helpful for the consultant to provide clear expectations for the site to the teacher and/or administration. The consultant should have systemic and individualized training plans and goals. Systemic goals address the structure of the educational environment (e.g., classroom set-up, staff and student schedules, etc.) and individualized goals address each of the teaching staff's area of needed growth (e.g., utilization of behavior management techniques and effective teaching strategies, etc.). By sharing this long-term perspective, it may reduce the pressure that comes from the expectation that change should be accomplished in short order. The training plan should include classroom intervention strategies to be targeted (e.g., reinforcement systems, reactive and proactive teaching plans, crisis management, etc.). These training objectives should be discussed with the teacher and administration to determine training priorities.

Team communication is key. In order to build a lasting program, time must be set aside for the team to come together as a group. By scheduling time to meet and discuss the day, plans can be adjusted, progress can be shared, concerns can be voiced, and the risk of burnout will be reduced. Ideally, teaching teams should have time at the end of each day to debrief, review plans and prepare for the next day. Additionally, at least one day a month (or a portion of day) should be set aside for the team to come together without students. This can be used for training, discussing behavior plans for the class, discussing individual student goals, and materials creation.

Once a behavioral culture is created in the classroom, it will help sustain the progress toward long-term goals. The culture itself however must be maintained through ongoing communication, training and support. To do this, the consultant should work with the administration to build this into the overall plan.

Maximize training time. Training can be conducted prior to the start of the school year. This can function to build momentum for the coming year and can allow any new team members to receive education regarding behavioral techniques and strategies prior to working hands on during the start of school. It can also provide an opportunity for trained staff to share their knowledge and build their skills with regard to training new staff. The eventual goal of the consultant should be to create an environment that is self-sustaining. Therefore, they must target and give feedback to individuals who can mentor future staff.

The Sixth Commandment: *Thou Shall Teach To Independence.*

In order to build self-sustaining progress, the consultant must provide instruction with the goal of independence in mind. This is true when working with students of any variety. Initially, a heavy prompting strategy may be required to help staff understand the expectations and goals. This may include modeling, verbal prompts, direct instruction, written protocols and other supports. The goal is to help them experience success in the application of behavioral techniques. When first attempting to apply a behavioral model to a classroom setting, the learning curve can be steep and teachers will need to be supported. As time goes on, it is the consultant's responsibility to fade the prompts and utilize a less directive approach in the process. If the consultant fades the prompts too soon, the teaching staff could feel put on the spot or unsuccessful. The consultant should sew the seeds of fading out support by providing rationales for their recommendations. Over time, the consultant can turn to the teaching staff and ask them to argue rationales during assessment. This process of generating hypotheses, developing a plan of action, and assessing the result of the plan is the basis for later independence.

The Seventh Commandment: *Thou Shall Be Willing To Make Mistakes.*

Working with children on the autism spectrum is often very challenging work. Teaching children, in general, requires adults to have a sense of humor about themselves. By not taking mistakes personally and by being willing to implement plans and take risks, the classroom environment will be better for it. As a presence in the classroom, the consultant should model the type of professional conduct you wish to encourage in the teaching staff. There should be a sense that you do not have to be perfect to be effective. It is the process of venturing into unknown territory that leads to advancement. Creative work often cannot be accomplished without making mistakes. There should also be a sense that genuine effort is supported and that mistakes can help shape future successes.

The Eighth Commandment: *Thou Shall Normalize The Difficulties In The Learning Process.*

It is important to make learners feel comfortable with the learning process. It is often difficult for teaching staff to feel at ease while being watched by others as they are learning new skills and techniques. By telling the teaching staff up front that learning new strategies may disrupt their sense of competency, you inoculate them against demoralization. It has been helpful to describe the process in terms of sports-related skills. Take for example, a person who has played tennis for years and wishes to improve his skills. During a lesson, the trainer might advise that the student should change his grip on the racket in order to improve his game. At first, the new grip feels wrong and skills that the student was once able to perform easily now feel awkward and ineffective. As with the skills involved in classroom teaching, when new behavior needs to be integrated with existing skills, a person's natural timing is frequently disrupted. It would be tempting to stop using the new grip and return to holding the racket the old way. If he truly wants to improve his skills, however, he needs to endure this period of discomfort in order to integrate new skills and become a better player.

The Ninth Commandment: *Thou Shall Be Generous With Your Praise.*

As consultants, it is easy to lose track of what is working in the environment because the purpose of the visit is usually to address problems. The big picture is to support the effectiveness and productivity of the classroom for all of its students. In order to achieve this, the staff needs to know what they are doing that is working as well as what may need alteration. It is important that comments be sincere. Disingenuous praise is insulting. There are numerous potential areas that deserve positive comments. Because a consultant comes in with an outsider's perspective, the consultant may often recognize changes that have occurred over time that might not be recognized by those working with the students day in and day out. It is, therefore, important to remind them of how student behaviors and classroom operations used to be and how much better they are today. If the staff does not know their strengths, they will be unable to exploit them and may get bogged down by focusing upon areas of weakness.

The Tenth Commandment: *Thou Shall Inspire.*

As a consultant, share in the teaching process knowing that there will be a direct impact on the lives of countless students and teachers. This opportunity is exciting and is an opportunity to share this perspective with the professionals you are training. Behavioral work, as it is applied to students with developmental disabilities, involves not only explaining concepts and procedures and training staff to use behavioral principles, but motivating adults to implement strategies that are frequently time consuming and intensive. It is also the role of the consultant to ultimately demonstrate the effectiveness of systematic behavioral intervention strategies. In order to be truly effective at using behavioral analysis, a person must be willing to change their behavior, trusting that there will be long-term payoffs for doing so. There is simply nothing more inspiring than watching a student learn and become more independent. Well-planned and executed behavioral strategies facilitate such learning, but gains may not be immediately observable. Even when profound, observable gains have been made, they may be overlooked. The consultant should develop ways to capture and record gains that students have made, including data collection and video recording. During group meetings, the consultant can use these tools to communicate to the team the results of their hard work and effort.

These ten commandments may be obvious. However, it is our experience that the consultation relationship is often overlooked or devalued. As an agency, we have had to learn some of the consultation strategies described here the hard way. Consultation relies heavily on the ability to develop relationships with teaching teams that produce openness and availability to the learning process. As experts in the field, we are not there to tell but to guide. In order to promote change in children with Autism Spectrum Disorder, we must first look to change our own behavior and when we do, student behavior will also change.

IT HAD TO BE SAID!!!

REFERENCES

Billington, T., McNally, B., & McNally, C. (2000). Autism: Working with parents, and discourse in experience, expertise and learning. *Educational Psychology in Practice, 16*(1), 59-68.

Caplan, G. (1970). Theory and practice of mental health consultations. New York. Basic Books. Cheseldine, S., Manders, D., & McGowan, C. (2005). The role of consultation clinics in services for children and young people with learning disabilities and/or autism. *Child Adolescent and Mental Health, 10*(3), 140-142.

Davis, B., Smith, T., & Donahoe, P. (2002). Evaluating supervisors in the UCLA treatment model for children with autism: Validation of an assessment procedure. *Behavior Therapy, 33*, 601-614.

Dawson, G., & Osterling, J. (1997). Early intervention in autism. 307-326.

Drotar, D., Palermo, T., & Barry, C. (2004). Collaboration with schools: Models and methods in pediatric psychology and pediatrics. In R. T. Brown (Ed.), *Handbook of pediatric psychology in school settings*. Mathaw, NJ: Lawrence Elrbaum Associates Publishers.

Gersten, R., & Woodward, J. (1990). Rethinking the regular education initiative. Focus on the classroom teacher. *Remedial and Special Education, 11*(3), 7-16.

Giangreco, M., & Broer, S. (2005). Questionable utilization of paraprofessionals in inclusive schools: Are we addressing symptoms or causes. *Focus on Autism and Other Developmental Disabilities, 20*(1), 10-26.

Handleman, J. (1990). Providing effective consultation to students with severe developmental disabilities and their families. *Journal of Educational and Psychological Consultation, 1*(2), 137-147.

Harchik, A. E., Sherman, J.A., Sheldon, J.B., & Strouse, M.C. (1992). Ongoing consultation as a method of improving performance of staff members in a group home. *Journal of Applied Behavior Analysis, 25*(3), 599-610.

Kamps, D. (1997). The behavior analyst's role in facilitating interventions in general educational settings. *Journal of Behavioral Education, 7*(1), 81-89.

Kirgin, K., Brukmann, C., Atwater, J., & Wolf, M. (1982). An evaluation of teaching family (achievement place) group homes for juvenile offenders. *Journal of Applied Behavior Analysis, 15*(1-16).

Leaf, R.B., & McEachin, J.J. (1999). A Work in Progress: Behavior Management Strategiesand a Curriculum for Intensive Behavioral Treatment of Autism. New York, NY: Different Roads to Learning.

Leaf, R.B., McEachin, J.J. & Taubman, M. (2008). Sense and Nonsense: It Has To Be Said. New York, NY: Different Roads to Learning.

Martens, B.K. (1993). Social labeling, precision of measurement, and problem solving: Key issues in the assessment of children's emotional problems. *School Psychology Review,* 22 (2), 208-312.

Martens, B. K., & Ardoin, S.P. (2002). Training school psychologists in behavior support consultation. *Child Behavior and Family Therapy, 24*(1-2), 147-163.

McGimsey, J. F., Greene, B.F., & Lutzker, J.R. (1995). Competence in aspects of behavioral treatment and consultation: Implications for service delivery and graduate training. *Journal of Applied Behavior Analysis, 28*(3), 301-315.

Noell, G. H., Witt, J.C., LaFleur, L.H., Mortenson, B.P., Rainer, D.D., & LeVelle, J. (2000). Increasing intervention implementation in general education following consultation: A comparison of two follow-up strategies. *Journal of Applied Behavior Analysis, 33*(3), 271-274.

Preece, D. (2002). Consultation with children with autistic spectrum disorders about their experience of short-term residential care. *British Journal on Learning Disabilities, 30*(3), 97-104.

Renty, J., & Roeyers, H. (2006). Satisfaction with formal support and education for children with autism spectrum disorder: The voices of the parents. *Child Care Health and Development, 32*(3), 371-385.

Robertson, K., Chamberlin, B., & Kasar, C. (2003). General education teachers' relationship with included students with autism. *Journal of Autism and Developmental Disorders, 33*(2), 123-130.

Ruble, L. A., & Dalrymple N.J. (2002). Compass: A parent-teacher collaborative model for students with autism. *Focus on Autism and Other Developmental Disabilities, 17*(2), 76-83.

Rush, K. L., Kee, C.C., & Rice, M. (2005). Nurses as imperfect role models for health promotion. *Western Journal of Nursing Research, 27*(2), 166-183.

Skinner, M. E., & Hales, M.R. (1992). Classroom teachers' "explanations" of student behavior: One possible barrier to the acceptance and use of applied behavior analysis procedures in the schools. *Journal of Educational and Psychological Consultation, 3*(3), 219-232.

Taylor, I., O'Riley, M., & Lancioni, G. (1996). An evaluation of an ongoing consultation model to train teachers to treat challenging behavior. *International Journal on Disability, Developmental and Education, 43*(3), 203-218.

Wakschlag, L. S., Leventhal, B. (1996). Consultation with young autistic children and their families. *Journal of American Academy of Child and Adolescent Psychiatry, 35*(7), 963-965.

Wilkinson, L. A. (2005). Supporting the inclusion of a student with Asperger syndrome: A case study using conjoint behavioral consultation and self-management. *Educational Psychology in Practice, 21*(4), 307-326.

Chapter 8

COACHES PRIMER

Assessing

Benefitting

Collaborating

By Ronald Leaf

FIRST CONSULTATION

The primary goals of the first consultation are to begin developing a collaborative working relationship, defining your role, and **indoctrinating** the teacher regarding the consultation. It is a critical meeting in establishing the teacher's expectations. Unfortunately, teachers are often given misinformation or just do not understand the consultation model. Additionally, they are often overwhelmed. Even though they may need and even want the support, having someone intrude into **THEIR** classrooms can be a burden. Often, they want you to quickly give them the magic bullet or show that you are no more competent than they are and to move on! This first meeting will provide them critical information that will hopefully facilitate reducing their resistance and make them eager for your return visits!

- Set up a time to meet that is convenient for the teacher. It is important that you have approximately 30 minutes when the teacher can be able to devote all her(*) attention to you. Ideally, it should be out of the classroom so as to reduce interruptions or distractions.

- After exchanging pleasantries (which of course is important to help develop a collaborative relationship), it is time to start building the relationship. Begin by getting to know her. Besides developing rapport, this information can be invaluable in gaining important information for you to help assess the teacher and therefore develop a consultation plan:

* We will use "her" since most teachers are females.

GETTING TO KNOW HER:

- How did she get into the field?

- Have her describe her experiences.

- Does she have any other job aspirations?

- What are her favorite things about teaching?

- What does she like least?

- What are her favorite "subjects" to teach?

- What are her least favorite "subjects" to teach?

- What are her favorite student types (e.g., younger vs. older; higher vs. lower functioning; aggressive vs. passive)?

- What are her biggest challenges?

- What behaviors bother her the most?

It is essential that you are absolutely not perceived as being judgmental in the slightest, just interested in getting to know her!

- Describe your experiences, be humble but let her know subtly and **quickly** what incredible experiences and talents that you have (be your best advocate, while maintaining humility)

DEFINING ABA

A great deal of resistance is because of the myths regarding ABA. Many teachers have either been exposed to rigid ABA through consultation or rumor. Therefore, they may be more than skeptical from the beginning. It is critical for you to define OUR brand of ABA:

- Initially focus on reducing interfering behaviors

- Proactive and positive in our approach

- Utilize natural reinforcers with the goal of internalization

- Focus on the whole child (i.e., functional academics, communication, social and play)

- Natural as possible (language, settings, materials)

- Structured flexibility

Acknowledge that a great deal of ABA is rigid and not child or teacher friendly. And you too would be resistant if someone was attempting to make you use it!

DEFINING THE RELATIONSHIP

Define your role as a CONSULTANT. You are there to:

- Help FURTHER develop staff's skills

- Provide advanced training in ABA and Autism

- Be an objective set of eyes

- Provide recommendations for staff and students

- Provide support as appropriate and necessary

- As a consultant you are NOT there to:

  - Be judgmental, which is different than helping her improve

  - Be an additional staff member! IN FACT, you will attempt to limit your interactions with the students so that you do not interfere and reduce the staff's authority and so that you can be an objective observer. The more you interact, the less likely you will observe what occurs when you are not there.

  - Intervene in parent or staff disputes

  - Be a therapist (e.g., "As much as I would like to help you with your frustration and stress, it isn't my role.")

INOCULATION: WHAT TO EXPECT

- Provide information so that you can prepare her for the consultation. Also raise problematic issues prior to observing them. This can reduce defensiveness because you have not observed them. Possibly it may change her perspective and avoid issues, conflict and resistance. This is commonly referred to as "inoculation."

- Your ultimate objective is to help her become as independent as possible by giving her the tools to make her job less stressful as well as enjoyable and to accomplish this goal as quickly as possible.

- Since your time is limited, it only makes sense for her to be able to become independent.

- She has far more day-to-day knowledge.

- Your approach to consulting with the teacher as well as with students is to be proactive and not reactive. Therefore, the majority of your time will not be spent addressing the crisis. Rather, it is more productive to focus on her skills and situations away from the crisis. If you can increase the non-crisis situations, you will naturally be reducing a crisis.

- Feedback is essential. You will be generous with your praise but corrective feedback is every bit as important. By providing corrective feedback, you are attempting to provide the necessary information so that rapid improvement will occur. It is absolutely not personal, hopefully just informative. If you were to only provide positive feedback, it would greatly prolong the time it would take for improvement to occur. She would understand what you would like her to continue to do, but would not necessarily figure out what not to do or what to do instead. Remember, one learns as much from mistakes and corrective feedback as they do from being correct. It is imperative that you absolutely believe this. If you are not comfortable with this, then you will be hesitant to provide corrective feedback.

- Initially, you will provide training primarily in one-to-one situations. This provides a more structured teaching situation so that both the student and teacher will be successful. Eventually, training for both will move to more group situations.

TEACHING THEM TO FISH!

■ Describe the two methods of consulting (i.e., prescriptive and psycho-educational). **PRESCRIPTIVE**: tell them exactly what to do.

The advantage is that it can result in rapid change. It can also make the teacher happy because it does not require thinking and it will make you look brilliant! Of course this will eventually become a disadvantage.

One disadvantage is that it does not develop independence. Moreover, if one is not part of the process, then it is less likely that they will truly understand the information. And it reduces buy-in. If someone tells you what to do, it is easier for them to reject your recommendation than if they helped come up with it (i.e., cognitive dissonance).

"Don't look for the big quick improvement. Seek the small improvement one day at a time. That's the only way it happens, and when it happens it lasts"

John Wooden

■ **PSYCHO-EDUCATIONAL**: provide them necessary information so that together you develop a plan.

■ The disadvantage is that this is not as quick a process. It can also be frustrating for the teacher because you may be perceived as withholding the answer.

■ The advantages are that it is a collaborative process and it develops independence (you can give someone a fish or teach them to fish; you can tie a student's shoes or teach them how to tie their shoes; you tell them what to do with an inattentive student or you could provide them some information and then you could collaboratively develop a plan).

■ This is by far a more difficult process for supervisors. It requires you to skillfully lead the teacher to the answer without sounding testing but by being informative and inspiring as subtly as possible (i.e., the least intrusive prompts necessary).

■ Acknowledge that while this approach will eventually result in tremendous growth, it is:

- **A PROCESS** – change may be slightly slower but "good things happen to those who wait!"

- Frustrating because they are not being rescued. And it can be aggravating not to be rescued! Furthermore, they will make mistakes, but learning occurs through mistakes.

- The more open and receptive staff are, the faster and the more successful the consultation.

PSYCHO-EDUCATIONAL: A NON-DIRECTIVE APPROACH???

- You can be quite direct without being prescriptive! For example, you can identify a problem quickly and help them identify the disadvantages. "Clearly you provide a great deal of praise and smiles. But do you think that this is enough for Cole? And if it's not powerful enough, what do you think you could you provide instead?"

- It is critical to develop a style that does not seem as if you are quizzing them to show that they are inadequate. But rather that you are helping them grow!

THE STRUCTURE

- Let her clearly know that you will not be able to have set appointments. First, you are consulting with so many teachers that it would not be possible. Also, you want to be able to drop by as often as possible. Sometimes if you are in the area, you may want to be able to provide coaching. Finally, it is helpful to be able to see a representative sample of the entire day. However, make an appointment for the second visit, so that you can observe at a time that the teacher feels is more representative.

- Your consultations will only be for a short amount of time, which usually provides a good enough time sample. Give examples: you do not need to test the whole cake to see if it is done; you do not usually need to have an hour-long conversation with someone to determine if you would be interested in dating them, etc. Also with shorter appointments, you can see them more often.

- Let her know that you will be as unobtrusive as possible. As discussed, this allows students and staff to be as natural as possible so that you are able to obtain a more valid observation. However, let her know that in a crisis (i.e., the student posses a danger to himself or others) you will certainly help intervene.

■ Only focus only on a few issues so as not to be overwhelming. With her input, you will choose the issues that you feel will ultimately be the most helpful.

■ Conclude by asking her that, prior to your next visit, you would like her to identify a few areas she would like to concentrate on.

Be sure to let the teacher know that you will be meeting with the school administrator so that they will be supportive of the process!

■ When you meet with the school administrator and summarize your session, it is critical that they understand that this will be a process (you are teaching them how to fish)! It is also important that they understand that you will not be prescriptive, the reasons for not being prescriptive and that staff will likely be frustrated. Hopefully, this will facilitate their support with the teacher. You are there to help and not to evaluate or provide additional stress!

FOOD FOR THOUGHT

1. Always attempt to provide rationales for every recommendation that you make. For example, do not just tell them to provide differential reinforcement, tell them why it is important. This will not only promote their understanding but it has the advantage of:

   ▪ Stimulating thinking

   ▪ Developing independence because they will better understand the concept and therefore be more likely to generalize to new situations

   ▪ Promoting the consultation model

   ▪ Inspiring

   ▪ It will also help YOU to better understand the concepts

2. Use examples as often as possible. This often helps to clarify information as well as making it more interesting. If you can provide real-life examples, it helps them to see that the principles of ABA are not exclusive to autism and promotes their generalization of learning. Additionally, it may help them remember the concepts.

3. It is better not to have a set agenda of topics. If you can, use what you observe as your material to discuss. It will be more relevant and seem less "forced" and therefore more natural. Typically, the issues and concerns will play out during your observation.

4. The number of topics and suggestions will be highly dependent upon the staff. If they are less skilled or overwhelmed, then you should probably limit the number of topics. However, if they are hungry and receptive, it might be advisable to increase the number of recommendations. Of course you will always be assessing! Also, the suggestions will be based upon a number of factors. You certainly want staff to experience success, so you may start by providing them with suggestions that will be most successful. Or you may begin by making recommendations in the teacher's area of priorities and interest. However, you may need to focus on reducing the on-going crises that are tremendously impacting the classroom.

5. When providing feedback, it is not suggested that you necessarily start with a list of positive feedback and then end up with more corrective feedback. This pattern often has a negative impact. Sometimes, staff will feel that they are so good that they will not listen to or discount the corrective feedback. More often, however, they will not pay attention to the positive feedback in anticipation of the corrective feedback. It can also convey the message that you are not comfortable providing corrective feedback and that you need to "butter them up" or dance. We recommend that you provide feedback in the chronological order that you observed to break this pattern.

6. Working with teachers as well as parents is very similar as working with students. It follows the guidelines of good teaching. That means providing feedback, both positive and corrective, with a high frequency of positive; using the least intrusive prompting as well as systematically fading prompts; not overwhelming (carefully selecting priorities) and making sure your level of instruction matches the "learners" level of comprehension; and of course making learning as enjoyable and natural as possible. It's just good teaching!

7. Your priority is the teacher and not the students. Ultimately, by helping further improve the teacher, you are actually providing more support to the students. Naturally, in a crisis the student becomes your priority.

8. When teachers ask questions, analyze the purpose of the questions (i.e., its function). Is it to:

   - Find out information

   - Challenge

   - Help to process the information

   - Show her knowledge

   The function will help you provide the better answer.

9. If you do not know the answer, it is time to stall!

   - Ask them to repeat the question

   - Have them clarify the question

   - You clarify the question

   - Paraphrase the question

   - Invite them to ask the question privately

   - Tell them to think about the question and you will discuss it next week and then get help!

   Once you have established credibility, it's fine to say you do not know!

EFFECTIVE COMMUNICATION GUIDELINES

1. **GOOD LISTENER**

   A. Stop talking

   B. Wait until speaker is done

2. **RECEPTIVITY**

   A. Facial expression

   B. Eye contact

   C. Body posture

   D. Personal space

3. **CLARIFY WHAT YOU HEARD**

   A. Paraphrase what you think you heard

   B. Ask for more information

   C. Ask questions to clarify issues

4. **PLEASANT ATTITUDE**

   A. Open

   B. Non-judgmental

   C. Accept difference of opinion

5. **CLEARLY & ACCURATELY STATE YOUR BELIEF**

   A. Utilize receiver's language

   B. Summarize your message

   C. Verbal and non-verbal messages must be consistent

6. **IDENTIFY POTENTIAL CONFLICT & DEVELOP EFFECTIVE CONFLICT RESOLUTION PROCESS**

   A. Decide the optimal time to discuss the conflict

   B. Define the problem

   C. Understand other's position

   D. Generate as many solutions as possible

   E. Choose the best alternative

   F. Accept the decision

SECOND CONSULTATION

The goal of the second consultation is to assess the strengths and weaknesses of the teacher and staff so that you can develop a "task analysis" of your consultation. You should focus your observations on the following areas:

- **Reinforcement**: Do they use reinforcers, are they powerful enough, contingent, varied, differential, etc.?

- **Behavior Strategies**: Do they have a systematic plan, are they primarily reactive, do they use proactive strategies, have they determined the function of the behavior, have they identified replacement skills, etc.?

- **Teaching Technique**: How closely do they follow DTT guidelines? Are they systematic, do they break down skills, use effective prompting procedures, fade prompts, make good timing decisions, build independence, etc.?

- **Style**: Do they enjoy teaching, are they calm, are they positive?

- **Structure**: Does the schedule promote quality programming and behavior control? Is there sufficient teaching time, is the classroom well managed, etc.?

- **Functional and Relevant Curriculum**: What percentage of the observation involved the teaching of important goals, is the curriculum functional, will the goals facilitate meaningful progress, etc.?

- **Does the Staff Appear to Be ABA Friendly**: Philosophically, do they appear to be a good match with ABA or are they more closely aligned with other approaches (e.g., TEAACH, "traditional education," etc.)?

Appendix B contains a checklist that you should use to help evaluate the classroom as well as provide a tool to assess progress. We would highly recommend that you do not fill it out while observing. The staff will feel as if they are being evaluated. Take simple notes that will assist you in completing the checklist IMMEDIATELY after you leave the class.

A secondary goal of this consultation is to reinforce the consultation process.

- After exchanging pleasantries, take on your role as an observer. Be as unobtrusive as possible. Find a good location that will give you the best observations. We would recommend sitting over standing. It helps you to more quickly blend into the woodwork. If you are taking notes, a smaller the pad the better. Once again, it will make you less obvious. If students talk to you, give simple answers or just smile if possible. Naturally, if there is a TRUE crisis, then assist as necessary. If the teacher or staff comes up to you to chat, be as pleasant as possible and assure them that you will talk in a little while and keep observing. Try as hard as you can not to make comments, ask questions or even give facial expressions.

- It is essential that you show as little emotion as possible. If you frown when the teacher does something you do not like, it will likely affect what she does in the future, thereby reducing the validity of your observation. Similarly, if you smile, it will also alter her teaching. You want as representative an observation as possible.

- When you feel you have as much information as necessary (e.g., the last five minutes did not give you any additional information and it is likely the next five minutes will not either) it is time to chat with the teacher. Ideally, you should have enough information within 20 minutes. Being "efficient" will reinforce the process (i.e., that your consultations will be short) and allow you to move on to your next classroom.

Ask to meet with the teacher for about 10 minutes. Ideally, you have already located a place to meet near the classroom so that you do not have to spend the time finding a room. The primary goal of this meeting is to find out if what you observed was "typical," and to review your previous session.

- I would begin by asking something like: "was today typical? Were the kids having an extra good day, a usual day, or a poor day?"

- If her answer was that it was not typical, ask how the students were different. Once she has answered, then ask why she thinks it was different. Finally, ask if the staff was different?

  - Do not be surprised if you are told that it was poorer because of your presence! It is a good way to excuse what occurred. It is representative of a potentially resistant teacher. Most likely it was not that the students who were directly affected, rather it was the staff who in turn affected the students! Or it really was not different but she was more sensitive to the challenges.

  - Resist the urge to comment or argue! I would simply respond that with time, everyone will get use to your presence.

  - If she shares that she was nervous, this can be a good sign that she cares.

  - If she says it was a bad, **WITHOUT EXCUSES,** it may be a good sign.

- If she says it was a good day, when it was horrible, you have your work cut out for you!

■ Let her know something that you felt she did particularly well (e.g., "I love the way you interact with the kids," "your classroom is well structured," "I really like the way you ..."). It has to be genuine and something that you can build on. If there really was not something, do not invent!

■ Ask her what areas would she like help with. **HERE IS THE TRICK!!!** Whatever she says, bring it back to the first objective on your task analysis. Most likely reinforcement, unless the reinforcement was outstanding! Reinforcement is most likely the foundation of any problem she raises or you observe. For example:

Teacher: "I need help with Jake's inattention."

Consultant: "I understand how getting Jake to pay attention would help him tremendously. Without knowing anything about Jake, I would imagine that he is not finding circle (worksheet, center, etc.) enjoyable. So we will need to develop a reinforcement system to improve his ability to pay attention. And eventually, the goal will be to fade the reinforcers so that he will find circle enjoyable without needing artificial reinforcement. So during my next visit we will focus on reinforcement."

OR

Teacher: "I need some free time so that I have time to prepare for centers."

Consultant: "That's understandable! I think perhaps the most effective way to be able to get you some time to prepare and breathe is to get the kids to work a little more independently. In that way you will have more free time. So I think the best way would be to develop reinforcers that we can then use to reward them for working independently...."

OR

> Teacher: "I really do not need help with anything!"
>
> Consultant: "The problem is that I have been assigned to collaborate with you, so we need to come up with something we can work on. I was thinking that if we could increase reinforcement then... (the finish to the sentence will be something that will help her, such as the kids can meet their goals quicker or they will be better listeners or they will be quieter)."

- Regardless of the teacher's perspective on reinforcement, it is most likely not being used effectively! Invariably,:

  - The reinforcers are not reinforcing (i.e., they are not increasing the desired behavior or skills).

  - They are not being provided frequently enough.

  - The behavior is not being labeled.

  - It is not contingent (they get it eventually, regardless of their performance) and they are most assuredly rarely, if ever, experiencing loss of opportunity of receiving reinforcement (eventually, they all get it because of fear of the student melting!).

  - There is not a variety of reinforcers being used.

  - They are not being provided differentially.

If effective reinforcement is not occurring, it will be very difficult for anything else to be effective (i.e., behavior programs, curriculum, and being able to use systematic teaching), The suggested order of priorities is based upon a task analysis of prerequisite skills:

- Reinforcement

- Reactive Behavior Strategies

- Proactive Behavior Strategies

- "Learning to Learn Skills"

- DTT guidelines

- User-Friendly Data

- Functional and Relevant Curriculum

- As "homework", I would ask her to do something regarding reinforcement before your next visit. For example:

  - See how many new reinforcers she can identify for one student

  - Try to spend 30 minutes a day reinforcing a student every five minutes for the absence of a disruptive behavior OR doing the right thing (e.g., staying on task). Help select a student that most likely will respond to the program, thereby reinforcing the teacher!

  - Select one behavior for every student that you feel would be important to reinforce.

  - Try to identify *A*, *B* and *C* reinforcers for a selected student.

- Conclude the session by reiterating your role and the process. "As we talked last time, my objective is to help you! I know by not giving you the answer, it can be a frustrating process. But I also know that with time it will be well worth it!"

- Let her know that during the following sessions, you will be providing feedback during your observation. The feedback will be limited in the classroom, but at the end of the visit, you will meet with her to provide more extensive feedback, support and training.

Thank her for letting you observe and acknowledge that it is never easy to have someone new in a class.

Resist the urge to have her evaluate if the session was worthwhile!

Complete the attached *Assessment of Consultation Issues* and *Successful Trainee Markers*.

ASSESSMENT OF CONSULTATION ISSUES

Teacher Expectations: _____

_____

_____

_____

_____

Teacher Management Style: _____

_____

_____

_____

Teacher Receptiveness: ❑ Yes   ❑ Somewhat   ❑ No

EXPLAIN: _____

_____

_____

_____

Accepts Consultation Model: ❑ Yes   ❑ Somewhat   ❑ No

EXPLAIN: _____

_____

_____

_____

Barriers to Consultation: _____

_____

_____

_____

SUCCESSFUL TRAINEE MARKERS

	Poor		Average		Outstanding
	1	2	3	4	5

Teacher Characteristics

Enthusiasm

Willingness to participate   ___ ___ ___ ___ ___

Excitement at the opportunity to learn   ___ ___ ___ ___ ___

Expectation for future application in own classroom   ___ ___ ___ ___ ___

Leadership Skills

Takes control of teaching situations   ___ ___ ___ ___ ___

Respected by Teaching Assistants and other service
  providers   ___ ___ ___ ___ ___

Jumps in during training opportunities   ___ ___ ___ ___ ___

Doles out classroom responsibilities effectively   ___ ___ ___ ___ ___

Rapport

Good working relationship with Teaching Assistants   ___ ___ ___ ___ ___

Good working relationship with other professionals
  in classroom   ___ ___ ___ ___ ___

Good working relationship with school administration   ___ ___ ___ ___ ___

Organized

Classroom set up functional   ___ ___ ___ ___ ___

Lesson plans established   ___ ___ ___ ___ ___

Goals/objectives for individual students   ___ ___ ___ ___ ___

Materials easily obtainable   ___ ___ ___ ___ ___

Daily schedule available   ___ ___ ___ ___ ___

Philosophical Buy-in

    Understands and believes ABA techniques are
        applicable and can be used successfully in the
        classroom setting   ___   ___   ___   ___   ___

Accepts consultation/outreach as an ongoing training
        process   ___   ___   ___   ___   ___

Classroom Characteristics

Materials

    Updated   ___   ___   ___   ___   ___

    Functional   ___   ___   ___   ___   ___

    Age appropriate   ___   ___   ___   ___   ___

    Rotated   ___   ___   ___   ___   ___

Physical Set-up of Classroom

    Functional   ___   ___   ___   ___   ___

    Age-appropriate   ___   ___   ___   ___   ___

Student Grouping (age, functioning levels, needs)   ___   ___   ___   ___   ___

Ancillary Services

    Pull out vs. within centers   ___   ___   ___   ___   ___

Staffing Ratio   ___   ___   ___   ___   ___

THIRD CONSULTATION

Start this session by having a short chat regarding what she identified as the target she selected regarding reinforcement. Then provide some suggestions of what you would like to see during the observation. For example: "Could you try to reinforce Jake every three minutes when he is paying attention?" Remind her that you will only be providing feedback as necessary, but at the end of the observation you will have time during the debriefing to answer questions and provide more extensive feedback. When giving feedback during the observation, the less intrusive the better (e.g., gestures). If that's not effective, then give simple comments. Try to avoid lengthy discussions.

You also need to decide whether it is more effective to provide feedback in the moment or if it is better to wait for a while. There are advantages and disadvantages to both. There are also personal preferences for staff and consultants alike. To complicate the issue, sometimes teachers say they prefer one style, when clearly it is not effective or they truly do not like it. For example, teachers may express the preference for immediate feedback, but when you follow their stated preference they appear annoyed that you interrupted them. Ultimately, your decision is based upon the best teaching tool.

Immediate Feedback	
Advantages	**Disadvantages**
■ More immediate feedback is usually a more effective learning tool ■ Avoids continuing ineffective intervention ■ More solid in memory	■ Interrupts flow ■ Does not allow self-correction ■ Teacher may say she was going to do it differently if you had given her a chance ■ Reduces opportunities to gather more information ■ Somewhat reactive

Delayed Feedback	
Advantages	**Disadvantages**
■ Allows you to process with the teacher ■ Allows you to gather more information ■ Allows you to prioritize ■ Teaches YOU to become more patient ■ Teaches YOU not to rescue	■ Situation may go out of control ■ Teacher may forget exactly what happened ■ Teacher may become more defensive if situation became worse ■ You may appear to be unhelpful and aloof

Another big decision is regarding your modeling. As with the timing of feedback there are several advantages and disadvantages:

Advantages of Modeling	Advantages of Not Modeling
- It may be perceived that you are being supportive - It can establish your credibility as a talented teacher - It might be easier for staff to understand and learn through observation - It might be easier for you to train than having to articulate what you are doing - It might help you figure out a program - It fulfills your need to work with students and look good–NOT REALLY AN ADVANTAGE!!!	- "Hands on training" is often a better learning process - It forces coaches to articulate - It may increase generalization for student - It is a more proactive approach and therefore reduces dependency - It reduces the possibility of teacher feeling helpless, that they are not as good as you! - It reduces the risk if you are not successful - The teacher may be able to successfully copy what you did, but may not understand what you did and therefore will not be able to generalize

Modeling is sometimes a necessary tool, but it is potentially risky. And it should not be used often! It is often a result of a staff challenge, *"well why don't you show me!"* If you fail, they may be happy. If you succeed, they may conclude that you were lucky or come up with excuses as to why it worked. Either way, it may be a lose/lose situation. Tread carefully!!!

At the end of your observation (e.g., 20 minutes or so) meet with the teacher to review the observation. This is also the time that you start providing specific training on the target. Let her know that there will not be time to thoroughly discuss the topics but over time you will be able to more fully address her questions and concerns. It is advisable to recommend that she writes down her questions between visits.

Staff will not always be open to your recommendations! Factors include: not agreeing philosophically, feeling evaluated, or feeling overwhelmed. Simply make your recommendations utilizing a psycho-educational approach. Provide plenty of rationales. In the first couple of sessions, we would not recommend being confrontational. This does not help build a collaborative relationship. However, always be honest.

- It is critical to identify the function of their resistance. For example, do they not understand, do they not want to change, or do they want you to go away?

- It is important that you are understanding:
    - Change is often difficult for everyone. They do what they do because either they learned to do it that way, it has worked, or they are comfortable with their approach.
    - Change will most likely require more time and effort.
    - It is critical to realize that most staff are not as talented as you are! The reason that you rose to the position is because you were a skilled teacher and had a good work ethic. Most teachers will not rise to your position. So you must not use yourself as a model or be judgmental.
    - Always remember that they are your students! Be supportive, patient and understanding.

- You most likely agree with the ultimate objective (e.g., students should be internally motivated, the importance of them not needing support, the need to learn academics, etc.) but you may disagree on how to get there. We recommend that you establish that you are on the same page (e.g., "I quite agree that it is critical that Cole does not need artificial reinforcement) and show how you plan to make it happen.

However if resistance persists, see the section entitled: The Last Session?

When staff tells you that they have tried it and it did not work, consider the following:

1. Ask for a detailed explanation of what they have tried previously. Do not be leading or evaluative. Get as much information in order to determine if indeed they followed what you recommended. Most likely they missed some key steps that will allow you to explain the differences between what they did and what you recommended.

2. Point out that effective intervention is a process and therefore unlikely to work the first time or rapidly.

3. Let them know that even if procedures did not work previously, it is a different time and situation and therefore perhaps this time it may work.

   Consultations will primarily remain the same:

   ▪ At the beginning of the observation, make suggestions of what you would like to see during the observation (this should be based on last sessions wrap up and discussion).

   ▪ During the observation, provide feedback as necessary.

   ▪ Wrap up sessions are for reviews, teaching and recommendations.

The following sections will include information most likely to be targets.

THE LAST SESSION?

A question that is often asked is, "When should a student stop receiving ABA intervention at home?" The assumptions being either that it should be time limited or that there is a certain point where there is little or diminishing progress. One could pose a similar question regarding: "When should a consultation stop?" The answers are both similar and different. Consultations are not necessarily time-limited. Similarly, sometimes a teacher can continue to benefit from years of consultation. And sometimes progress is not being made to warrant continuation.

Whereas we would continue to work with a student regardless of his resistance (e.g., non compliance, aggression, avoidance) with a teacher, we may decide not to continue consulting because it becomes a matter of priorities. There are just too many other teachers willing and eager to receive consultation. Therefore, we cannot spend our time once we conclude that it is highly unlikely for them to become available to receive consultation.

Naturally, it is necessary to do everything possible to reduce their resistance. However if the teacher remains resistant then it's probably time to make one last ditch effort! **Now, it's time to confront!!!**

Confrontation does not mean being aggressive. It simply means you need to more directly address the teacher's attitude by making some of the following statements:

- I feel that you are not finding our time beneficial (e.g., you often are too busy to meet; your body language indicates dissatisfaction, you rarely seem to be able to follow my recommendations, etc.).

- Is there something that I have said that I can clarify because it seems that either you do not understand or that you do not agree?

- I understand this is a difficult process. Is there something I can do differently so that I can better help you?

- I know that change is difficult. I also understand much of what I have asked may be placing more burden on you and is stressful, but if I did not feel you have the ability or if it was not worth it for the children, then I would leave you alone!

If you feel the teacher's resistance may melt because of your brilliant clinical skills, then try a couple more visits to confirm if the resistance is diminishing. If not, it's time for a break!

NOT THE TIME!

When it is abundantly clear that this is not going to work, then it's time to tell the teacher as well as the site administrator that it's time for a break! Simply say that it is clear at this time that the consultation is not productive. However, in the future if the teacher feels it could be beneficial, then by all means contact you. Make one or two practical suggestions (e.g., "catching them being good," only provide instructions if you can follow through, pick your battles, etc.).

Try not to take it as a personal defeat! First, you cannot win them all! Second, you are most likely inheriting loads of issues. Third, it is a process and sometimes you have sewed the seeds that someone else will reap. However, regularly evaluate what you did, what perhaps you could have done differently, and add this to your ever increasing tools.

NOT RESISTANT, BUT TIME???

Back to the analogy of the child terminating services. There will be lots of times when the teacher is receptive and/or the consultation is beneficial regardless of how long you have been consulting. So the questions becomes do you continue? Just like serving children there are no easy answers. It is encouraged that you to consider the following:

- How significantly will the teacher improve with your continued consultation?

- Will the teacher experience significant regression if you stop?

- Is **THIS** teacher likely to improve more students, staff or administration than other teachers?

- Does the teacher have longevity?

- Is the teacher improving **YOUR** skills?

- Can you reduce your consultation while still maintaining significant impact?

- Are there other teachers that are on the waiting list?

If, based upon these considerations, you decide to stop or provide limited consultations, then I would recommend providing a number of recommendations. But be sure to prioritize and of course let them know that they should contact you if necessary.

REINFORCEMENT

DEVELOPING REINFORCERS

1. Some very small and ordinary things can be made into reinforcers with good "packaging" or a good job of "selling" them with your own enthusiastic responses to them.

2. High frequency behaviors, such as listening to music or playing on the computer would constitute likely reinforcers. Anything a student would select in a free choice situation will probably work as a reinforcer.

3. The first step in developing reinforcers is simply exposing students to potential reinforcers.

4. Giving free access to potential reinforcers can also create new reinforcers.

5. It is necessary to sometimes make a reinforcers unavailable, so as to increase its value as well as to avoid satiation.

6. An effective way to develop reinforcers is to associate potential reinforcers with established reinforcers (e.g., if they like music, have them read while they are listening to music so that by association reading will become a reinforcer).

7. Ask the student.

REINFORCEMENT GUIDELINES

1. **REINFORCERS SHOULD BE REINFORCING**: Often staff provide what they think are reinforcers (e.g., "good job," a high five, or a toy they have played with for a year) when it does not serve to increase appropriate behavior or performance and therefore by definition it is not a reinforcer. Even if the student likes it, it may not be powerful enough to serve as a reinforcer. Even though you may like praise, it probably would not be effective enough to serve as your paycheck!

2. **REINFORCEMENT SHOULD BE CONTINGENT:** This is perhaps one of the most violated guidelines. There should be established criteria on how the student earns the reinforcer. In other words, the reinforcer is earned. Consequently, there should be times when the student does not receive reinforcement. In this way, the student will learn what needs to occur in order to receive reinforcement. It will make rein-

forcement far more powerful. It should be so clear that anyone observing for five minutes could identify the criteria. If the school principal, school nurse, or custodian cannot figure it out, it's likely the student will not either. Therefore, the reinforcer will not have limited or no impact on the behavior or performance.

If the student always receives reinforcement, either he does not need external reinforcement or more likely it is not contingent.

3. **USE A VARIETY OF REINFORCERS:** So as to avoid satiation and to be able to develop new reinforcers. As long as the same reinforcer is provided it reduces the student's willingness to accept new reinforcers.

4. **PAIR SOCIAL REINFORCERS WITH PRIMARIES**: So that social reinforcement will become powerful, thereby allowing the fading of external reinforcement.

5. **CONTINUOUSLY DEVELOP & IDENTIFY REINFORCERS**: So as to develop a variety of reinforcers and avoid satiation.

6. **USE AGE APPROPRIATE REINFORCERS**: To help with inclusion as well as increase expectations.

7. **UNPREDICTABILITY & NOVELTY GREATLY ENHANCE REINFORCEMENT**: It simply makes reinforcement more exciting. It can also help in the fading of reinforcement.

8. **INITIALLY, REINFORCEMENT SHOULD OCCUR IMMEDIATELY**: This helps the student better understand contingency. It also reduces inadvertently reinforcing disruptive behaviors.

9. **FADE REINFORCEMENT AS QUICKLY AS POSSIBLE**: So that student's reinforcement occurs at a more natural frequency. This helps in including students in general education experiences.

10. **INITIALLY, LABEL THE BEHAVIOR BEING REINFORCED**: So as to increase the student's understanding of the contingency. It also greatly helps to facilitate a classroom culture of reinforcement. It may also serve as social reinforcement.

11. **DO NOT USE AS BRIBERY!!!**: Bribery or "bribery land" serves to reinforce the disruptive behavior. It also reduces independence because it is difficult, if not impossible, to fade bribery. It also requires the adult to negotiate! Remember, reinforcement occurs after the exhibition of appropriate behavior and/or performance.

12. **UTILIZE DIFFERENTIAL REINFORCEMENT**: It helps increase the student's understanding of the most desirable behavior or performance. It also serves as motivation to progress.

WHAT STAFF SHOULD KNOW ABOUT REINFORCEMENT

■ A reinforcer is anything that will increase behavior. Normally, most things a student likes or would consider a reward will work as a reinforcer. However, you can only be sure it is a reinforcer by observing the effect it has on behavior. If it improved behavior, then it is a reinforcer. Otherwise it is not!

■ Premack Principle:

You can increase non-preferred behaviors by making preferred activity contingent on performance of non-preferred behavior. For example, playing on the computer is preferred and sitting doing a math worksheet is less preferred. To increase the completion of worksheets, implement the following rule: first you do your worksheet, then you play on the computer.

■ Satiation vs. Deprivation
   ▪ Reinforcers are most effective if the student has been deprived of that item for a while. The longer the delay, the greater the potential reinforcing effect.
   ▪ Satiation occurs when a student has had enough of the item to satisfy him for now. The reinforcer temporarily loses its reinforcing value.

■ Relativity
   ▪ Potential reinforcers may be placed along a continuum of least to most reinforcing.
   ▪ You can only determine how reinforcing an item is by knowing what the alternatives are. Items that are not "typically" viewed as reinforcers may be while those that are traditionally thought of as reinforcers may actually be punishing!

- Schedules of Reinforcement

    - *Continuous*. Every response is reinforced, produces a high rate, and extinguishes rapidly. Use for new behavior (e.g., paying attention, being calm, or communicating appropriately) but rapidly move to intermittent.

    - *Intermittent*. Produces more behavior per reinforcer and is more resistant to extinction. Use for maintaining old behavior.

- Generalization

    - Shift from frequent to occasional rewards.

    - Shift from artificial to natural reinforcers.

    - Eventually shift from reward to avoidance schedule. That is, the student no longer receives reinforcement but would receive corrective feedback or consequences if he did not behave or perform.

- Differential Reinforcement

    - Definition: Using varying levels of reinforcement according to the quality of the behavior. Excellent behavior gets an 'A', very good gets a 'B', and good gets "C".

    - **DRO**: Differential Reinforcement of Other behavior. All other behavior except the target behavior will be reinforced. In order to earn the reinforcement there must be zero occurrences of the target behavior (e.g., reinforcing all behavior EXCEPT aggression).

    - **DRI**: Differential Reinforcement of Incompatible behavior. Reinforcement is provided for specific behavior that is incompatible with the target behavior (e.g., reinforce play or attending which is incompatible with self-stimulation).

BEHAVIOR STRATEGIES

1. Two ways to change behavior:

A. REACTIVE

    a.   Provide an effective consequence at the time the target behavior occurs

        1. To increase a behavior provide a positive (+) consequence

        2. To decrease a behavior provide a negative (-) consequence

    b.   The primary assumption is to eliminate the disruptive behavior – the problem, however, is if the behavior serves a need, wiping out the behavior does not wipe out the need. Therefore, unless you teach an appropriate alternative, either a new disruptive behavior will evolve, or the disruptive behavior will eventually return.

    c.   Reactive programming is typically what is used BUT it is far less effective

        1. Does not teach what you want, only what you do not want. For example, if a student has poor social skills, the reaction of others may punish poor social skills, but this does not teach the student good social skills.

        2. Emotional reaction for adults and peers may reinforce student for acting out.

B. PROACTIVE

    a.   To successfully reduce a disruptive behavior, you must teach an appropriate alternative behavior (**NOT WHEN THE TARGET BEHAVIOR OCCURS**)

    b.   It requires precise teaching (DTT).

    c.   Proactive intervention requires careful analysis and sophisticated teaching strategies.

    d.   In order to teach alternative behaviors, you must first identify the function of the disruptive behavior.

    e.   Based upon the function of the disruptive behavior, you then select the replacement skill to be taught.

IDENTIFYING THE FUNCTION OF THE DISRUPTIVE BEHAVIOR

1. What is the pattern of the disruptive behavior (e.g., under what circumstances does it occur and what are the payoffs)?

2. If the student was able to effectively communicate what he is attempting to gain from his behavior?

3. Take an **EDUCATED** guess.

    a. Observe behavior.

    b. Ask what do the teachers first think when they observe the behavior.

    c. Ask what they attempt to do to resolve the difficulty (e.g., if they try to calm their student, it is most likely attention or frustration based).

ASSESSMENT FORM

BEHAVIOR:

_____

_____

_____

_____

OPERATIONAL DEFINITION:

_____

_____

_____

_____

ANTECEDENTS:

_____

_____

_____

_____

RATE OF BEHAVIOR:

_____

_____

_____

_____

CURRENT CONSEQUENCES:

_____

_____

_____

_____

PREVIOUS METHODS EMPLOYED:

_____

_____

_____

_____

APPROPRIATE ALTERNATIVE BEHAVIOR DISPLAYED:

_____

_____

_____

_____

CONSEQUENCES FOR ALTERNATIVE BEHAVIOR:

_____

_____

_____

_____

IDENTIFYING APPROPRIATE ALTERNATIVE BEHAVIORS

1. This is extremely difficult for people. They know what they do not want but they do not know what they want.

Behavior	Alternative Behavior
Aggression	More Appropriate Avoidance Responses Waiting Stress Management Increase Skills in Deficit Areas
Self-Stimulation	Play Skills Staying on Task
Non-Compliance	Errorless Compliance Appropriate Negotiation
Inattention	Observational Learning Staying On-Task

PROACTIVE STRATEGIES

Shaping

- Identify what behavior the student now performs that comes closest to the target behavior

- Reinforce performance that meets the current criterion

- Do not reinforce performance that is below the criterion

- Reinforce successive approximations

- Use differential reinforcement in order to maximize the difference between levels of reinforcement–if performance exceeds criterion, give greater reinforcement

Modeling

- Have a model to demonstrate behavior (either peers or staff)

- The model should emphasize relevant cues

- Learner should observe model receiving reinforcement

- Learner should perform immediately after model

- Prompt as necessary to ensure success

- Reinforce target learner for correct imitation

PROMPTING & PROMPT FADING

- Definitions
  - Prompt: additional stimulus which facilitates responding
  - Fading: systematic reduction of intensity of prompt

- Kinds of Prompts
  - Physical
  - Demonstration
  - Verbal instruction
  - Modeling (indirect demonstration)
  - Nonspecific: gesture; pointing; glance
  - Voice inflection
  - Recency (reduced time delay; no interference)
  - Position/proximity/natural propensity
  - Order of presentation
  - Linking to previously learned response (e.g. receptive as prompt for receptive)

- How To Do It

- Select response that is a little higher than present level

- Choose prompt that <u>facilitates</u> response

- Establish prompt sequence

- Use within-stimulus prompts when at all possible

- Make sure prompt is "fadeable"

■ Present prompt simultaneously with instructions (SD)

■ Start with full prompt and 100% reinforcement

■ Gradually fade prompt

■ Use differential reinforcement

■ Once step is learned, **DO NOT** reinforce prompted trials

TASK ANALYSIS: BREAKING SKILLS INTO SMALLER PARTS

■ Why do a task analysis?

■ It is much easier for students to learn tasks if they are broken down into component parts

■ It is much easier for teachers as well

■ It also allows consistency between staff

■ EXAMPLE: Tooth Brushing Task Analysis

　　▪ Some individuals wet the toothbrush prior to putting toothpaste on the brush

　　▪ Some individuals wet the toothbrush after putting toothpaste on the brush

　　▪ Some individuals wet the toothbrush both before and after placing toothpaste on the brush

■ How to do a task analysis

■ Do task yourself

■ Have others complete the task

■ Locate manuals that have task analysis

■ Have students attempt task

■ Number of steps

■ Partially dependent upon functioning level

■ Arrange so that student will be maximally successful

"LEARNING TO LEARN"

Teachers are often eager to teach their students academic and language skills. Clearly, these are important objectives that are essential for student's well being. It is generally recognized that in order for students to be successful in learning these skills that their disruptive behaviors must not interfere in the learning processes. Therefore, behaviors such as aggression, non-compliance and self stimulation must be targeted prior to teaching more formal skills. However, there are other critical perquisite skills that are essential in order to maximize learning success. Acquiring "learning to learn" skills is absolutely pivotal in a student's success. It is really teaching students the process of learning. It is the foundation, perhaps the pivotal skill, necessary for them to acquire all other skills. Often when a student is struggling to learn beginning or even advanced skills, it is often because the student is deficient in this area. "Learning to learn skills" include some of the following skills:

- Attending

- Returning reinforcers

- Hands still

- Waiting

- Responding to instructions

- Changing behavior based upon feedback

- Learning from prompts

- Remaining calm

- Persistence

- Staying on task

- Leaving materials alone

"Learning to learn" skills often are not directly targeted. By the time "typically developing students" participate in more formal instruction, they have learned these behaviors through maturation, casual observations, or their interest in learning. However, the majority of students with ASD require direct teaching to understand these critical skills. Therefore, systematic programs designed to teach these critical skills are essential.

See Work In Progress 2 (McEachin, Leaf, Taubman, In Preparation for Publication)

DISCRETE TRIAL TEACHING (DTT)

One of the most commonly used teaching techniques employed by ABA practitioners is Discrete Trial Teaching (DTT). DTT is a specific instructional methodology based on the principles of ABA. It is a teaching process that can be used to develop critical skills, including cognitive, communication, play, social, coping and self-help skills. Additionally, it is a strategy that is used to maximize learning and is effective for all ages and populations.

DTT involves:

1. Teaching functional skills

2. Breaking a skill into smaller parts

3. Teaching one component skill at a time until mastered

4. Allowing repeated practice within a concentrated period of time

5. Providing prompting and prompt fading as necessary

6. Using reinforcement procedures

7. Facilitating generalization of skills into the natural environment

The basic teaching unit, called a *trial*, has a distinct beginning and end, hence the name "discrete." When teaching a new skill in DTT, the new skill is broken into small parts and each part of the skill is presented separately and mastered before more information is presented. Consequences are provided immediately after the student performs the skill or provides a response to the instruction. Reinforcement in the form of social praise or preferred item or activity is given for performing the skill correctly, while corrective feedback is provided if the skill is performed incorrectly. Teaching often involves numerous trials in order to strengthen learning. The student and teacher must be active and engaged during learning the learning process.

Example: If you are teaching a student to tie his shoes, you would first break the skill into several parts (e.g., putting the shoe on the foot, pulling up the tongue, tightening the laces, crossing one lace over the other, etc.). Once you have conducted a task analysis (e.g., breaking the skill into small steps or sub skills), then you would work on the first sub skill (e.g., putting the shoe on the foot). Perhaps in a 10- minute teaching session, you would have the student practice placing the shoe on their foot several times. The student would receive prompting (e.g., verbal, pointing, demonstration, etc.,) as much as necessary.

Prompts would be faded (i.e., discontinued) as quickly as possible. Throughout the session, the student would receive both positive and corrective feedback. Once the sub skill is mastered, then the next sub skill would be taught utilizing the same process. Finally, once the sub skills are learned in the teaching session, the skill should be practiced under less structured situations. The process would be repeated until all the sub-skills were learned and thus the student learns to tie his shoe independently.

Coaches and instructors commonly use DTT, without knowing the terminology or being explicitly trained. For example, when learning to swim, the skill is broken into many steps. First, the objective may be for the student to just play on the steps until they feel comfortable (e.g., they have conquered/"mastered" the skill of being comfortable in shallow water). Then they may practice repeatedly to place their face into the water. After multiple opportunities (e.g., trials) and mastery, the student would proceed to the next steps (e.g., kicking on the side of the pool). Systematically and gradually, the students learn more steps; they do not proceed to the next skill until the previous step is learned. Naturally, the lesson provides multiple opportunities for practice. Good swim instructors know how to make learning fun and filled with reinforcement (e.g., bobbing for rings). They also provide assistance (prompts) as necessary and fade those prompts as quickly as possible. Through good DTT (breaking skills down, teaching individual skills to mastery, providing prompts/feedback/ reinforcement, making learning fun, helping the student be comfortable in the learning environment), the student learns to swim!

DTT can be contrasted with continuous trial or more traditional teaching methods that present large amounts of information to students without having clearly identified or defined target responses. Traditional teaching often involves delayed, minimal to no feedback and/ or delayed opportunities for the teacher to evaluate how much learning has occurred. In addition, traditional teaching does not allow for the generalization of skills or measuring the use of newly acquired information into the natural environment. While this approach works for most students, it is typically not effective for students with ASD at the beginning of their education.

Although it is an intensive approach, DTT involves abundant reinforcement and students usually come to quickly enjoy the learning process. We have found that students can tolerate and thrive on a surprisingly large number of hours of DTT throughout the day **GIVEN** that staff are fun, respectful, energetic and enjoy being with the students.

See Appendix C for DTT Guidelines.

FUNCTIONAL AND RELEVANT CURRICULUM

Because of the belief that the more goals the better, IEPs all too often contain hundreds of goals. Not only is this not necessary, it actually seriously interferes with the teaching process. There can be a number of problems associated with too many goals:

1. Are the goals meaningful? When there are too many objectives, they are often trivial! Often goals are selected that are not very functional and therefore do not teach students the skills that are most critical in their learning or help improve their quality of life. As an example, a student may not know the labels of fingernail and eyebrow and could certainly learn it but maybe there are other skills that might prove to be more functional and useful. Typically, with five year olds, IEPs will include objectives to learn shapes and colors. However if a student has severe behavior problems or has limited functional labels, they may not be the most relevant skills. Although one could identify hundreds of goals to teach a student pre-academic skills, perhaps it is more relevant to develop just a few observational learning and socialization goals.

   For example, goals are often selected because other "four-year-olds know their shapes, colors, or numbers." Well, the reality is that other four-year-olds know hundreds of concepts. We are not going to teach them to have a "potty mouth" because other 4 year olds do! We will need to be selective and choose those that are most functional and will have the greatest impact.

2. Often mastering numerous goals is a false indicator of success. If a student learns all the programs contained in a book, it does not necessarily mean that they will achieve the "best outcome." We know many adults, who have mastered all the programs contained in books, that are still ASD and have restrictive lives because they did not learn behavior control or functional skills. More tragically, their quality of life has been seriously compromised because of their deficiencies in social skills and therefore not having friendships or functional academics so they cannot buy groceries or go to a fast food restaurant.

3. It is quite easy and therefore not very meaningful to create thousands of goals. For example, one could identify 25 goals (and really hundreds) in teaching non-verbal imitation:

Object	Large Body	Out of Chair	Fine Body	Chain
Roll Car	Wave	Turn off Light	Point to Nose	Stand Up and Turn Around
Throw Ball	Clap	Close Door	Point to Eyes	Touch Head and Clap
Wave Flag	Stomp Feet	Retrieve Item	Touch Elbow	Retrieve Ball and Car
Beat Drum	Touch Tummy	Throw Trash Away	Touch Ankle	Turn on TV and Sit Down
Spin Top	Touch Head	Stand Up	Point to Finger	Stand Up and Wave

Or one could identify five goals (i.e., object, large body, out of chair, fine body, chain, etc.) or identify just one goal: non-verbal imitation! The programs in books like *"A Work in Progress," "The Me Book,"* or *"Teaching Autistic Students"* have been broken down into very small parts. **IT IS NOT NECESSARY FOR EVERY STUDENT TO FOLLOW THE SAME TASK ANALYSIS.** Some students may need a more detailed task analysis than provided in the books to learn effectively, whereas others benefit from a broader approach that does not seek to teach everything in such tiny steps and looks to teach overall concepts. The teaching should be based on the learning ability of each student.

4. By having too many goals, it is often impossible to run every program. Teachers simply cannot run hundreds of programs. Therefore, program non-compliance is facilitated!

5. If indeed all the programs are run, then there is most likely not enough concentration on any particular program to ensure enough practice of the skill to learn it. So although the student may be taught hundreds of different programs, the student may master very few.

Remember the IEP is not supposed to contain all the student's objectives. It is a road map, but it is fine to deviate!

WHAT'S YOUR SUPERVISORY STYLE?

Consultant: _____

FEEDBACK

IMMEDIATE	1	2	3	4	5	DELAYED
SPECIFIC	1	2	3	4	5	GENERAL
SUCCINCT	1	2	3	4	5	COMPREHENSIVE
COUCHED	1	2	3	4	5	STRAIGHTFORWARD

STYLE

SERIOUS	1	2	3	4	5	PLAYFUL
DEMONSTRATIONS	1	2	3	4	5	VERBAL
DIDACTIC	1	2	3	4	5	INTERACTIVE
REACTIVE	1	2	3	4	5	PREDICTIVE
STRUCTURED	1	2	3	4	5	FLEXIBLE
QUIET	1	2	3	4	5	VOCAL
ERRORLESS LEARNING	1	2	3	4	5	MISTAKES
CREATE COMFORT	1	2	3	4	5	CREATE DISCOMFORT

MONTHLY CONSULTATION NOTES

Consultant: _____   Consultation Dates: _____

Primary Topics: _____

_____

_____

Secondary Topics: _____

_____

_____

Teacher Receptiveness: ❏ Yes   ❏ Somewhat   ❏ No

EXPLAIN: _____

_____

Accepts Training Model: ❏ Yes   ❏ Somewhat   ❏ No

EXPLAIN: _____

_____

Accepts Recommendations: ❏ Yes   ❏ Somewhat   ❏ No

EXPLAIN: _____

_____

Rate of Progress: ❏ Good   ❏ O.K.   ❏ Poor

EXPLAIN: _____

_____

Barriers to Consultation: _____

_____

Concerns: _____

_____

Chapter 9

DATA CAN AND SHOULD BE YOUR FRIEND!

By Mitch Taubman

ABA AND MEASUREMENT

Applied Behavior Analysis (ABA) is a psychological and educational discipline concerned with positively impacting the disorders and difficulties of human behavior, including challenges associated with autism. ABA is behavioral in that it focuses on observable phenomenon, such as actions and statements, as opposed to speculating about internal psychological states or processes (Baer, Wolf, & Risley, 1968; Baer, Wolf, & Risley, 1987). It also focuses on observable factors that control behavior and features of an individual's environment that encourage or discourage particular behaviors. These serve as verifiable explanations for behavioral difficulties as opposed to speculations about past experiences or hypothetical intrapsychic causes. It is very optimistic in its approach, proposing that with constructive changes in an individual's environment, skills can be learned and desirable alternatives to problem behavior can be strengthened.

ABA is applied, as opposed to theoretical, in that it addresses significant problems of human behavior in communities, homes, schools, and other natural settings, rather than in artificial settings like laboratories (Baer, et.al., 1968; Baer, et.al., 1987; Fawcett, 1991). It is concerned with practicality, user friendliness, and consumer satisfaction. It pays attention to the social importance of goals, the social acceptability of procedures, and the social and clinical significance of results. Finally, ABA is analytic in that it utilizes the scientific method and directs the practitioner to examine interventions in relationship to their measurable outcomes (Baer, et.al., 1968; Baer, et.al., 1987).

Objectivity of measures and the use of scientific methodology in ABA has meant that its principles and procedures are empirically supported, more thoroughly so than in other psychological disciplines. It also means the data collection is an important part of behavioral intervention. Behavioral assessment, centrally including objective measures, allows accurate and meaningful data collection to be a significant part of behavioral treatment. Data can assist in identifying children's needs, examining treatment procedures, and evaluating the effects of those efforts with such analyses giving straightforward guidance to treatment decisions. Finally, data can be collected in ways that are practical and do not compromise our clinical goals.

BALANCE OF APPLIED AND ANALYTIC: SOMETIMES LESS IS MORE

Over time, the definition of behavioral assessment has evolved (Haynes, 1998; Ollendick, Alvarez, & Green, 2003) and has come to include more than observational measures. This represents a positive change as it not only allows for multiple methods to be utilized (see below) but it allows measurements to be used that fit the interventional need. Data is a tool. It is utilized in support of interventional efforts. This is true whether the intervention is in a home, school or other center-based setting, in the community, or in a clinical laboratory. Data collection should not take precedence over or interfere with the clinical effort, but serve it. We like to say, "Data is your friend." If data feels more like an enemy then a friend, then there is a problem. There needs to be balance between practical realities and the interventional needs that data is intended to serve.

In research, rigor in data collection is essential. These are efforts that are not only intended to demonstrate the effectiveness of a procedure or program, but also establish experimental control (Sulzer-Azaroff, & Mayer, 1991). The findings of experimental efforts are then to be disseminated through peer reviewed journals throughout the field, hopefully leading to replication and confirmation of findings. Such rigor is just not necessary and may even be counterproductive in interventional efforts. One drawback to highly rigorous data collection systems is that it is extremely difficult to make them sensitive to the nuances of behavior that are of greatest clinical interest in everyday applied settings, i.e., outside of the experimental laboratory. And just because the procedure comes from a study, it does not at all mean that the investigation's complicated data collection system that was necessary for the study will prove to be necessary in clinical application. Clinical data requirements are most often remarkably lower then those of research. Additionally, we are confronted with practical limitations on how teachers and clinicians can spend their time (e.g., in classrooms serving many students with incredible demands upon staff). Balance means getting sufficient information to serve your instructional or treatment effort, within a system that is doable.

It would be possible in most interventions to establish data collection systems that are amazingly involved, elegant, and comprehensive. Yet most often in applied and community settings, the more complex and time consuming the design of the data system, the less likely it will actually be implemented. Paradoxically, a more simple system that gets used will produce more information then a complex one that does not get used. Furthermore, complicated systems often yield voluminous amounts of data. This produces two possible results: either no one looks at the data because it is too overwhelming to digest or it is collapsed, meaning data is averaged or otherwise summarized to make some sense of it. If second-by-second data is collapsed into minutes, and minutes into hours, and hours into days, and days into weeks, etc., we probably did not need to take second-by-second data and could have much more sensibly (and practically) taken data at a less fine-grained level.

If data collection is too oppressive and the information it yields too unwieldy, then data is unlikely to be collected, and most importantly, not likely to be examined. Besides, ABA really is not about data collection, it is about data analysis. Data is collected to be reviewed and used. It is used to make decisions about treatment and teaching, to help in planning by identifying what is working and what is not. If data is not examined and employed, it is truly a wasted effort. The primary directive then, in creating data forms and in specifying collection and analysis protocols, is to have data taken in a way that is practical, user friendly, reviewable, and meaningful to the intervention effort. In that way, data can be your friend.

MULTIPLE METHODS AND SOURCES

In the area of psychological assessment it is broadly accepted that multiple sources of evaluation are necessary to capture the range of information essential to measurement of status, progress or interventional planning (Vance & Awadh, 1998; Cone, 1998; Merrell, 1998). This is no less applicable to assessment in Autism Spectrum Disorder (ASD) (Eaves & Awadh, 1998). Since individuals with ASD present with a variety of symptoms and needs, from small to global, a battery of assessments can provide the necessary range and breadth of information. Also, since "hard" testing, *i.e.*, medical exams such as blood tests and MRI's, are not currently available as sources of relevant information on performance or progress in ASD, confidence in findings is strengthened through the use of aggregated multiple sources. Multiple sources can provide corroboration between each specific area of assessment, breadth of information, and an integrated picture of performance, functioning, and/or progress. Their use can also assist efforts to explain discrepancies in performance.

Multiple measurement can include, but may not be limited to, a contemporaneous objective scoring of instructional and/or behavioral performance, tangible product, structured observation, observation in naturalistic settings, questionnaires and rating scales, direct testing, structured and unstructured interviews, self generated devices, curriculum-based assessment, standardized tests, criterion-referenced testing, and norm referenced testing. Multiple sources can be within and/or between types of assessment.

OBSERVATIONAL DATA

One of the hallmarks of ABA research and intervention is the collection, analysis, and utilization of objective data, gathered primarily through direct observation (Sulzer-Azaroff, et.al., 1991). Though not the only form of behavioral assessment, observational data collection involves the simple recording of what is observed, rather than the scoring of subjective impressions, recollections, or interpretations of actions or behaviors. It does not involve assumptions about internal process, past occurrences or unseen forces. It is concerned with phenomena that can be observed and are such that everyone who is observing can agree that a certain phenomenon is occurring and to what extent it is occurring (Hall, 1999; Miltenberger, 2001).

Observational data collection involves in-vivo measurement, which is "live" observing or the scoring of video taped records. Measurement must be as contemporaneous as possible. That is, data is recorded when the behavior occurs or immediately after its appearance, rather than through recollection. Accuracy and objectivity is reduced when information is conveyed through recall. Observational assessment might be conducted by an individual while providing behavioral services or by an independent observer. Recording might be in naturally occurring circumstances or artificial ones (often called analogue conditions). Natural circumstances might consist of observing a student in the class he attends every day. It would be an analogue if the student was observed in a clinic where certain features of the classroom situation were replicated (e.g., sitting at a desk receiving instruction).

For behaviors that are to be observed, clear definitions are created so that there will be consistency between observers and the information they record (Haynes, 1998; Bailey & Burch, 2002). These are called operational definitions. They should be clear and sufficiently detailed for someone to be able to duplicate the behavior by reading the definition (Baer, et.al., 1968; Baer, et.al., 1987, Sulzer-Azaroff, 1991). Important dimensions of the behavior are identified, such as the frequency, duration, rate, intensity, correctness, or percentage of opportunity for occurrence of the behavior and serve as the focus of the measurement. Data may be taken on a continuous basis, that is every occurrence of the behavior is observed and scored, or representative samples may be taken (Bailey & Burch, 2002; Sulzer-Azaroff, et.al., 1991).

In ASD, it is common for observational data to be collected on correctness of performance during instructional (often discrete trial teaching) tasks and frequency or other important dimensions of disruptive behavior (such as aggression, non-compliance, inattention, or self-stimulatory behavior). Typically, observers are trained in an observation system until they meet a specified criterion for competence, which means that their recordings are consistent with other observers. This increases our confidence in the measurement and the "believability" of the information (Green, 1996).

OBERVATIONAL VS. GLOBAL ASSESSMENTS

Observational data collection is central to behavioral assessment as it is more objective, providing information containing fewer guesses, judgments, recollections, and interpretations, and thereby promoting greater confidence in the information. However, it is not the only form of measurement performed in ABA. As with any single data source, there are limitations to observation data (Romanczyk, Kent, Diament, & O'Leary, 1973; Pfadt, & Wheeler, 1995). For example, since observation data tends to focus on specific behavioral areas, information on global functioning is not easily derived from observational assessment. Functioning in such global areas as communication, social skills, or adaptive living are better captured on standardized tests (Watson, 1951). Since standardized tests are norm referenced, the test results for a child can be compared to the performance of other children of the same age. While some comparisons can be made with observational data (for instance, cross-referencing observations to what is developmentally or socially typical), standardized norms are not generally available. On the other hand, global tests do not typically involve direct, non-reactive observation and contemporaneous recording of those observations AND therefore do not typically yield information on naturalistically occurring phenomena. Also, information on performance in specific, critical skill or behavioral areas, directly related to particular needs and objectives, could not be provided by global assessment alone. Obviously the best approach is to combine observational data with a global measure of functioning. One important example of how this has been done in the field of ASD is the results from

UCLA Young Autism Project. This study used multiple sources including objective measurement of specific behaviors as well as various types of longitudinal global assessment, which yielded comparison data with typically developing children. Such a combination of data provided compelling evidence of the progress children made within the intensive treatment program.

OTHER ASSESSMENTS

Although observational and global assessments provide important information, there are additional types of measures that are useful and deserve to be considered. Naturalistic assessment, interviews, and questionnaires, for example, may give information on generalization and functional application of skills. Curriculum assessment may provide direct information on acquisition of targeted skills, and rating scales might furnish data on the clinical relevance of the skills taught or degree of change achieved (Campbell, Kafantaris, Malone, & Kowlaki, 1991; de-Bildt, Kraijer, Sytema, Minderaa, 2005; Matson, Dixon, Matson, & Logan, 2005; Mayes, Calhoun, 2004).

With multiple sources of information augmenting keystone and essential objective assessment, the validity of each source can be established, and a comprehensive picture of functioning, performance and progress can be derived.

INSTRUCTIONAL DATA COLLECTION

Trial-by-trial data collection involves the recording of the student's performance immediately after each trial, during the inter-trial interval. It is a form of continuous data collection. Contemporaneous scoring, as done in trial-by-trial data collection, reduces the effects of degraded recall and thereby provides more objective behavioral data. However, such data collection is often cumbersome, interfering with the flow and focus of instruction and interaction with the child. We have witnessed many therapists and teachers allegedly taking trial-by-trial data. But what they are really doing is **estimation data** on trial-by-trial sheets. That is, because they are rightly involved in the momentum of therapy, they stop and record data at a natural break point, not after each trial. But even though they record the information based on each trial, they are really doing so retrospectively, therefore sometimes complex information is recorded after some time has elapsed. Such a process strikes us as misleading. Only contemporaneous, continuous information should be reported as trial-by-trial data, and retrospective reconstruction should be reported clearly as such. The fact that such practices occur speaks to the practical, even counter-instructional difficulties encountered in attempting to take trial-by-trial data.

Retrospective, summarization, and estimation data are forms of measurement in which data is recorded at some point subsequent to the actual instruction and typically involve the scoring of several trials at once. Such data collection is often less labor intensive and may be minimally interfering with instructional efforts. However, estimation type data collection, while offering practical benefits, presents some difficulties. When data is taken retrospectively, especially data that requires observation on and recording of multiple pieces of information (e.g., correctness or incorrectness, prompts, no response, number of trials, behavioral information, and, in the case of rotated trials, information on several targets all for a number of trials), accuracy is adversely impacted.

DATA SAMPLING

In some cases, sample data is taken. That is, data is taken on only a portion or sample of the occurrences of what is being measured. In the case of discrete trial teaching, this means that data is collected on only a portion of the trials, teaching sessions, or instruction days. There is much research on the pros and cons of time-sampling and similar data collection systems, although much of this research concerns contrived circumstances created to measure the comparative accuracy of various measurement techniques (Alevizos, 1978; Birkimer, & Brown, 1979; Miltenberger, Rapp, & Long, 1999; Repp, 1976). Sampling can be practical, and when care is taken, an accurate representation of the larger phenomenon can be assessed. A familiar example is conducting opinion polls. It is not necessary to interview every registered voter to get an idea of which candidate is favored by the electorate. Similarly, one does not have to eat an entire cake to get a representative sense of how it tastes. However, if the slice is only of the top layer, as opposed to a cross section of all the layers of the cake, then the sample may not be representative. Therefore, when using sample methods, samples should be taken frequently and broadly (e.g., not always on Mondays) to get a representative picture. Another potential problem with sampling in applied settings is that it is sometimes difficult to remember to periodically take samples when the data is not collected according to a predetermined schedule, thereby resulting in a potentially skewed sample. To illustrate this point, consider a teacher who intends to record samples of a noncompliant student's behavior. If the instructor records data at various times based mainly on when she remembers to do it, the moments that are chosen are likely to over-represent the occurrence of uncooperative behavior and under-represent the occurrence of cooperation. The reason for this is that when the student is being compliant, the teacher is less likely to remember to record data samples. In order to counteract this tendency, the timing of the recordings needs to be based on some external factor that is truly random or at least not correlated with the student's behavior. For example, a timer could be set to signal the moment when the behavior should be observed, thereby eliminating the common problem that we are more likely to notice (and therefore more likely to remember to record) undesirable behavior.

We conducted a study at Autism Partnership's clinic to examine the comparative strengths of the three different forms of data collection; continuous/trial-by-trial, estimation, and time sample (Papovich et al., 2002). Each type was compared in terms of its accuracy (relative to an accuracy standard), efficiency (how many trials were accomplished in a teaching session and how many trials were required to master a skill), and preference (we hypothesized that preference would be related to likelihood of usage). Continuous/trial by trial was the most accurate (though the other methods were not inaccurate when used by trained recorders), estimation was the most efficient (followed by time sample), and time sample was ultimately the most preferred. The study points to the discrepant strengths of the various approaches.

Given the different strengths and weakness of the various forms of data collection, we typically recommend that data be taken based upon need as well as the particular benefits of the various forms of data collection. When practical considerations are most prominent, retrospective data is most routinely taken, with objective, trial-by-trial data being taken only on an intermittent basis. In so doing, not only is objective information on performance available on a sampled basis, but also objective data can be used as an accuracy standard against which the estimation data can be compared. Should the two data forms prove comparable, then confidence in the estimation data is strengthened. If there are inconsistencies, then efforts (e.g., additional training in estimation techniques) are directed at promoting comparability to increase the believability of the retrospective data.

When accuracy is most important, contemporaneous trial-by-trial data should be taken more frequently. Such cases may include circumstances where responding is unclear, behaviors are changing rapidly, or mastery needs to be established. Even in such cases, some amount of sampling may be possible, thereby adding the practical benefits of such measurement.

With modeling-practice-feedback types of instruction with persons with ASD, such as with Teaching Interactions, task analysis (rather than trial-by-trial) oriented data collection is typically used. With this measurement, the task is broken into its component steps and measurement of the correct or incorrect performance of each step is conducted. The percentage of correctly performed steps is then reported. As with discrete trial data, such measurement can occur on a continuous, sampled, or estimation basis. As before, the technique or combination of techniques utilized should reflect the information needed and a balance between the accurate and the practical.

BEHAVIORAL DATA COLLECTION

Examples of problematic or disruptive behavior of individuals with ASD are aggression, non-compliance, tantrums and self stimulation, for which there are several types of data collection. These include: **frequency counts** (how many times the behavior occurred); **rate** (frequency divided by time span); **duration** (how long it lasted); **latency** (how long of a delay before the behavior began); **intensity or severity**; and **ratio** (how many times out of how many opportunities) (Sulzer-Azaroff, et.al., 1991). The type of data collected largely depends on consideration of the important dimensions of the problem behavior. For example, the number of times tantrums occur during a day may be critical. Frequency counts would be taken on such responding. However, with a particular individual, tantrums may be infrequent but last for incredibly long periods of time. In such a case, duration recording would be important. For another person, how often or how long may be less important than how severe (how loud, how much is broken, level of force used, etc). As another example, straight frequency on compliance may be misleading. A child may comply five times on Monday and 20 times on Tuesday, and based on frequency information alone, we may conclude that he or she improved by Tuesday. However, if we learn that on Monday only five instructions were given and on Tuesday 50 were given, by taking ratio data we discover that Monday's 100% compliance is vastly superior to Tuesday's 40%.

Just as with instructional data, continuous sample and estimation data can be recorded on problematic behaviors. And just as with instructional data, it is recommended that the data collection protocol fit the informational needs of the effort. Most typically, we recommend that estimation data be taken on a regular basis for practical reasons, with periodic continuous data taken as an objective standard. Comparisons of the information between the two sources should regularly be made to ensure corroboration of the estimation data from the continuous data.

OTHER TYPES AND SOURCES OF INFORMATION

Information on the interventional performance or progress of a person with ASD may be collected in other ways and from other sources. For example, within school settings, information on the attainment of Individualized Educational Plan (IEP) goals might be useful. In all interventional settings, including home, school, and clinic, data on the introduction and mastery of instructional targets may provide meaningful information on progress. Rate of acquisition could be derived from knowing the number of trials required for a student to master a targeted item. Information on other areas of goal achievement (e.g. amount of spontaneous language, amount of time in less restrictive class placements, number of playmates, degree of successful toileting, amount of time successfully spent in community settings) may provide information on important areas of advancement.

Fading of programming (e.g., ending of a contingency contract, reduction of instructional time, longer periods before cash-in within token economies) might provide direct and indirect evidence of progress. Specifying the level of stressors or the difficulty level of tasks to which a student is exposed provide a meaningful context for interpreting frequency data. For example, the number of tantrums could remain unchanged but if the student is tolerating a higher level of stressors, we would be assured that progress is nevertheless occurring. Ratings from relevant respondents (e.g., parents and teachers) may be obtained as information supplemental to core observational data (Wolf, 1979). Ratings may include information on individuals' progress, the sufficiency of such progress, and consumers' satisfaction with services and their impacts. As noted above, augmentative information from standardized tests may provide information on progress and functioning in global areas.

GENERALIZATION

Data reflective of efforts and progress in the area of generalization is critical to documenting meaningful success. Generalization pertains to the appropriate, independent, and functional performance of learned skills, and consistency of behavior change, across a range of circumstances and settings, with a variety of individuals, and sustained over time (Baer, et.al., 1968; Baer, et.al., 1987, Sulzer-Azaroff, et.al., 1991). ABA is not merely concerned with a child's acquisition of targets, but with the development and independent utilization of meaningful and functional skills and capabilities. Further, it is not uncommon among children with ASD for generalization to be problematic. With spontaneous generalization so commonly lacking in ASD, there is a need for systematic programming specifically designed to promote generalization and for data that examines the success of such efforts. Therefore, information of the transfer of skills from specific individuals and situations to a range of people and circumstances, from the structured and contrived to the unstructured and natural, from a learning situation to functional and meaningful independent usage is of critical importance. This means data, of the various types we have discussed, should be collected outside of structured teaching and programmatic arrangements. Information should be available on the independent, functional and meaningful employment of learned skills, and on the consistency of behavioral improvement in natural situations and everyday contexts.

DATA ANALYSIS

As noted above, what we are really talking about is not so much data collection but data usage. Data must be relevant to assessment questions and intervention purposes, and collected in doable ways. We have found that taking data from the beginning (or as close to the beginning as possible) within interventional efforts helps staff develop an expectation and rhythm regarding data collection. It often helps to increase data collection responsibilities in stages. Starting perhaps with only estimation data and adding in periodic objective data collection over time and as interventional efforts are established. When data collection makes sense, then people are more likely to take it. Taking data that is user friendly and at levels at which the information is digestible helps here. When data is examined and progress is observed in graphic form, interventionists tend to get excited about the work they are doing, and the data that documents it. This in turn motivates data collection and analysis practices.

As part of developing practical data collection systems, we have also found that developing forms which contain a week's worth of information all on one sheet tend to be easier to use and manage. Such sheets also provide a broader picture of performance, all on one form. Further, these forms allow for easy summarization and this in turn allows for easy access and quick review of an individual's performance and progress. Forms can be designed in a manner that results in a graphic representation that allows easy analysis without having to take the additional step of transferring information to an actual graph. For example, when taking a frequency count, each day can be recorded in a column that consists of empty boxes. For each episode, staff can record an '**X**' in the next open box starting at the bottom of the column. At the end of the day, the height of the column of **X**'s can be instantly compared to the height of the previous days' columns, effectively yielding a bar graph with no extra work. We have found that the depiction of summary information in a graphic manner on the forms promotes easy data review on a week to week basis, even in the absence of charts or summary tables.

REFERENCES

Alevizos, P. (1978). "The behavior observation instrument: A method of direct observation for program evaluation." *Journal of Applied Behavior Analysis* 11(2): 243-257.

Alvero, A. M., & Austin, J. (2004). "The effects of conducting behavioral observations on the behavior of the observer." *Journal of Applied Behavior Analysis* 37(4): 457-468.

Austin, J. L. (2004). "Preparing Tomorrow's Behavior Analytic Researchers: A review of research methods in Applied Behavior Analysis by Jon Bailey and Mary Burch." *Journal of Applied Behavior Analysis* 2(243-248).

Baer, D. M., Wolf, M.M., & Risley, T.R. (1987). "Some current dimensions of applied behavior analysis." *Journal of Applied Behavior Analysis* 1(1): 91-97.

Baer, D. M., Wolf, M.M., & Risley, T.R. (1987). "Some still current dimensions of applied behavior analysis." *Journal of Applied Behavior Analysis* 20(4): 313-327.

Bailey, J. S., & Burch, M.R. (2002). *Research Methods in Applied Behavior Analysis.* Thousand Oaks, CA, Sage Publication.

Birkimer, J. C., Brown, J.H. (1979). "Back to basics: percentage agreement measures are adequate but there are easier ways." *Journal of Applied Behavior Analysis* 12(4): 535-543.

Campbell, M., Kafantaris, V., Malone, R.P., Kowalik, S.C., et.al. (1991). "Diagnostic and assessment issues related to pharmacotherapy for children and adolescents with autism." *Behavior Modification* 15(3): 326-354.

CARD Website (2002). Progression through the CARD Curriculum: Joey: A Case Study. WWW.centerforASD.com/whatiscard/progression.asp

Cone, J.D. (1998). Psychometric considerations. Concepts, contents, and methods. In A. S. Bellack & M. Hersen (Eds.) *Behavioral Assessment. A practical handbook.* (pp. 22-46). Boston, MA: Allyn and Bacon.

de-Bildt, A., Kraijer, D., Sytema, S., Minderaa. R. (2005). "The psychometric properties of the Vineland Adaptive Behavior Scales in Children and Adolescents with Mental Retardation." *Journal of Autism and Developmental Disorders* 35(1): 53-62.

Eaves, R. C. & Awadh, A. M. (1998). The diagnosis and assessment of autistic disorders. In H. B. Vance (Ed.) *Psychological Assessment of Children. Best Practices for school and clinical settings.* (pp. 385-417). New York, NY: John Wiley & Sons, Inc.

Fawcett, S.B. (1991) Social Validity: A note on methodology. *Journal of Applied Behavior Analysis,* 24 (2), 235-239.

Galizio, M. (1987). "Interpretation versus experimentation in the experimental analysis of human behavior." *Psychological Record* 37(1): 11-15.

Green, G. (1996). Evaluating claims about treatments for ASD. In C. Maurice, G. Green, & S. C. Luce (Eds.), *Behavioral intervention for young children with ASD* (pp. 15-28). Austin, TX: Pro-Ed.

Hall, R. V. (1999). Behavior Modification: *The Measurement of Behavior.* Austin, TX: Pro-Ed.

Handleman, J. S. (1990). "Providing effective consultation to students with severe developmental disabilities and their families." *Journal of Educational and Psychological Consultation* 1(2): 137-147.

Hanley, G. P., Iwata, B.A., & McCord, B.E. (2003). "Functional analysis of problem behavior: A review." *Journal of Applied Behavior Analysis* 36(2): 147-185.

Haynes, S. N. (1998). The changing nature of behavioral assessment. In A. S. Bellack & M. Hersen (Eds.) *Behavioral Assessment. A practical handbook.* (pp. 1-21). Boston, MA: Allyn and Bacon.

House, A. E. (1978). "Naturalistic Observation: Formal and informal difficulties." *Child Study Journal* 8(1): 17-28.

Johnston, J. M. (1996). "Distinguishing between applied research and practice." *Behavior Analyst* 19(1): 35-47.

Kelly, M. B. (1977). "A review of the observational data collection and reliability procedures reported in the Journal of Applied Behavior Analysis." *Journal of Applied Behavior Analysis* 10(1): 97-101.

Leaf, R.B. (1982). Outcome and predictive measures. Paper presented at the Annual Meeting of the American Psychological Association. Washington, D.C.

Lovaas, O.I., & Smith, T. (1988). Intensive behavioral treatment for young autistic children." In B.B. Lahey and A.E. Kazdin (Eds.), *Advances in Clinical Child Psychology*, Volume 11 (pp. 285-324). New York: Plenum.

Matson, J. L., Dixon, D.R., Matson, M.L., & Logan, J.R. (2005). "Classifying mental retardation and specific strength and deficit areas in severe and profoundly mentally retarded persons with the MESSIER." *Research in Developmental Disabilities* 26(1): 41-45.

Mayes, S. D., & Calhoun, S.L. (2004). "Similarities and Differences in Weschsler Intelligence Scale for Children-Third Edition (WISC-III) Profiles: Support for Subtest Analysis in Clinical Referrals." *Clinical Neuropsychologist* 18(4): 559-572.

Merrell, K. W. (1998). Assessing social skills and peer relations. In H. B. Vance (Ed.) *Psychological Assessment of Children. Best Practices for school and clinical settings.* (pp. 246-276). New York, NY: John Wiley & Sons, Inc.

Miltenberger, R. G. (2001). *Behavior Modification. Principles and Procedures.* Belmont, CA: Wadsworth/Thomas Learning.

Ollendick, T.H., Alvarez, H.K., & Green,R.W. (2003). Behavioral assessment: History of underlying concepts and methods. In E.M. Heiby & S. Haynes (Eds.), *Comprehensive handbook of psychological assessment*: Vol.3. Behavioral Assessment (pp. 16-37). New York: Wiley.

Miltenberger, R. G., Rapp, J.T., & Long, E.S. (1999). "A low tech method for conducting real time recording." *Journal of Applied Behavior Analysis* 32(1): 119-120.

Moore, J., & Cooper, J.O. (2003). "Some proposed relations among the domains of behavior analysis." *Behavior Analysts* 26(1): 69-84.

O'Leary, K. D., Kent, R.N., & Kanowitz, J. (1975). "Shaping data collection congruent with experimental hypotheses." *Journal of Applied Behavior Analysis* 8(1): 43-51.

Ollendick, T.H., Alvarez, H.K., & Greene, R.W. (2003). Behavioral assessment: History of underlying concepts and methods. In E.M. Heiby & S. Haynes (Eds.), Comprehensive handbook of psychological assessment: Vol. 3. Behavioral assessment (pp. 16-37). New York: Wiley.

Papovich, S., Rafuse, J., Siembieda, M., Williams, M., Sharpe, A., McEachin, J., Leaf, R., & Taubman, M. (2002). An Analytic Comparison of Data Collection Techniques Used with Discrete Trial Teaching in an Applied Setting for Persons with Autism. Paper presented at the Association for Behavior Analysis Annual Convention, Toronto, Canada.

Paul, R., Miles, S., Cicchetti.D., Sparrow, S., Klin, A., Volkmar, F., Colfin, M., & Booker. S. (2004). "Adaptive Behavior in Autism and Pervasive Developmental Disorders Not Otherwise Specified: Microanalysis of scores on the Vineland Adaptive Scale." *Journal of Autism and Developmental Disorders* 34(2): 223-228.

Pfadt, A., Wheeler, D.J. (1995). "Using Statistical process control to make data based clinical decisions." *Journal of Applied Behavior Analysis* 28(3): 349-370.

Repp, A. C. (1976). "A comparison of frequency, interval, and time sampling methods of data collection." *Journal of Applied Behavior Analysis* 9(4): 501-508.

Ringdahl, J. E., Vollmer, T.R., Borrero, J.C., & Connell, J.E. (2001). "Fixed-time schedule effects as a function of baseline reinforcement rate." *Journal of Applied Behavior Analysis* 34(1): 1-15.

Romanczyk, R. G., Kent, R.N., Diament, C., O'Leary, K.D. (1973). "Measuring the reliability of observational data: A reactive process." *Journal of Applied Behavior Analysis* 6(1): 175-184.

Smith, T, Groen, A.D., & Wynn, J. W. (2000). Randomized trial of intensive early intervention for children with pervasive developmental disorder. *American Journal on Mental Retardation*, 105, 269-285

Sturmey, P. (2006). "In Response to Lindsay and Emerson." *Journal of Applied Research in Intellectual Disabilities* 19(1): 125-129.

Sulzer-Azaroff, B. & Mayer, G. R. (1991). *Behavior Analysis for lasting change.* Fort Worth, TX: Harcourt Brace.

Vance, H. B. & Awadh, A. M. (1998). Best practices in assessment of children: Issues and trends. In H. B. Vance (Ed.) *Psychological Assessment of Children.* Best Practices for school and clinical settings. (pp. 1-10). New York, NY: John Wiley & Sons, Inc

Watson, R. I. (1951). The Vineland Social Maturity Scale. *The clinical method in psychology.* R. I. Watson. New York, NY, Harper and Brothers: 313-329.

Wolf, M. M. (1979) Social validity: The case for subjective measurement or how applied behavior analysis is finding its heart. *Journal of Applied Behavior Analysis, 11*(2), 203-214.

Chapter 10

FUNCTIONALITY IN BEHAVIORAL ASSESSMENT: A New Approach

By Tracee Parker, Andrea Waks, Ron Leaf & Craig Kennedy

INTRODUCTION

Behavior problems greatly impact the lives of children with autism by increasing family stress, restricting educational placement, and decreasing the child's overall quality of life. In an effort to improve outcomes for children with autism as well as other disabilities, researchers over the last 40 years have been attempting to determine effective means of intervention to reduce these behavior problems. The result of this substantial research effort indicates successful interventions for reducing problem behavior must be assessment driven.

Assessment results provide critical insight into the functions of problem behavior. That is, what need does the behavior serve to meet? What are the environmental circumstances maintaining unwanted behavior? Determining these functions enables us to alter the circumstances by establishing new contingencies and pinpointing replacement skills to be taught. Acquisition of new skills should enable the student to fulfill the need in an adaptive and socially acceptable manner.

TERMINOLOGY

As in many scientific disciplines, the field of applied behavior analysis (ABA) has diverse terminology and technical jargon. While there is general agreement in the application of some terms (e.g., positive reinforcement, extinction, and motivating operations), there is not consensus among behavior analysts regarding the terminology for many types of assessment procedures. Authors in the field of ABA have used various terms, including Behavioral Assessment, Functional Analysis, Functional Assessment, Functional Behavioral Analysis, Structural Analysis and Behavioral Analysis. To add to the confusion, the same terms may be used differently by those outside the field of ABA, such as legal and educational professionals.

In an effort to avoid confusion over terminology, we will follow the guidelines established in the 1997 Individuals with Disabilities Education Act (IDEA). In IDEA, the assessment process is generically referred to as Functional Behavioral Assessment (FBA) which covers the range of empirically derived behavioral assessment techniques in wide use. As the name implies, FBA refers to a methodology for assessing patterns of behavior using objective, quantifiable data. This is considered the foundation for developing effective intervention programs to reduce or eliminate problem ("target") behaviors.

The interventions resulting from an FBA will be referred to as Behavior Intervention Plans (BIP). The BIP commonly includes procedures to reduce the behavior in the short term (e.g. elimination of events that trigger, motivate, or reinforce the problem behavior) and teach replacement skills for the long term. While a broad range of BIP strategies are available, it is critical that the strategies utilized are evidence-based and logically follow from the findings of the FBA.

TRADITIONAL APPROACHES TO CONDUCTING A FBA:
Description and Comparison

Differing Perspectives on Functional Behavioral Assessment

Although there is agreement that determining functions is critical for assessment and successful intervention, there is division between professionals within the field as to the most effective and valid procedures for this process. One approach emphasizes the rigor and precision of the assessment process, using highly controlled and structured protocols that essentially meet the standards required for scientific studies. Another approach focuses on conducting naturalistic observations in those settings where the student normally functions day to day. While the efficacy of each of these procedures is the subject of ongoing debate and controversy, to date neither one has been empirically validated as superior to the other. Instead, it is likely that each approach has its place in the FBA process (Ellingson, Miltenberger, & Long, 1999).

There are three general categories of behavioral assessment, which are distinguished based on methodological approach and control of conditions under which data is collected.

The following section describes and compares these methodological approaches. For the sake of clarity, we will use the following terms in the context of a three tiered (level) system:

TIER I: INDIRECT MEASURES (RECORD REVIEW, INTERVIEWS & QUESTIONNAIRES)

These measures include the review of student records and/or obtaining information from individuals who are familiar with the student through interviews or questionnaires. Because this information is often gathered using varied methods and different sources, it can offer a comprehensive profile of the student and current conditions under which the student is functioning.

Record Reviews: A retrospective review of student records may include evaluations, progress reports, IEPs, behavior intervention data, standardized test results, or anecdotal and subjective reports. Sometimes past or current observational data regarding student behaviors is contained in these records. Student records can provide valuable information on the outcome of current and previous interventions, student functioning and skill level, history of school placement, types of services received, and relationships between the student and individuals (e.g., parents, teachers, or school staff) currently involved with the student.

While this information does not precisely reflect current patterns of behavior, it offers relevant background about factors that have contributed to and maintained problem behaviors over time. Utilized in conjunction with current information, this can assist the behavior analyst in developing a "road map" for planning and designing subsequent steps of assessment and treatment. It enables the behavior analyst to identify individuals who are most knowledgeable about the student, and thus prioritize the inclusion of follow-up interviews and/or questionnaires.

Interviews and questionnaires: This method involves soliciting information from individuals who are familiar with and regularly spend time with the student, as well as from the student himself/herself. Data may be collected through interviews or self-administered questionnaires. These measures provide first hand descriptions of behaviors, environmental correlates (i.e., conditions under which the target behaviors are most and least likely to occur), general factors influencing behavior, history of treatment, etc.

Non-standardized approaches may include interviews or questionnaires that are developed by the behavior analyst specifically for a particular student's profile and circumstances. The design and focus of the inquiry is often based on information gathered from the records review.

Standardized approaches use a number of formal instruments that have been developed for gathering anecdotal information in a structured and organized format. Many of these measures can be conducted as either interviews and/or self-administered questionnaires. Some examples include: Motivation Analysis Rating Scale (MARS) by Wiesler, Hanson, Chamberlain, & Thompson (1985), Behavioral Diagnosis and Treatment Information Form, (BDTIF) by Bailey & Pyles (1989), Stimulus Control Checklist (SCC) by Rolider & Van Houton (1993), and Functional Analysis Interview Form, (FAIF) by O'Neil, Horner, Albin, Storeyand Sprague, (1990).

Advantages

- Information obtained using these methods incorporates multiple perspectives from a variety of professional disciplines and provides insight into the current conditions under which the student is functioning.

- Review of records can offer information that was contemporaneously documented.

- Records help narrow the focus on relevant sources and highlight additional information needed (e.g., sources to interview).

- With standardized methods, it will be relatively easy to organize and compare information across and between varied sources.

- Indirect methods can be conducted in advance of an onsite visit.

Limitations

- Documents can be ambiguous and difficult to understand and interpret.

- The original sources (who produced the records)may not be available to clarify information contained in records.

- Interviews and questionnaires have the disadvantage of inaccurate recall.

- Depending on the amount and variability of sources, collection and integration of the information obtained can be extremely time consuming and complex.

- Indirect measures are limited by the subjective bias of the individual sources, as compared to direct observations.

- And most importantly, indirect measures alone are insufficient for determining behavioral functions. However, even proponents of more rigorous approaches report utilizing indirect measures as an initial step in the assessment process.

TIER 2: DESCRIPTIVE ASSESSMENT

This process utilizes direct, naturalistic observations of student behavior as a method for assessing and generating hypotheses regarding functions. Observations are usually conducted in one or more environmental contexts and target behaviors are recorded in relation to the events that precede and follow them. Tier 2 assessments generally include the following components: (1) objective definitions of behavior and environment, (2) coding system and rules for observations, (3) quantitative methods for summarizing data, and (4) assessment of inter-observer agreement.

Data Collection: During this process, the observer directly (but passively) observes and records objective data on the student's behavior patterns. The type of data collected includes both quantitative (e.g., frequency, intensity, and/or duration) and descriptive (e.g., antecedent, behavior and consequence patterns) for each target behavior.

Procedures: There are a number of observational measures utilized and recommended for conducting Tier 2 assessments. Three commonly used methods are: Continuous Observation (e.g., frequency, ratio, or duration recording), Antecedent-Behavior-Consequence (ABC) Measures, and Narrative Recording. Unlike a Tier 3 assessment, data may be collected for more than one target behavior simultaneously.

Duration/Time frame: The duration and number of sessions needed to complete this type of assessment depends on the variety and complexity of target behaviors and patterns. However, in actual practice, Tier 2 assessment is considered ongoing.

That is, once pre-treatment baselines are established, intervention is initiated and the assessment process continues indefinitely throughout the course of the treatment program, including generalization and maintenance phases. In such a manner, information on behaviors and their functions continues to be refined.

Observers: Data is gathered by one observer most of the time, with a second observer (periodically) for inter-observer reliability checks. The observations are generally conducted by individuals who have little or no history with the student. However, as more teachers and school staff are trained in this methodology, it may be possible for those who are familiar to conduct observations, thereby reducing subjectivity.

Context: Refers to Individuals, Setting and Conditions.

<u>*Individuals:*</u> It is common practice to observe both the student and individuals who typically interact (e.g., staff, parents, etc.) with the student.

<u>*Settings*</u>: Observations are usually done in natural settings where the student typically functions day-to-day. Of particular interest are settings in which target behaviors are most likely and least likely to occur (for comparison).

<u>*Conditions:*</u> Generally, there is no intentional change in the typical conditions and the observer is unobtrusive. Depending on degree of social awareness, the observer's presence may or may not alter the student's typical behavior. Of course, the observer's presence may impact how others (e.g., staff, parents, etc.) interact, and indirectly alter the student's behavior. Repeated observations typically reduce such reactivity.

Advantages

- Proponents assert this method is less costly and time consuming, as compared to Tier 3 assessments.

- Use of direct, contemporaneous observational measures avoids errors due to retrospective recall and subjective bias.

- Because it is conducted in natural settings, it is less intrusive, disruptive and restrictive to the student and offers greater ecological validity (represents what naturally and typically occurs).

- Observing multiple target behaviors simultaneously offers insight as to the interrelationship between target behaviors (e.g., pattern/cycle of escalation).

- Since assessment occurs in natural setting, it allows for comparison of pre-intervention verses post-intervention behavior, within the same setting.

- It is suggested that non-experts can be trained to utilize this method in a relatively short time, in comparison to Tier 3.

Limitations

- Tier 2 assessments do not afford systematic, precise control in manipulating variables or measuring behaviors. Thus, results do not necessarily demonstrate the same degree of experimental rigor, or convincingly establish causative relationships, as compared to Tier 3.

TIER 3: ANALOG OR EXPERIMENTAL ANALYSIS

This approach involves controlled manipulation of environmental events that serve as antecedents and positive and/or negative reinforcement for problem behavior using single-case designs.

Data collection: Tier 3 assessments commonly involve very precise and elaborate data collection procedures, similar to those in experimental research studies (at times using very sophisticated equipment). The degree of precision and complexity depends on the student's profile and the specific target behaviors being assessed. To date, there are no established methods for determining the best instruments or strategies for collecting or integrating data (Bellack & Hersen, 1998), and none has been definitively demonstrated as superior. Descriptions of the wide variety of complex data collection and analysis procedures is beyond the scope and focus of this chapter.

Procedures: These assessments utilize different types of single-case experimental designs to establish a functional relationship between behavior and environmental events (Kennedy, 2005). During this process, antecedents and consequences are presented or withdrawn in a precise manner, to establish the specific impact of these variables on each of the target behaviors. The procedure is performed as separate and distinct analyses for each individual target behavior. Once the procedure is initiated for a given target behavior, it continues until the behavior stabilizes. Once stabilized, the analysis for that behavior is considered complete. The same procedure may then begin for another target behavior. This type of assessment has a distinct beginning and end for each behavior being assessed.

Duration/Time frame: As with Tier 2, the duration of time required to complete a Tier 3 may vary considerably, depending upon the number of target behaviors and variables introduced. Reports in the literature are inconsistent regarding comparison of durations for Tier 3 and Tier 2. Tier 3 (like Tier 2) may be conducted prior to, during and following intervention.

Observers: The observers are usually unfamiliar (e.g., have limited or no history) with the student. Due to the complexity, conducting Tier 3 assessments requires a high level of expertise. It is common to utilize at least two full time observers.

Context: Refers to Individuals, Setting and Conditions.

<u>Individuals:</u> The individuals who conduct the protocol (interact) with the student, and are usually unfamiliar (e.g., have little or no history) with the student.

Setting: Assessment generally occurs in a clinic or laboratory, requiring removal of the student from the natural environment where the target behaviors typically occur.

Conditions: Assessment is conducted under simulated (highly controlled and standardized) conditions.

Advantages

■ Use of direct observational measures avoids errors due to retrospective recall and subjective bias.

■ This method is considered more precise and accurate for the identification of environmental determinants of behavior through demonstration of functional relationships.

■ Proponents suggest that this analysis allows for the development of truly individualized treatment plans based on sound assessment data.

Limitations

■ It may increase the risk of behavior problems beyond acceptable limits.

■ Some behaviors are not amenable to this type of assessment because:

1) They are maintained by alleviation of painful conditions (not ethical);

2) Low frequency behaviors may not be elicited under these procedural conditions (Austin & Carr, 2000).

■ A variable may be selected and/or identified using this type of assessment that is not in fact the maintaining variable in the natural environment.

■ Opponents suggest this is more costly and time consuming than Tier 2 assessments.

■ As Tier 3 is typically conducted in a lab or clinic, reactivity due to intrusive procedures in these artificial environments may affect behavior, thereby reducing assessment validity.

Tier 3 appears to be an extremely precise and therefore accurate assessment. However, because of the issues and limitations mentioned, it may, under a range of circumstances, not be the most accurate assessment approach.

FOUNDATIONS FOR AN ALTERNATIVE APPROACH

Given comparative advantages and limitations of different FBA methods we propose an approach to assessment process that maximizes the following considerations:

- Validity: Inclusion of multiple sources, methods & contexts.

- Systematic: Flexible yet structured application of procedures in an individualized manner.

- Efficiency & Efficacy: Interventions determined in relation to viability of success across settings and interventionists.

The following sections highlight these premises, along with clinical and behavioral rationales that support them.

MULTIPLE SOURCES, METHODS & CONTEXTS

Any professional who conducts FBA can attest to the variability in information obtained from different sources, methods and contexts.

- Parents often present a very different picture than teachers when reporting about the same behavior.

- By the same token, observations by one staff member may vary considerably from another staff member, even in reference to the same context.

- Subjective verbal reports compared to documented records can be widely divergent, even when the source and timeframe are the same.

- Similarly, objective behavior observations and subjective reports during the same time may look like two different students were observed.

- The underlying causes of this variance include: difference in individual perspectives, professional training/orientation, knowledge of student and their history, and subjective bias. Review and comparison of these variations offers important clues and insight for delineating functions, as well as potentially effective interventions.

The importance of utilizing multiple sources, methods and contexts for valid assessment is well established (Bellack & Hersen, 1998). The more diverse the sources, methods and contexts, the closer to "reality" (more valid) our theories about the functions will be.

SYSTEMATIC DETERMINATION OF INDIVIDUALIZED ASSESSMENT PROCEDURE

Maximizing experimental rigor and precision via highly controlled conditions are suggested/considered benefits of Tier 3. Similarly, minimizing intrusion and preserving what is typical through naturalistic observation is assumed an advantage of Tier 2 assessments. We would argue that neither statement is necessarily or absolutely true. In contrast, we propose that control, precision, intrusion and other assessment parameters be individually determined based on the student clinical profile.

Assume that cost, time, and expertise required for Tier 2 and Tier 3 are equivalent. We propose the following questions in determining the optimum assessment protocol warranted:

. . . Is it based on systematic evaluation of individual clinical needs?

. . . Is it flexible in adapting procedures to identify the primary functions?

. . . Is it in the best interests of the student?

Our contention is in many cases these questions are neither asked nor answered prior to beginning an assessment. Systematic consideration and progression to include advantages of all three FBA tiers in each particular case is not standard practice. More typical is the application of a preferred methodology regardless of the child's needs or circumstances.

FLEXIBILITY

Flexibility in design and implementation of assessment protocol is not standard practice. The adherence to a cookbook approach to assessment negatively compromises the quality of all types of assessments, leading to poor outcomes as well as wasted time and money.

Traditionally, Tier 2 and Tier 3 assessment procedures are considered to have distinct characteristics. While this may appear true, we assert that these distinctions are not inflexible and need not be viewed and used as such. Failure to adjust Tier 2 procedures for greater control may result in an unnecessary referral for a Tier 3. If in fact a Tier 3 is warranted, adherence to an unduly rigorous protocol may result in substantial control and precision, but may not be necessary or representative of the specific needs. We suggest conceptualizing FBA procedures along a continuum.

While factors commonly cited to distinguish Tier 2 and 3 tend to fall on one end of the continuum versus the other, common practices and scientific studies drift in both directions. Consider the traditional descriptions for Tier 2 and Tier 3 assessments as "anchors" on each end of a continuum.

Tier 2 (Descriptive Assessment): One end of the continuum is the textbook Tier 2 method. Behavior functions are assessed via direct, naturalistic and objective observations of behavior patterns. It is conducted in one or more settings (home, school, *etc.*), while student follows typical daily routines with the same people they normally interact with. There is no intentional alteration in the usual circumstances (e.g., activities, practices or interactions with the student). This end of the continuum represents minimum experimental control, under highly natural, non-contrived conditions.

Tier 3 (Analog Functional Analysis): On the other end of the continuum is the "textbook" Tier 3 methodology. Assessment requires highly controlled, standardized conditions, using systematic manipulation of variables and precise and elaborate data collection procedures. This end of the continuum represents maximum experimental control, under extremely contrived and artificial conditions.

To illustrate, examples of variations within and across these methodological anchors are described.

PHYSICAL LOCATION/SETTING

It is not uncommon that some behaviors and patterns occur only in particular settings, but not in others (the playground vs. the classroom, the grocery store vs. at home, etc.).

- In a Tier 2, specific changes in the natural environment can be made in order to increase control of factors that impact target behaviors. For example: Altering the physical arrangement, increasing or decreasing accessibility to certain items or objects, changing where the student is seated, etc.

    - Theoretically, a Tier 3 procedure could be conducted within more natural settings (e.g., classroom or home), where target behaviors normally occur. This would require cooperation of others (e.g., teachers or parents) as it would disrupt the normal routine. Disruption could be minimized by conducting the assessment at a specific time (e.g., before or after school) or at a different location within the natural setting (e.g., an empty room).

INDIVIDUALS

Behaviors may vary considerably, depending on who is interacting with the student (e.g., presence of a particular staff member versus another), even when all other conditions are the same. Comparing these differences offers insight for understanding behavior functions. Both Tier 2 and Tier 3 assessments could benefit from systematic variation of this person factor.

- Observations of a familiar versus unfamiliar person working with the student can be compared.

- Observations with and without peers may be relevant, as some student behaviors are rarely observed if peers are not present.

- An unfamiliar person can be introduced in the context of normal routine in a Tier 2.

- A variety of individuals who typically interact with the student (e.g., peers, school staff, etc.) could be systematically introduced and removed from the setting during observation.

- A familiar person could implement the structured protocol with the student under the guidance and direction of a Tier 3 assessor.

PROCEDURE

Observations collected under structured versus unstructured conditions often reveal significant differences in behavior patterns.

■ The degree of control in a Tier 2 can be increased by structuring conditions in particular ways. For example, the assessor can guide staff or parents to change instructions, feedback or other responses. Such variations can be systematically introduced and withdrawn while behavior changes are recorded.

Suggestions to staff or parents to engage in responses that might increase problem behavior are frequently an uncomfortable proposition to those parties (often an understandable position in applied settings). Recommendations to probe responses that may promote alternative desirable behavior may be a satisfactory alternative which will also provide valuable information for the assessment.

Tier 3 assessments often adhere to a level of experimental rigor that meets the requirements for publication in scientific journals. Thus, it is not surprising that the literature reflects a wide variety and quantity of Tier 3 studies. However, in contrast, relatively few of these studies include data demonstrating successful generalization of the intervention outside of these clinic or laboratory settings. In general clinical practice there is less concern with empirically proving whether the hypothesized variables did in fact cause the undesired behavior. To put it simply, the doctor will be satisfied if the patient recovers and remains healthy. What more could one ask for in terms of a successful outcome?

Formal Vs. Informal FBA: For many experienced practitioners, it becomes almost innate to apply the FBA process anytime we observe or work with a student, regardless of current phase of assessment or intervention. After thousands of observations and hundreds of students, this ability is refined such that lengthy observations using formal protocols are unnecessary to assess and recommend highly effective treatment programs. The accuracy of this proficiency has been validated through many exceptional student outcomes. This is not to suggest throwing out formal FBA, which may be clinically, legally or procedurally warranted. Our contention is to consider rationales (desired outcome and circumstances) before embarking on costly, time consuming formal assessment.

Instead of a pre-determined standardized Tier 3 protocol, elements of the student's normal routine and activities can be incorporated within the structured procedure. For example, familiar routines, instructions, materials, etc., associated with target behaviors, can be used in the protocol. This may include presentation of familiar tasks or denial of particular items that commonly result in exhibition of target behaviors.

CENTRAL CONSIDERATIONS

It is ironic that as systematic and individualized as FBAs are intended to be, the overall clinical approach is often neither. Practitioners do not generally utilize a stepwise progression, or objective criteria in deciding on the type of FBA or individualizing the protocol. Adherence to cookbook protocols can lead to useless results, unwarranted rigor and intrusion, and wasted resources. Students may be subjected to disruption and removal from normal routines and environment to undergo unnecessary restrictive procedures that may not be in their best interests or characteristic of what is typical. Systematic and individualized selection of assessment procedures and protocol affords the gathering of optimal information based on the needs of the students in an efficient, representative, and effective manner.

Successful intervention requires implementing programming in the necessary settings that will effectively impact and change the student behavior as intended. Determining optimal intervention requires bearing in mind factors that influence viable application across settings and interventionists.

Any intervention plan, regardless of assessment procedure, remains a work in progress. Design and implementation of intervention is a continuous, dynamic and fluid process, requiring ongoing evaluation of its impact on behaviors. As is common knowledge within our field, progress and change in student behavior patterns requires regular revision of the intervention program (Scott et al., 2004). Given that a Tier 2 process continues indefinitely, errors in the initial (pre-treatment) assessment phase will likely be revealed relatively quickly through ongoing evaluation of target behaviors. This affords opportunities to adjust and revise the treatment program as needed.

An experienced clinician is often able to make reasonably accurate estimates about the variables to be quantified and calculated guesses about the functions of targeted behaviors.

CONCLUSION

Our intent was presentation of evidence and rationales for utilizing a more flexible, individualized and hierarchical approach to conducting FBA . The goal is to limit data gathered to that which is necessary to effectively formulate a viable intervention plan. The process highlights inclusion of multiple sources, methods and contexts. It is strongly suggested that the student team be involved and consulted throughout this process. We recommend a sequential progression for collection and evaluation of data. This progression begins with general questions and information and systematically proceeds to specific focus of inquiry. At each phase, the compiled data is reviewed and evaluated to make decisions regarding necessity, purpose and goals for the next phase. Decisions are based on knowledge gained as well as efficiency, necessity, representativeness, and utilization of least intrusive and restrictive procedures whenever possible, in the best interest of the student.

REFERENCES

Austin, J., & Carr, J. E. (2000). *Handbook of applied behavior analysis.* Reno: Context Press.

Axelrod, S. (1987). Functional and structural analysis of behavior: Approaches leading to the reduced use of punishment procedures? Research in Developmental Disabilities, 8, 165 178.

Bailey, J. S., & Pyles, D. A. M. (1989). Behavioral Diagnostics. In E. Cipani (Ed.), *The treatment of severe behavior disorders: Behavior analysis approach,* (pp. 85-107). Washington D. C.: American Association on Mental Retardation.

Bellack, A. S., & Hersen, M. (1998). *Behavioral assessment: A practical handbook* (4th ed.). Boston: Allyn and Bacon.

Carr, J. E., Taylor, C. C., Wallander, R. J., & Reiss, M. L. (1996). A functional analysis approach to the diagnosis of a transient tic disorder. *Journal of Behavior Therapy and Experimental Psychiatry, 27,* 291-297.

Ellingson, S. A., Miltenberger, R. G., & Long, E. S. (1999). A survey of the use of functional assessment procedures in agencies serving individuals with developmental disabilities. *Behavioral Interventions, 14,* 187-198.

Foster, S. L., & Cone J. D. (1995). Validity issues in clinical assessment. *Psychological Assessment.* 7, 248 260.

Individuals with Disabilities Education Act Amendments of 1997, 20 U.S.C. 1400 *et seq.*

Iwata, B. A., Pace, G. M., Dorsey, M. F., Zarcone, J.R., Vollmer, T. R., Smith, R. G., Rodgers, T. A., Lerman, D. C. Shore, B. A., Mazaleski, J. L., Goh, H., Cowdery, G. E., Kalsher, M. J., & Willis, K. D. (1994). The functions of self-injurious behavior: An experimental-epidemiological analysis. *Journal of Applied Behavior Analysis, 27,* 215-240.

Kennedy, C. H. (2005). *Single-case designs for educational research.* Boston: Allyn & Bacon.

Lalli, J. S., Casey S., & Kates, K. (1995). Reducing escape behavior and increasing task completion with functional communication training, extinction and response chaining. *Journal of Applied Behavior Analysis, 28,* 261-268.

Messick, S. (1993). Validity. In R. L. Linn (Ed.), *Educational measurement* (2nd ed.). Phoenix: American Council on Education and the Oryx Press.

Nezu, A. M., & Nezu, C. M. (1989). *Clinical decision making in behavior therapy: A problem solving perspective.* Champagne, IL: Research Press.

O'Brien, S. N., & Haynes, S. N. (1995). Functional analysis. In Gualberto Buela-Casal (Ed.), *Handbook of psychological assessment.* Madrid: Sigma.

O'Neill, R. E., Horner, R. H., Albin, R. W., Storey, K., & Sprague, J. R. (1990). *Functional analysis: A practical assessment guide.* Sycamore, IL: Sycamore, Publishing Co.

Persons, J. B., & Fresco, D. M. (1996). Assessment of depression. In M. Hersen & A. S. Bellack (Eds.), *Behavioral assessment: A practical handbook* (4th ed.). Boston: Allyn and Bacon.

Piazza, C. C., Hanley, G. P., & Fisher, W. W. (1996). Functional analysis and treatment of cigarette pica. *Journal of Applied Behavior Analysis, 29,* 437-450.

Rojahn, J., & Ebsensen, A. J. (2002). Epidemiology of self-injurious behavior in mental retardation: A review. In S. R. Schroeder, M. L. Oster-Granite, & T. Thompson (Eds.), *Self-injurious behavior: Gene-brain-behavior relationships* (pp. 41-78). Washington, DC: American Psychological Association.

Rolider, A., & Van Houton, R. (1993). The interpersonal treatment model. In R. Van Houton & S. Axelrod (Eds.), *Behavior analysis and treatment*, (pp. 127-168). New York: Plenum.

Schroeder, S. R., Oster-Granite, M. L., Berkson, G., Bodfish, J. W., Breese, G. R. et al. (2001). Self-injurious behavior: Gene-brain-behavior relationships. *Mental Retardation and Developmental Disabilities Research Reviews, 7*, 3-12.

Schulte, D. (1992). Criteria of treatment selection in behavior therapy. *European Journal of Psychological Assessment, 8*, 157-162.

Scott, T. M., Bucalos, A., Liaupsin, C., Nelson, C. M., Jolivette, J., DeShea, L., et al. (2004). Using functional behavior assessment in general education settings: Making a case for effectiveness and efficiency. *Behavioral Disorders, 29*, 189-201.

Sisson, L. A., & Taylor, J. C. (1993). Parent training in A. S. Bellack & M. Hersen (Eds.), *Handbook of behavior therapy in the psychiatric setting* (pp. 555-574). New York: Plenum.

Vollmer, T. R., Marcus, B. A., Ringdahl, J. E., & Roane, H. S. (1995). Progressing from brief assessments to extended experimental analyses in the evaluation of aberrant behavior. *Journal of Applied Behavior Analysis, 28*, 561-576.

Vollmer, T. R., Northrup, J., Ringdahl, J. E., LeBlanc, L. A., & Chauvin, T. M. (1996). Functional analysis of severe tantrums displayed by children with language delays: An outclinic assessment. *Behavior Modification, 20*, 97-115.

Wiesler, N. A., Hanson, R. H., Chamberlain, T. P., & Thompson, T. (1985). Functional taxonomy of stereotypic and self injurious behavior. *Mental Retardation, 23*, 230-234.

Wincze, J. P. (1982). Assessment of sexual disorders. *Behavioral Assessment, 4*, 257-271.

Appendix A

COURSE CONTENT FOR TRAINING ABA PERSONNEL

TRAINING OUTLINE

I. Overview: ABA and Autism

II. Classroom Environment

III. Curriculum

IV. ABA Instruction

V. Reinforcement

VI. Behavior Programming

VII. Data

VIII. The Classroom Team, Professionalism, Liaisoning

PART I
OVERVIEW: ABA AND AUTISM

This section outlines material on Applied Behavior Analysis (ABA) and autism to provide basic understanding in these areas and to serve as a foundation for other learning. Material in these areas could comprise of complete courses unto themselves, so it should be clear that only basic information, necessary to provide philosophical underpinnings and core material, is provided.

Historical roots of ABA and the empirically-based nature of the discipline is considered. That ABA deals with an observable, measurable phenomenon concerned with an individual's behavior and controlling environmental conditions is also covered. The nature and theories of operant behavior, which is behavior controlled by its consequences and respondent behavior, and responding controlled by antecedents, are also addressed.

The history of the origins of the diagnostic label of autism is provided. Autism is defined from an ABA perspective, that is, in terms of its behaviors. Behavioral excesses (e.g., aggression, tantrums, self stimulation, non compliance) and deficits (e.g., in language/communication, social skills, play and leisure skills, self help, cognitive capabilities) and their exhibition along a continuum are spelled out. The behavioral nature of the disorder is compared to the abundance of past and current myths and speculation about causes and cures, as well as to the current clinical diagnostic definition of autism and related disorders in the Diagnostic and Statistical Manual (DSM IV TR) used by psychological and psychiatric practitioners. Current understanding about possible etiology is covered and a template for critical analysis of hypothesis about the causes of autism is offered.

Following this is a discussion of ABA research in autism (covering facts and fictions about the approach) and included are the seminal efforts of Dr. Ivar Lovaas and the long term outcome investigation of the UCLA Young Autism Project. Other behavioral methods including Pivotal Response Training, incidental teaching, verbal behavior, activity schedules, and Project TEACCH are compared. Finally, evolutions in the ABA approach, including a movement to greater naturalness and flexibility, are detailed.

OVERVIEW: ABA AND AUTISM

I. What is ABA?

    A. History

    B. Basic Theory/Tenets

        1. Outside Skin—Behavior and Environment

        2. Behavior as Learned

        3. Observable, Objective

        4. Empirically Supported

    C. Operant Behavior

        1. ABCs

        2. Functions of Behavior

    D. Respondent Behavior

        1. Defined

        2. Contrasted with Operant

II. Autism from ABA perspective

    A. Mythology

    B. Continuum/Spectrum

    C. DSM IV TR definition and PDDs

D. Deficits

E. Excesses

F. Speculation on Causes

G. Speculative/Alternative Treatments

H. Current Genetic and Neurobiological Understanding

I. Awareness, Critical Analysis, and Consumerism

III. ABA and Autism

A. Early Interventions

B. Procedural Research

C. Outcome Research

D. Other ABA Approaches

   1. PRT/NLP

   2. Verbal Behavior

   3. Incidental Teaching

   4. Activity Schedules

   5. TEACCH

E. Current Evolutions

How

■ *Presentations*

■ *Discussion*

■ *Readings: "A Work in Progress" by Leaf & McEachin; Behavioral Intervention for Young Children with Autism", by Eds. Maurice, Green, & Luce; "The World of the Autistic Child" by Siegel; "Let Me Hear Your Voice" By Maurice.*

PART II
CLASSROOM ENVIRONMENT

This section is concerned with the physical setup of a self contained classroom for students with autism. The focus is on the interplay and interdependence between the programmatic and instructional content of a class and the actual classroom environment.

Emphasized is the attention paid to the functionality of the way the classroom is designed. This includes consideration of the way areas are labeled, space is used, furniture is arranged, transitions are facilitated, and students' specific needs are taken into account. Storage, organization, appropriateness, and accessibility of stimuli, curriculum, and reinforcement materials are also covered. In terms of the classroom decor, it is emphasized that the environment should have instructional purpose, approximate a regular education classroom as much as possible, and be thematically relevant, attractive, and age-appropriate. Supportive rationales are provided regarding the instructional value of such arrangements, and the generalization benefits accrued through the naturalistic nature of the environment.

Much time is spent on the classroom schedule. Such important factors as classwide aspects, individualization, pacing, range of instructional arrangements and formats, practical considerations, and ongoing review of the schedule are underscored. Division of the self-contained classroom into centers, subject areas, or periods as appropriate as a means to cover core curriculum and to approximate regular education is also covered.

Finally, this section addresses the critical area of classroom organization. Staff scheduling and assignments, preparation, documentation, and lesson planning and the relationship of these considerations to classroom organization and efficient operation is discussed.

CLASSROOM ENVIRONMENT

1. **Design and setup is functionally appropriate**

   A. <u>Rationale</u>: There are numerous physical layout considerations that can greatly impact the classroom environment for children with autism. A classroom that is attractive, cheerful, orderly and interesting indicates to children that this is a place where they want to be. They should feel comfortable, safe, and motivated to learn. The setup of the classroom is an important component in setting the tone and occasion for learning, accommodating and supporting students' behavioral needs, and facilitating independent and smooth transitions from area to area

B. Areas are clearly defined

C. Limited space is maximized

D. Furniture arrangement serves a purpose

    1. Defines learning areas

    2. Blocks access to unauthorized areas, but permits free movement to learning areas

E. Consideration is given to transition areas/systems, "traffic flow" during rotations, and dual purposes for learning areas

F. Room arrangement decisions include considerations of individual student needs

    1. Behavioral concerns

    2. Distractibility

    3. Typically developing peers

    4. Other needs specific to class' students

G. Classroom setup should be viewed as an evolutionary process

H. Materials are organized and displayed in appropriate learning areas for functionality, care and safety, and accessibility

I. Materials are clean, complete, and in good working order

J. Materials are appropriate for desired skill acquisition

How

■ *Readings: Chapter 4 Creative Curriculum*

■ *Presentation*

■ *Examples/Models*

■ *Exercises: Evaluate two sample classroom setups considering the first five classroom design components. Discuss positive aspects observed and possible solutions for areas of need; apply these components to trainee classroom design. Identify positive aspects and identify possible solutions for areas of need; use scaled classroom model to assist in rearranging the setup if desired*

- *Followup, in-class consultation should involve application, review, and feedback in this area*

2. **Classroom environment is cheerful and age appropriate**

   A. <u>Rationale</u>: A cheerful, clearly positive environment sets the tone for learning. Cheerful skill-oriented materials are not only attractive to look at, but are also more motivating for children to respond to. Thematic units provide a motivational, high-interest template for teaching new information and skills in a meaningful context. Teaching new skills with age-appropriate materials assists in fostering pro-social opportunities by providing students with more socially acceptable participation options

   B. Classroom décor serves a purpose (skill oriented, numerals, alphabet)

   C. Classroom décor and materials are thematically linked to instruction

   D. Classroom décor is age appropriate

   E. Classroom should reflect a literacy rich environment

   F. Classroom environment should be presented in an attractive, tidy, and orderly way

   G. Materials are age-appropriate

   H. Materials are attractively displayed

How

- *Review attached list of suggested materials*

- *Discussion*

- *Examples are viewed and evaluated according to necessary components*

- *Exercises: Trainee identifies materials in own classroom which are not age appropriate*

- *Identify age-appropriate materials, which could serve the same educational purpose*

- *Brainstorm with staff for additional replacement ideas; "design a wall activity"*

- *Followup, in-class consultation should involve application, review, and feedback in this area*

3. Structure/Schedule

A. <u>Rationale</u>: Establishing schedules and routines are critical for creating consistency and predictability. Consistency and predictability are important for students' comfort, independence, and success in participating in the activities presented throughout the day. An established schedule does not mean lack of flexibility and should eventually be used to teach deviations, spontaneity, tolerance and adaptation. A clearly established schedule is also critical in maximizing opportunities for instructing students

B. Schedule is established and posted in a visible area of the room for easy reference

C. Schedule is designed to meet the dynamic needs of the students

D. Schedule is evaluated and modified to reflect changes in student needs

E. Individualization within the schedule is established

    1. For unique variations from master schedule:

        a. Specific Goals for Student's Involvement

        b. Varied Activities/Routine

        c. Specific Duration of Participation

    2. Individual schedules are created and posted as needed

F. Stations/Centers/Subjects/Periods/Activities are varied and balanced to promote active learning, breadth of focus, and engagement

    1. For younger students, Station/Center areas may be defined by activities and targets

        a. Group/Circle Time

        b. House Keeping/Imaginary/Role Play/Make Believe

        c. Table Toys/Manipulatives

        d. Language Center

        e. Library

        f. Art

        g. Computer

        h. Indoor Gross Motor Play

    2. For older students, areas may be defined by subjects or periods

G. Individual, small group, and whole group instruction are represented

H. Individual student needs should be considered when time is allocated to instructional options (e.g., need for one on one instruction vs. need for transitioning skills to small and large group activities

I. Movement activities, indoor vs. outdoor are represented

J. Goals to be addressed within activities can be included in the schedule or posted separately in the area

    1. Target areas such as language/communication, socialization, play, gross motor, and academic can be listed

    2. Individualized curricula, or curricular layers can be noted (see Curriculum section)

K. Staff assignment/rotation schedule can be included or presented separately in the area

L. Minimize down time and maximize teachable moments and active engagement

M. Schedule is maintained and implemented by staff

How

- *Discussion*

- *Example schedules*

- *Exercises: Review demonstration class schedule. Identify positive aspects of scheduling, as well as areas that appear to require adjustment based on hypothetical changes in student needs. Provide rationale for the above determinations; Trainee evaluates own schedule with regard to class' instructional needs. Identify areas schedule that need modification. Provide rationale for making those changes*

- *Collaborate with itinerant intern classroom teacher for replication in your classroom*

- *Followup, in-class consultation should involve application, review, and feedback in this area*

4. Organization

    A.   Rationale: Organization is the foundation of a successful classroom. Preparation, organization of materials and documentation, and clearly defined roles of classroom staff create an atmosphere of efficiency, productivity, and confidence for the staff that significantly impacts the instruction of the students. In an organized classroom, down time is minimized and instructional time is optimally spent systematically teaching students individually targeted skills

    B.   Preparedness is critical

        1.   Necessary teaching materials are prepared

        2.   Structural/setup arrangements are made

        3.   Instructional activities are planned

        4.   Behavioral expectations are identified ahead of time

    C.   Data/documentation is organized (see Data section)

        1.   Accessible

        2.   Easy to utilize

        3.   Easy to read/interpret

    D.   Instructional themes should be age-appropriate, reflected in lesson planning, and meaningfully tied to the curriculum (See Curriculum section)

    E.   Lesson plans should identify students' individual goals, corresponding curriculum, behavior targets, activities, materials, and embedded reinforcers (See Curriculum section)

    F.   Transitions and rotation of students and staff through out the day are smooth and maximize learning

    G.   Staff responsibilities, student assignments, and rotations are established and clearly communicated to all staff

    H.   Rotations of students and staff assignments are designed to reflect the specific needs of the class

    I.   Staff assignments and responsibilities should also reflect staff strengths and weaknesses

How

- *Discussion*

- *Observation in demonstration classroom with discussion*

- *Exercises: Trainee reviews sample staff assignment schedules. Identifies staff duties, rotation of duties and student/staff assignment rotations and provides rationales. "Organization Inventory for own classroom"*

- *Follow-up and in-class consultation should involve application, review, and feedback in this area*

SAMPLE PRE-SCHOOL SCHEDULE

8:00 - 8:30   **OPEN PLAY**

PLAY SKILLS/SOCIAL SKILLS/REINFORCEMENT ASSESSMENT

8:30 - 9:00   **OPENING CIRCLE**

WHOLE GROUP INSTRUCTION

9:00 - 10:00   **CENTER ROTATIONS**

PRE-ACADEMIC AREA W/LAYERED INDIVIDUALIZED IEP
CURRICULUM — SMALL GROUP OR ONE-TO-ONE AS NECESSARY

10:00 - 10:30   **RECESS**

EMBEDDED SOCIAL, PLAY, ETC. INSTRUCTION

10:30 - 11:00   **SNACK**

EMBEDDED COMMUNICATION, SOCIAL, SELF-HELP, ETC.
INSTRUCTION

11:00 - 12:00   **CENTER ROTATIONS**

PRE-ACADEMIC AREAS WITH LAYERED INDIVIDUALIZED IEP
CURRICULUM — SMALL GROUP OR ONE-TO-ONE AS NECESSARY

12:00 – 12:45   **LUNCH**

EMBEDDED SELF-HELP, COMMUNICATION, SOCIAL, PLAY,
SCHOOL ROUTINE, ETC. INSTRUCTION

12:45 - 1:30   **CENTER ROTATIONS**

PRE-ACADEMIC AREAS WITH LAYERED INDIVIDUALIZED IEP
CURRICULUM — SMALL GROUP OR ONE-TO-ONE AS NECESSARY

1:30 – 2:00   **CLOSING CIRCLE**

WHOLE GROUP INSTRUCTION

PART III
CURRICULUM

This section begins with an acknowledgment that, within and outside of education, there are many definitions of the term. For the purposes of this discussion, curriculum refers to instructional content. At the core, for educational programs for students with autism, is the ABA curriculum. These are the instructional targets, broken down into teachable components (often derived from IEP objectives) and phases of instruction that comprise the content of the systematic ABA instruction (See the curriculum in "A Work in Progress").

In addition to the ABA curriculum State or District grade level core curriculum, thematic elements, behavioral programming, instructional subject areas (or stations, centers, or periods), and the instructional projects or activities may all constitute layers (in educational vernacular, scaffolding) of instructional content. For example, State guidelines may recommend a grade level competency in computers, and work with computers would therefore be part of the center, based within the classroom daily schedule. Thematic work on undersea life would mean a program involving sea creatures would be part of the day's lesson plan activity on navigating the program's menus successfully. Most regular education students' instructional content would end there. However, for the student with autism, additionally layered within this scaffolding of curriculum would be a behavior program reinforcing on task attention, and an ABA curriculum regarding the following two-step receptive instructions provided in a small group learning arrangement.

This layering of curriculum is contrasted with what would typically be found in one-to-one intensive teaching, which would just be the inclusion of the unadorned ABA curriculum. While there are clearly benefits to such an arrangement within in-home, center-based, or even pull-out setups in schools, the layering of the curriculum more closely approximates what is found in educational settings and therefore promotes generalization. Further in a study on the layering of curriculum (Taubman, Soluaga,...2002), it was found that with the scaffolding of curriculum, incidental acquisition of layered (in the case of the study, thematic) elements occurred without direct instruction. When possible, and for reasons similar to those supporting scaffolding in regular education, layering of the curriculum can be a useful and success-promoting element of ABA classrooms.

The section emphasizes the rationales for structured instructional content, including its importance in providing systematic teaching, allowing for individualization and implementation of IEPs and assessing progress. Familiarity with the areas covered by ABA curriculum in addition to cognitive and academic areas are also covered. These include communication, social, leisure and play, school-related (e.g., hand raising, lining up, cafeteria routines, freeze bells), and learning to learn areas. The use of prepared curricula as guidelines rather then cookbooks is also emphasized.

Finally, the section emphasizes how the ABA curriculum is objective-driven, how this determines curricular development and content, how curricular elements are integrated, how a student may progress through or within a curriculum, and how progress is assessed.

CURRICULUM

1. **WHAT is Curriculum?**

    A. Lack of consensus on a definition for the term curriculum

    B. Definitions range from a narrow perspective of subjects taught to a broad perspective of all the experiences of learners in school and out, directed by the school

    C. Can include State or District Core Curriculum, Grade Level Frameworks, Classroom Instructional Plan, Lesson Plans, Instructional Strategies, Programs, Individual (Modified) Curriculum

    D. Curriculum in this section refers to ABA Instructional Content (e.g., Curriculum from "Work in Progress"). This includes skills targeted for systematic instruction, description of requisites and sub-components of skills, and objectives

    E. Integration of various levels of curricula (e.g., the imbedding of an individual curriculum within center-based instructional content, thematic overlays, and core curricula) and the relationship of the curriculum to IEP are essential considerations

How

- *Presentation/Discussion*

- *Material to read/consider: Catherine Maurice's Manual/Chapter on Curriculum and District Core Curriculum. EASIC (Evaluating Acquired Skills and Communication) by Riley. Teach Me Language by Freeman and Dake*

2. **WHY Do We Need/Utilize Curriculum (ABA Instructional Content)?**

    A. It is a "tool" designed to assist in teaching essential skills

        1. Is a guide

        2. Not rigidly adhered to but adapted as indicated

    B. It can be highly individualized and designed to meet the needs of the student

        1. Programs are selected and modified to target an individual student's deficits and replacement skills for behavioral excesses

        2. Areas of need are prioritized and functional curricula identified

        3. New programs are developed as necessary

    C. It translates overall objectives into specific instructional content

    D. It gives a sense of instructional progression

        1. Includes requisites, phases, and expansions

        2. Not always linear but shows interrelationships between content areas

        3. Promotes systematization of instruction

    E. It provides for criterion (curriculum-based) referenced assessment of progress

    F. It is comprehensive

        1. Programs are within various learning areas: learning readiness, language and communication, play and socialization, self help, fine and gross motor, pre-academic and cognition, and whatever a child needs!

    G. It promotes planned teaching since it contains already developed instructional content (precludes "re-invention of the wheel")

3. **Familiarity with Curriculum (ABA Instructional Content)**

    A. Format of Curriculum

    B. Skill Areas

        1. Learning to Learn: Requisite Skills

        2. Language/Communication

        3. Social/Emotional

        4. Play

        5. Self Help

6. Cognitive

7. Setting Relevant

   a. Home/Family

   b. Community Based Instruction

   c. School Demands and Routines, pre-academics and academics

8. Learning to Learn: Generalized Learning Processes

C. Familiarity with Curriculum and Skill Areas

   1. Identifying programs within the curriculum

   2. Identifying phases/components within a program

How

■ *Presentation/Discussion*

■ *Reading: Work in Progress*

■ *Exercises: a) Pick a few frequently utilized programs (i.e., NVI, Matching, Receptive Instructions, Expressive Labels) and have the Trainees read the program descriptions. Demonstrate various programs and have the Trainees identify/label each program (i.e., role play, video, centers). When Trainee has demonstrated proficiency in specified programs, introduce new programs to target. b) Demonstrate various phases of a program and have them identify if it's early, middle or advanced. Have them demonstrate the various phases of a particular program*

4. Objective Driven: Understanding the Purpose Behind Curriculum

A. Objective-driven nature of the curriculum

B. Fit and Functionality

C. Simultaneous Targeting of Multiple Objectives

   1. Micro/Immediate Objectives

   2. Macro/Pivotal Area Objectives

D. Familiarity with Curricular Objectives

   1. Identifying objective(s) behind program(s)

   2. Determining program/phases necessary to meet an objective

How

- *Discussion*

- *Exercises: a) Have Trainees identify objectives for specified programs. Discuss (e.g., expand upon, re vise, etc.). b) Assign the Trainee an objective (e.g., "to increase attending") and have her identify all the programs that could help meet that objective. c) Have them individualize it for a specified student—address programs at various stages (NVI –>Describing) and students at various functioning levels (Non-verbal–>Conversational)*

5. **Curriculum Progression**

    A. Linear Perspective on Curriculum

    B. Interrelated Perspective on Curriculum

    C. Sequential aspect to phases within programs

        1. What—sequential and/or developmental progression

        2. How to move up, down and through progression

    D. Sequential aspect of Curriculum

        1. What—sequential and/or developmental progression

        2. How to move up, down and through progression

    E. Mastery

        1. Not absolute criteria

            a. 80%

            b. Across therapists and sessions

            c. Random rotation

    F. Not all students follow specified sequence

        1. Often there is a lot of scatter and we must fill in the gaps

        2. Individualization essential

How

- *Discussion*

- *Present Curriculum perspective models (circle vs. tree)*

- *Exercises: a) "Beat the Clock" Game: Have the Trainees put various phases of a program in order (e.g., worksheet, flashcards, etc.) before the timer goes off. Have them demonstrate an early and later phase of a specified program. b) Have them put various programs in order. What's the problem? Give them phases...it is any easier? Why is it hard? Point out that it is not entirely sequential but that there is a lot of overlapping*

6. Curriculum Assessment

    A. Rationale

    B. Curriculum Assessment

        1. What

        2. How

    C. Functional Assessment (See Behavior section)

    D. Task Analysis

        1. What

        2. How

    E. Other Assessments (See Data section)

    F. Individualized Curriculum

How

■ *Discussion*

■ *Exposure to assessment protocols and examples of completed assessments*

■ *Portion of curriculum assessment from video*

■ *Exercises: Partial Curriculum assessment on student in demonstration class. "Perform a task analysis for one program in a Work in Progress." "Write up a task analysis for a specific skill in these areas: Self Help, fine motor, play, Social." Independently generated task analyses for student in demonstration class by trainee and trainer compared*

■ *Follow-up and in-class consultation should involve application, review, and feedback in this area*

7. Curriculum Development: Working Towards Goals and Benchmarks

    A.   Dynamic between Curriculum and IEP

        1.   Each informs the other

        2.   Reciprocal fit and adaptation as necessary

    B.   Skill and Behavioral Assessments Conducted

    C.   Current Target Skills to be Taught must be Identified

        1.   What are the student's skill needs? (deficits)

        2.   What replacement behaviors to be taught? (behaviors)

    D.   Student Benchmarks and Goals Determined

    E.   Curriculum necessary to teach current target skills and to address commensurate benchmarks and goals generated and specified

        1.   Listing of all programs/phases

        2.   Detailing of relation of programs to target skills, benchmarks and goals

        3.   Prioritization of programs

            a. Immediacy of need

            b. Necessary prerequisites

            c. Pivotal and domain considerations

            d. Practical considerations

    F.   Application of Curriculum (See Instruction and Behavior Sections)

    G.   Ongoing Curriculum Review and Refinement

        1.   Evaluate and modify as is needed

        2.   Association between Curriculum and IEP evaluated

How

- *Discussion*

- *Exemplars*

- *Exercises: Develop curriculum and associated benchmarks and goals, for area of need (not complete curriculum) for student in demonstration class. Same process (for complete curriculum) for student in trainee's class*

- *Follow-up and in-class consultation should involve application, review, and feedback in this area*

8. How We Imbed Curriculum: Infusing Curriculum Into the Instructional Day

    A.   Rationale for Integration/Layering of Curriculum

        1.   IDEA—Exposure to core Curriculum

        2.   Amplification of learning through integration

        3.   Enhanced motivation

        4.   Efficiency and incidental learning

        5.   Approximation to naturalistic arrangements

        6.   Benefits to typical peers and reverse mainstreamed students

    B.   Layers of Curriculum include:

        1.   Grade level core/academic curriculum

        2.   Thematic overlays and instruction

        3.   Station/center/subject area/period

        4.   Activity within #3

        5.   Individualized Curriculum

    C.   Instructional Approach (See ABA Instruction)

    D.   Lesson Plans

        1.   Planning, structure, materials, and being systematic

        2.   Ongoing evaluation and adaptation

How

- *Discussion*

- *Observation with Discussion*

- *Exercises: Trainee leads classroom activity (e.g., group song, art project, recess activity, math competition, etc.) and infuses individual curricula at various points (initially for one student, then for several)*

- *Follow-up and in-class consultation should involve application, review, and feedback in this area*

PART IV
ABA INSTRUCTION

1. ABA Instruction for Students with Autism

    A. Rationale (See Overview section)

    B. Integration with other Elements/Sections

        1. Curriculum

        2. Behavior programming

        3. Reinforcement

        4. Materials and environment

        5. Team

        6. Data

    C. Direct relation to student needs

2. Initial Phase of Instruction

    A. Tolerance and Adjustment

    B. Rapport/Reinforcement Value Building

    C. Assessment

    D. Probing

    E. Gradual Initiation of Instruction

3. Later Phases of Instruction

    A. Continued Introduction of Instruction and Instructional Formats

    B. Full Implementation of Necessary Individualized Instructional Program

    C. Fading of Individualized Instructional Program as Appropriate

How

- *Presentation*
- *Discussion*
- *Reading: "A Work in Progress"*
- *Video and In Vivo Modeling*

- *Exercises: Instructions—Examples evaluated in terms of guidelines, practice at varying instructions. Prompts—Video or in vivo presentation of prompts with prompt type and inadvertent prompt identification. Reinforcers—Alphabet listing of varied reinforcers and feedback*

- *Hands-on experiences focusing on performance of components and guidelines*

- *Follow-up and in-class consultation should involve application, review, and feedback in this area*

4. **Instructional Techniques and Systems**

   A. Discrete Trial Teaching

      1. Discrete Trial Teaching is good teaching

         a. Elements of Good Teaching (see "Work in Progress")

      2. Components

         a. Instruction

         b. Response

         c. Feedback/Reinforcement (See Reinforcement Section)

         d. Prompt

         e. Inter Trial Interval

      3. Guidelines (See "Work in Progress")

   B. Teaching Interactions

      1. Components

         a. Initiation and Labeling

         b. Rationale

         c. Demonstration/Description

         d. Practice

         e. Feedback

         f. Reinforcement (optional)

         g. Continuation Statement

      2. Graduated Teaching/Generalization Plans

   C. Shaping

   D. Chaining

1. Forward
2. Backward

E. Behavioral Momentum

F. Fluency

G. Priming

H. Modeling

    1. Direct

    2. Observational Learning

    3. Video

    4. Pictorial

    5. Adult and Peer

I. Augmentative and Alternative Communication

    1. PECS

    2. WECS

    3. Signing

    4. Devices

    5. Visual Strategies for Communication

J. Incidental Teaching/Capture of Teachable Moments

K. Respondent Techniques

    1. Desensitization/Neutralization/Counter Conditioning

    2. Tolerance and Management

How

- *Presentation*

- *Discussion*

- *Observations of video and in vivo models*

- *Role Playing and/or hands on experiences focusing on performance of techniques and systems and their components*

- *Follow-up and in-class consultation should involve application, review, and feedback in this area*

5. Formats and Modalities of Classroom/School-Based Instruction

    A. Individual

        1. Intensive

        2. Individualization

        3. Promotes being systematic

        4. Works on skill or component in isolation (specific, concentrated attention)

    B. Small and Large Group

        1. Rationale

            a. Opportunity for social exposure, awareness, interaction, and skill development

            b. Opportunity for observational learning

            c. Group instruction-related skills

            d. Naturalistic/Generalization

            e. Efficiency

        2. Types of Group Instruction

            a. Sequential

            b. Choral

            c. Overlapping

            d. Utilization and integration of types

        3. Levels/Progression of Student Targets

            a. Proximity/Presence

            b. Learning readiness

            c. Participation

            d. Generalization of already acquired skills

            e. New skill acquisition

        4. Arrangements

            a. Small Group

                (1) Teacher in front

                (2) Two or three students

                (3) No aide or aide to side of students

  b. Large Group

   (1) Teacher in front

   (2) Aides behind students

 5. Responsibilities

  a. Everyone

   (1) Know individualized and group objectives/targets necessary for systematic teaching

   (2) Know prompt strategies and current prompt level

   (3) Know current phase and level of complexity

   (4) Know behavior strategies/programs

  b. Instructor

   (1) Sequence, elements, activities, themes

   (2) Pace and timing

   (3) Instructional lead

   (4) Reinforcement

   (5) Balance and integration of types of group instruction

   (6) Behavior Programming

   (7) Orchestration of aides

  c. Aides

   (1) Coordination with and responsiveness to instructor

   (2) Monitoring

   (3) Modeling

   (4) Prompting

   (5) Reinforcing

   (6) May involve teaching concurrently with Instructor

   (7) May involve behavior programming with Instructor

How

■ *Discussion*

■ *Reading: "Group Discrete Trial Instruction" article*

■ *Exercise: In vivo or from video, identification of types of group instruction; observe video discuss coordination between teacher and aides*

■ *Observation of video and in vivo models, sitting in participation, hands on participation as aide, experience leading group*

■ *Follow up, in class consultation should involve application, review, and feedback in this area*

6. Integration/Inclusion

1. Rationale

2. Continuum and individualized application

3. Readiness

    a. Scales for Predicting Successful Inclusion (SPSI)

    b. Exit Criteria Checklist

    c. Administrative Supports/Campus Attitude/Culture

    d. Special Education Teacher

    e. Regular Education Teacher

    f. Placement

    g. Resources and Supports

4. Where (setting)

5. How long

6. When (subject, activity, part of schedule)

7. Levels of inclusion

    a. Exposure

    b. Participation

    c. Modified/Parallel instruction and curriculum

    d. Assisted and Augmentative Instruction

    e. Integrated Instruction

8. Typical Peers

    a. Characteristics

    b. Roles

        (1) Models

        (2) Tutors/Teachers

        (3) Catalysts for social interaction

           (4) Initiators of social interaction

           (5) Informed recipients of social interaction

           (6) Playmates

9.   Transition Plan

10. Shadow Aides

    a. Who and Training

    b. Assessment Responsibilities

    c. Input into Necessary Requisite and Augmentative Instruction

    d. Prompting and Assisting

    e. Behavioral Programming

    f. Instruction

    g. Coordination with Regular and Special Education Instructors

    h. General Antecedent Manipulations

    i. Acting as Catalyst with Peers

    j. Balancing Intervention with Guided Natural Occurrences

    k. Fading toward Independence

11. Mixed Classrooms and Reverse Mainstreaming

How

- *Discussion*

- *Exemplars*

- *Handouts: SPSI and Exit Criteria Checklist*

- *Exercise: Scenarios with determination of inclusion readiness and plan*

- *Follow-up and in-class consultation should involve application, review, and feedback in this area*

7. Stylistic Elements

A. Rapport Building

B. Rapport Maintenance

C. Positive as Possible and Appropriate

D. Neutral as necessary

E. Energy and Enthusiasm as appropriate

F. Fun/Natural Balance

G. Development of natural, individual style

H. Distinct approach to each student

I. Age-appropriate

J. Dignifying and Respectful

K. Professional (See Professionalism Section)

How

■ *Discussion*

■ *Exemplars*

■ *Exercise: Viewing of videos with discussion/assessment of stylistic components*

■ *Hands on experiences focusing on performance of components*

■ *Follow-up and in-class consultation should involve application, review, and feedback in this area*

8. Instructional Strategies and Overarching Considerations

A. Being Systematic

1. Objectives

2. Progression

3. Monitoring and Assessment

B. Pervasiveness of Teaching

1. Throughout the day

2. In Between Times and Capture of Teachable Moments

3. Intensity and Pacing

C. Integration of instructional elements

1. Classroom elements

2. Students with each other

3. Classroom with campus and district

    4.   Between instructional formats

    5.   Within instructional formats (targeting skills in multiple ways concurrently)

D.   Isolated/pull out instruction (not necessarily in physical sense)

    1.   Requisite

    2.   For concentrated teaching or refinement

    3.   Coordinated with imbedded

E.   Imbedding

    1.   Rationale and benefits

    2.   Challenge of remaining systematic

    3.   Where and when

    a.   In group

    b.   In Stations/Centers/Periods/Subjects

    c.   Within in-class and outside activities

    d.   In various venues/setting

F.   Layering of Instruction (see Curriculum Section)

G.   Balance of Instruction

    1.   Activity-Related Assistance and Actual Teaching

    2.   Individual and Group

    3.   Isolated and Imbedded

    4.   Structured/Planned and Capture of Teachable Moments

    5.   Guided Natural Occurrences and Direct Instruction/Intervention

    6.   Intensity and Pacing

How

- *Presentation/Discussion*

- *Observation*

- *Exercise: Viewing of instructional strategies, video or in vivo and identification and evaluation of critical components*

- *Hands on experiences focusing on performance of components*

- *Follow-up and in-class consultation should involve application, review, and feedback in this area*

PART V
REINFORCEMENT

1. WHAT is Reinforcement? WHY Do We Utilize It?

    A.   Reinforcement is the process of presentation or removal of a stimulus that results in the increased likelihood of the performance of a behavior

    B.   We use it because it is a means for establishing, strengthening, and maintaining behaviors

    C.   Reinforcement motivates learning and is the backbone of teaching

    D.   Positive, ethical, and preferred modality

    E.   Much empirical support for its usage

2. HOW Do We Use it?

    A.   Types of Reinforcement

        1.   Positive Presenting a stimulus to increase a response

        2.   Negative Removing a stimulus to increase a response

        3.   Primary

        4.   Secondary/conditioned and generalized

    B.   Rules of Reinforcement (see "A Work in Progress" and Hand Out)

How

- *Trainee(s) should be given the "Reinforcement Chapter" from A Work in Progress to read.*

- *When completed, a debriefing session should be conducted using the "Rules of Reinforcement"*

- *Handout as an outline...have intern(s) tell you the why behind each rule.*

3. Assessment and Identification Process

    A.   List observable student preferences

        1.   What does the student do during his/her free time?

        2.   What items in the environment does he/she gravitate towards and seems to enjoy? How does the student engage with his/her preferred

item?

3. What are the salient points of preferences?

   a. Example: You observe a child "turn on/off the lights" repeatedly during his free time. What about this act is the child enjoying? Does he like the light flickering or the sound the switch makes when you move it. Perhaps it is the up and down movement that he enjoys. Maybe it is the reaction he gets from the classroom that he likes. It needs to be assessed in order to effectively identify potential rein forcers.

B. Identify potential reinforcers based on observations of preference.

C. Considerations:

   1. Appropriately making use of existing preferences. Preferences are transferred to appropriate items, activities, and actions.

      a. Example: You observe a child enjoying the lights flickering when he turns the light switch on and off so you identify the following potential reinforcers: light up spinners, light up bouncing ball, a flashlight, glow in the dark toys, etc.

   2. Using slight variations/permutations of existing preferences.

      a. Example: You observe a student who enjoys "to run," so you identify the following potential reinforcers: he could earn a superman cape (he/she gets to run when wearing it), or a chase card that he gets to cash in during recess.

   3. Incorporating aspects of self stimulatory behaviors.

      a. Example: You observe a student enjoying running a koosh ball across his/her face (tactile sensation) so you identify the following potential reinforcers: a feather pen, a book with different textures, a silk scarf, etc.

D. Sample the potential reinforcers you selected (does the student like it?) and develop and enhance reinforcement values.

   1. Present potential reinforcers during "play" time sandwiching in between stronger reinforcers

   2. Present the items you selected non contingently. Give free access

   3. SELL your reinforcement with your own enthusiastic response to them.

   4. Associate potential reinforcers with established (primary and conditioned) reinforcers (PAIRING)

5. When sampling potential reinforcers, you may want to limit access to stronger reinforcement, as targets may be less enjoyable in the presence of more powerful reinforcers.

6. Rate the student's level of preference (none, low, medium, high)

E. Develop a reinforcement hierarchy

1. List reinforcers to be used contingently based on level of enjoyment: A level (to die for), B level (likes more than loves), C level (mild reinforcers).

How

■ *Watch video and conduct a reinforcer assessment.*

■ *Assign trainee(s) a student to focus on. Have them list observable preferences and potential reinforcers based on the day's events (i.e., "Free Play": list observations. "Circle": list observations. "Centers," "Snack," "Recess," "Gross Motor/APE"). Set up a specific time for sampling to occur during that day (i.e., Center Rotation # 2). Have them rate the student's level of preference and develop a reinforcement hierarchy for the student they are assigned to, based on their day's assessment.*

■ *Handouts: Reinforcement Survey (classroom specific), Creative Reinforcement, Reinforcement Hierarchy, Developmental Play Ideas.*

4. Selection Process: Factors to Consider

A. Age appropriateness

1. Example: Two students differing in age both enjoy watching things fall/sifting.

a. Student A (age 3) is reinforced with Elephon, where he sees butterflies drop

b. Student B (age 10) is reinforced with Kerplunk, where he sees marbles drop

B. Practicality

1. Example: Utilizing Gak as a reinforcer in Circle may be difficult to deliver and utilize due to its messiness, but at the Art/Sensory Center where messiness isn't an issue and less children are involved it may be more practical of a reinforcer.

C. Level of interference

   1. Example: One student's reinforcer can be an antecedent to another student's behavior problems.

D. Immediacy

   1. Example: Some reinforcers require time to set up and deliver...this can be problematic for students who need it to be immediate; it can interfere with momentum; Imaginationetc.

E. Group Effect

   1. Example: You have two reinforcers you can utilize at Circle, Bubbles & Balloon. Two out of ten of your students like bubbles. Seven out of ten of your students like the balloon. Which do you choose? Balloon because more students like this.

F. Time in the day/Activity (Schedule)

   1. Example: You may more readily use special foods (i.e., candy, goldfish) as reinforcers during Snack; sensory toys (i.e., Gak, Shaving Cream) during Art Center, etc.

G. Thematic relatedness to instruction/lesson

   1. Example: If the lesson is on "Underwater Sea Life," you may select to use the following reinforcers: a talking fish, water tube with fish on it, fish stickers, etc.

H. Power

   1. Example: You may want to sparingly and commensurately use reinforcers that are very weak (minimally motivating) or regulate access to ones that are very strong (so powerful they may be interfering).

How

- *Didactic Session: go through the reinforcement hierarchy/list that the trainee has developed and determine which reinforcers would be best to weave in throughout the day taking into consideration the various factors discussed.*

5. Implementing Reinforcement

A. Timing and Contingency

   1. Reinforcement should be utilized immediately (at least in the beginning), should be contingent, and should be used consistently.

B. Frequency/Schedule

1. Reinforcement should be applied as indicated by the students needs.

2. Initially, a continuous schedule of reinforcement should be used.

3. Over time, an intermittent schedule of reinforcement should be used

   a. Ratio Schedules

   b. Interval Schedules

C. Labeling

1. Explicit, descriptive feedback given as indicated by the student's needs to help the aide in the establishment of contingencies

D. Differential

1. Better reinforcement should be utilized for better responses

E. Concurrent

1. Reinforcement should be utilized within and between trials, in conjunction with existing criteria, to reinforce additional behavior, and not just for correctness of performance

F. Imbedded

1. As part of an activity/lesson

G. Availability/Scheduling

1. Opportunities for reinforcement should be identified and planned for ahead of time

H. Variety

1. Variation/rotation of reinforcers to enhance novelty and minimize satiation and maximize the establishing operation of deprivation

I. Engagement

1. Instructor should be providing social reinforcement and actively involved in reinforcement/reinforcing event, enhancing social reinforcement value and/or value of tangible reinforcement (selling reinforcer) as well as capturing social interactional opportunity

How

■ *Have trainee(s) practice utilizing reinforcement throughout the day. Utilize the reinforcement performance evaluation checklist*

6. Fading Reinforcement

    A. Thinning Reinforcement Schedules: Continuous to Intermittent Schedules

        1. A continuous schedule refers to reinforcement that is given each time a desired/target behavior is displayed.

        2. An intermittent schedule refers to reinforcement that is periodic and often less predictable.

        3. Moving from a continuous schedule to an intermittent schedule of reinforcement is a critical step in the direction of fading.

    B. Transfer of Reinforcement: Moving towards the natural and the practical.

        1. By developing the reinforcement value of and exposure to more natural type reinforcers (e.g., toys instead of food; people/social instead of toys; social instead of tangibles etc.) while diminishing use of added consequences, you are fading.

        2. See Reinforcement Development Exercise

    C. Delaying Reinforcement: Moving away from immediacy.

        1. Waiting a few seconds after the desired response to deliver reinforcment instead of .5 seconds after it was given; Token economies as a delayed reinforcer; etc.

How

- *Have trainee(s) observe a student's schedule of reinforcement and develop a plan to fade reinforcement, taking into consideration the above strategies*

- *Trainee Develops Reinforcer identification, selection, establishment and utilization plans for students in own class*

- *Follow-up and in-class consultation should involve application, review, and feedback in these areas*

7. Reinforcement Systems (See Behavior Programming section)

RULES OF REINFORCEMENT

- Reinforcers should be reinforcing and individualized
- Reinforcement should be contingent.
- A variety of reinforcers should be used.
- Socials should be paired with primaries.
- Reduce reinforcer satiation.
- Continuously develop and identify reinforcers.
- Use age appropriate reinforcers.
- Unpredictability and novelty greatly enhance reinforcement.
- Initially, reinforcement should occur immediately.
- Initially, reinforcement should be provided consistently.
- Reinforcement schedule should be faded as quickly as possible.
- Initially, label the behavior that is being reinforced.
- Eventually, reinforcement should be practical and natural.
- Utilize differential reinforcement.
- Do NOT use bribery!!!

REINFORCEMENT SURVEY

	Rating Scale			
Potential Motivators	**None**	**Low**	**Med**	**High**

REINFORCEMENT DEVELOPMENT PROGRAM

Objectives

1. To establish effective reinforcers for the student

2. Motivate behavior change

3. Improve quality of life

Pointers to Facilitate Development of Reinforcers

■ Observe what the Student selects in a free-choice situation (e.g., What does he choose to do during his free time? Self stimulatory behaviors?) and identify potential motivators.

■ Expose the Student to potential reinforcers. You never know until you try it!

■ Give the Student free access to potential reinforcers.

■ To guard against satiation and to ensure maintenance of reinforcement value, it is necessary to ROTATE preferred activities/items with other same level reinforcers.

■ Limit access to strong reinforcers so that they are only available at certain times (e.g., structured teaching sessions only) and/or for specific behaviors (e.g., compliance, calmness, etc.). Ask parents to lock up some reinforcers; make sure you take your A level reinforcers home with you.

■ Associate potential reinforcers with established reinforcers (PAIRING).

■ Present potential reinforcers to the Student during "play" time. Sandwich in strong reinforcers with identified reinforcement targets.

■ SELL your reinforcement with your own enthusiastic response to them.

■ Good "packaging" can turn very small and ordinary things into reinforcers. Be creative and vary your presentation of reinforcement.

> "If you do not have good reinforcers and are not working to establish them, you might as well just go home."

CREATIVE REINFORCEMENT

Potato Chip   1. Drive the chip to the student in a match box car.

2. Use a puppet to give the chip to the student.

3. Put the chip in a "magic" box.

4. Feed the student the chip using a special airplane spoon.

5. Put the chip in the student's pocket.

Bean Bag   6. Put the bean bag in the student's shirt.

7. Put the bean bag on the student's head.

8. Throw the bean bag to the student.

9. Plop the bean bag in the student's hand and make a funny noise.

10. Rub the bean bag on the student's arms.

(Staff finishes filling out this form)

Markers   11. _____

12. _____

13. _____

14. _____

15. _____

Sound Tube   16. _____

17. _____

18. _____

19. _____

20. _____

Construction Paper

21. _____

22. _____

23. _____

24. _____

25. _____

Bubbles

26. _____

27. _____

28. _____

29. _____

30. _____

Stickers

31. _____

32. _____

33. _____

34. _____

35. _____

CREATIVE REINFORCEMENT
(Circle Time Activity)

Today is ...

Monday: **Green Beans**...

    1. long green balloon

    2. _____

    3. _____

Tuesday: **Spaghetti**...

    1. pop out snakes (aka "noodles")

    2. _____

    3. _____

Wednesday: **Zoup** (Soup)...

    1. bowl with a treat inside

    2. _____

    3. _____

Thursday: **Roast Beef**...

    1. brown slap of putty

    2. _____

    3. _____

Friday: **Fresh Fish**...

    1. singing/talking fish

    2. _____

    3. _____

Saturday: **Chicken**...

    1. rubber chicken

    2. _____

    3. _____

Sunday: **Ice Cream**...

    1. vibrating ice cream pen

    2. _____

    3. _____

All you hungry children get to eat it up!!!

REINFORCEMENT EVALUATION

	Obs. 1	Obs. 2	Obs. 3
Reinforcers utilized were effective.			
Reinforcement occurred after the desired behavior (timing).			
A variety of reinforcers were utilized.			
Socials were paired with tangible reinforcers.			
Attempts were made to develop reinforcers.			
Age appropriate reinforcers were utilized.			
Reinforcement occurred as immediately as was needed by the student.			
Reinforcement was provided consistently.			
Staff did not utilize bribery.			
Staff utilized differential reinforcement.			

Comments

_____

_____

_____

_____

_____

_____

REINFORCEMENT HIERARCHY

A Level:

1. _____
2. _____
3. _____
4. _____
5. _____
6. _____
7. _____
8. _____
9. _____
10. _____
11. _____
12. _____
13. _____
14. _____
15. _____
16. _____
17. _____
18. _____
19. _____
20. _____

B Level:

1. _____
2. _____
3. _____
4. _____
5. _____
6. _____
7. _____
8. _____
9. _____
10. _____
11. _____
12. _____
13. _____
14. _____
15. _____
16. _____
17. _____
18. _____
19. _____
20. _____

C Level:

1. _____
2. _____
3. _____
4. _____
5. _____
6. _____
7. _____
8. _____
9. _____
10. _____
11. _____
12. _____
13. _____
14. _____
15. _____
16. _____
17. _____
18. _____
19. _____
20. _____

PART VI
BEHAVIOR PROGRAMMING

1. Overall Considerations

    A.   Rationale for Behavioral Approach to difficult responses of autism

    B.   Team Approach/Continuity

    C.   Overarching Nature of Behavior Programming

    D.   Balance of Reactive and Proactive Intervention

2. Problematic Behaviors

    A.   Definition and Issues as relate to Autism

    B.   Challenges of Disruptive Behavior

    C.   Behavior as Learned

    D.   Behavior as Functional

    E.   Operant and Respondent Considerations

    F.   Operational Definitions

3. Functional Assessments/Behavior Programs

    A.   Functions of Behavior

    B.   Antecedents

    C.   Consequences

    D.   Methods of Functional Assessment

        1.   Observation

        2.   Interview

        3.   Functional Analysis

    E.   Transfer of FA to behavior plan

How

   ■   *Presentation*

- *Discussion*

- *Developing Concept and Rationales through Reading Materials: Behavior Modification: Principles and Procedures by Miltonberger, Chapters 13,15,20,22,23; Behavior Analysis for Lasting Change by Sulzer Azaroff & Mayer, Chapters 9,10,12,13,24*

- *Exemplars: Targets, Functional Assessments, Resultant Plans/Programs*

- *Observation of Functional Assessment, Development and Transfer to Behavior Plan*

- *Vignettes for practice of Functional Assessment*

- *Exercises: Practice Portion of Functional Assessment for student in the Demonstration Class. Compare with existing or Trainer generated Functional Assessment*

- *Trainee does Functional Assessment for the student in his own class*

- *Follow-up and in-class consultation should involve application, review, and feedback in this area*

4. Reactive Programming

A. Escalation Cycles

   1. What they are and phases

B. When to intervene and when not to

   1. The earlier the better

   2. Avoid intervening once escalated

   3. Practical Considerations

      a. Safety

      b. Making things less worse (Do no harm—keep problem from worsening)

C. Power struggles and round & rounds

   1. Limited long-term benefit

   2. Inadvertent Reinforcement

D. Cutting losses

   1. When

      a. No absolute criteria

      b. The earlier the better

   2. Why

    a. Prioritization of Immediate/Practical Issues

    b. Limiting Inadvertent Reinforcement

    c. Limited long-term benefit

E. Reference Management of Assaultive Behavior Type Courses (e.g., CPI, MAB, MANDT, PART)

F. Limiting Inadvertent Reinforcement

    1. How

        a. Minimal attention to attentionally motivated disruptive behavior

        b. Minimal delay in response to escape/avoidant

        c. Minimal reactivity to provocation motivated behavior

        d. Minimal communicative response to behavior with communicative intent

        e. Minimal power to control motivated behavior

        f. As much as is practically possible

    2. Why

        a. Reinforcement is individualized ("No" may mean "Yes!!")

        b. Avoids strengthening undesirable behaviors

        c. Supports strengthening of desirable alternatives

G. Working Through

    1. Defined

    2. When and when not to

        a. Often apropos for avoidance, control, or disruption-motivated behavior

        b. May be less appropriate for attentionally motivated behavior when high degree of engagement is necessary

        c. Cautions regarding potential for escalations

H. Reactive techniques for addressing behavioral disruptions

    1. Techniques

        a. Re-directions

        b. Distractions

        c. Interruptions

        d. Building and utilizing momentum

    2.   Prompts and assists

    3.   Opportunity makers

    4.   Situation Management vs. Behavior Management

    5.   Reactive advantages

    6.   Reactive disadvantages: reactive programming may present for proactive programming

I.   Shaping De-escalations

    1.   Differential reinforcement of de-escalated behavior

    2.   Avoiding fanning the flames—Easing forward and back

    3.   Learning over time—Teaching the skill of turn arounds

J.   Discouragers

    1.   Reframing toward the positive approach

    2.   What they are vs. aversives

    3.   Withholding reinforcement

    4.   Interrupting/Discontinuing preferred activity (when behavior problem occurs in context of preferred activity)

    5.   Response cost

    6.   Observational and vicarious learning

    7.   Extinction vs. Reinforcement reduction

K.   Reinforcement (See Reinforcement Section)

    1.   Catch them being good

    2.   Catching absences of disruptive behavior

L.   Respondent oriented responses

    1.   Identifying

    2.   Judgment calls

How

■ *Observation and Discussion*

■ *Vignettes: Hypotheticals and based on actual students in class requiring anticipation of reactive strategies*

■ *Role play of Reactive Circumstances*

■ *Stepping in during situations in the Demonstration classroom requiring reactive response as appropriate and with direct supervision*

■ *Exercises: Develop Reactive strategy for student in Demonstration Class and apply*

■ *Develop Reactive strategy for student in trainee's class and eventually apply*

■ *Follow-up and in-class consultation should involve application, review, and feedback in this area*

5. Proactive Programming

   A. Replacement Skill Instruction

      1. Functions of Replacement Behavior

         a. Replacement Behaviors controlled by similar contingencies vs. Replacement Behavior controlled by other reinforcers

         b. Customary need for Replacement Behaviors

      2. Task Analysis (See Data Section)

      3. Instructional techniques (See Instruction Section)

      4. Timing and frequency of instruction

      5. Progressive programs

         a. Hierarchies

         b. Generalization plans

      6. Respondent programming

         a. Desensitization/Neutralization

         b. Stress/Anger/Frustration Management

   B. Behavior Management Plans and Arrangements

      1. Systematic reinforcement of Replacement Skills

      2. Systematic reinforcement of Absences

      3. Differential Reinforcement programs

        a. DRL

        b. DRO

        c. DRA

        d. DRI

4. Behavior Management Plans Systems, and Arrangements

        a. Item exchange plans/Direct Reinforcement

        b. Token Economies

        c. Time In

        d. Contingency Contracts

        e. Self-Management

How

- *Discussion*

- *Exemplars of Proactive Programs*

- *Observation of Proactive Program Development*

- *Observation of Proactive Programming*

- *Vignettes: Hypotheticals and based on actual students for practice of Proactive Program Development*

- *Practice Proactive Program Development for student in Demonstration Class*

- *Application of Proactive Plan in demonstration class (Trainee engages in Replacement Skill instruction/Programming and Application of Proactive Behavior Management Plan as appropriate and with direct Supervision)*

- *Trainee develops Proactive Program for student in own class*

- *Eventual Application of Proactive Plan for student in own class with direct Supervision*

- *Follow-up and in-class consultation should involve application, review, and feedback in this area*

6. Antecedent Manipulation Plans

A. Establishing operations (e.g., satiation & deprivation)

B. Response Effort (e.g., increase of necessary effort for some undesirable behaviors, decrease of necessary effort for some desirable behaviors)

C. Opportunity Reduction Plans (e.g., less opportunity or occurrence of a problem behavior)

D. Opportunity Maximization Plans (e.g., greater opportunity for utilization of desired behaviors, new, and for reinforcement).

E. Creation of options, choices

How

■ *Discussion*

■ *Exemplars of Antecedent Manipulation Plans*

■ *Observation of Antecedent Manipulation Plans*

■ *Observation of Antecedent Manipulation Type Programming*

■ *Vignettes: Hypotheticals and based on actual students for practice of Antecedent Manipulation Plan Development*

■ *Antecedent Manipulation Plans Development for student in Demonstration Class*

■ *Application of Antecedent Manipulation Plans in demonstration class as appropriate and with direct Supervision*

■ *Trainee develops Antecedent Manipulation Plans for student in own class*

■ *Eventual Application of Antecedent Manipulation Plans for student in own class with direct Supervision*

■ *Trainee does Functional Assessment and develops Complete, Integrated Behavior Program for student in own class*

■ *Eventual Application of Complete, Integrated Behavior Plan for student in own class with direct Supervision*

■ *Follow-up and in-class consultation should involve application, review, and feedback in this area*

PART VII
DATA

1. **Rationale for Data Collection and Analysis**

    A. Objectivity/Observation core to what makes ABA unique

    B. Reduce subjectivity and enhance objective support

        1. Documentation and protection

        2. Defensibility: "If there is no documentation, it didn't happen"

    C. Assessment and problem identification

    D. Controlling variables (Functional Assessments)

    E. Treatment variables (Integrity Measures/Staff Characteristics)

    F. Effectiveness–Treatment Planning

    G. Cost/Benefit/Side Effect Evaluation

    H. Social Validity and Consumer Considerations

    I. Practical/Operational/Administrative Assessment

    J. Long Term Overall Outcome

2. **Overall Considerations**

    A. Data is a tool

    B. Process/Fidelity Measures

    C. For skill acquisition

    D. For Qualitative (including learning to learn) aspects

    E. For Behaviors

    F. Need for relevance to IEP

    G. Baseline and Intervention

    H. Independent Mastery considerations

    I. Generalization Considerations

    J. Practical considerations must be balanced with objectives

    1.   Comprehensiveness (How much)

    2.   Pervasiveness (How often)

    3.   Balance of Objectivity and Subjectivity

  K. User-friendliness key

    1.   In Data Collection

    2.   For Data Compilation and Analysis

  L. Documentation

    1.   Confidentiality

    2.   Storage and Access

        a. Hard Copy

        b. Computer

  M. Data Collection Schedule

    1.   What

    2.   When

    3.   By Whom

  N. Data Protocols and forms should fit need

  O. Flexibility and dynamic of data collection process

3. Basic Components of Data Collection

  A. Rationale for use

  B. Operational Definition of Behaviors

  C. Data Collection Forms

  D. Data Collection Protocol (Type, Form, and Schedule)

  E. Direct Observation

  F. Video Tapes

  G. Subjective Assessment

How

■ *Discussion*

- *Readings Miltonberger: Behavior Modification, Principals and Procedures, Chapters 2 & 3; Bellack and Herson: Behavior Assessment , A Practical Handbook, Chapter 1*
- *Exemplars/Samples*

4. Types of Data Collection

A. Continuous

　　1. Definition

　　2. Rationale

B. Interval

　　1. Definition/Types

　　2. Rationale

C. Time Sample

　　1. Definition/Types

　　2. Rationale

How

- *Discussion*
- *Exercises: Clapping Exercise; Observational Measurement Experiences (Tape and In Vivo)*

5. Forms of Data Collection

A. Skill Acquisition

　　1. Trial by Trial

　　　　a. Definition

　　　　b. Use/Application

　　　　c. Corresponding Data Collection Forms

　　2. Task Analysis

　　　　a. Definition

　　　　b. Use/Application

　　　　c. Corresponding Data Collection Forms

　　3. Introduction/Independent Mastery

    a. Definition

    b. Use/Application

    c. Corresponding Data Collection Forms

  4.   Attainment of IEP Goals

B. Qualitative Aspects During Skill Acquisition

  1.   As appropriate and indicated by need

  2.   Includes Readiness and Learning to Learn Elements

    a. On Task Attention/Off Task

    b. Responsivity/No Response

    c. Momentum/Clustering

    d. Engagement/Intent/Connectivity

    e. Processing

    f. Fluency/Response Latency/Pace of Responding

    g. Generalization

    h. Naturalistic Quality

    i. Spontaneity/Initiations

    j. Generalized Abilities

C. Behaviors

  1.   Frequency

    a. Definition

    b. Use/Application

    c. Corresponding Data Collection Forms

  2.   Opportunity/Ratio

    a. Definition

    b. Use/Application

    c. Corresponding Data Collection Forms

  3.   Duration

    a. Definition

    b. Use/Application

    c. Corresponding Data Collection Forms

4.   Intensity

    a.   Definition

    b.   Use/Application

    c.   Corresponding Data Collection Forms

5.   Ratings/Scales (Subjective Assessment)

    a.   Rationale for use

    b.   Definition

    c.   Use/Application

    d.   Corresponding Data Collection Forms

How

■   *Discussion*

■   *Exposure to Examples of Forms*

■   *Witnessing of Actual Behavioral Measurement*

■   *Exercises: Activities (e.g., Jump rope, bop it, sweatin' to the oldies, putting, hula hoop) Exercise (selection of most fitting form of data collection); Data Collection Exercises: Actual observation and recording/scoring of various forms of data collection (tapes, as in vivo observer, as interventionist and observer)*

6.   Data Analysis

A.   Rationale and Considerations

B.   Collapsing, Condensing, Compiling

C.   Graphic Representation

    1.   Graphs

    2.   Tables

D.   Interpreting Data

    1.   Decreasing Inferences and Raising Confidence

    2.   Effects vs. artifacts and anomalies

    3.   Data as factor in treatment decisions

How

■   *Discussion*

■ *Modeling and Practice, with previously recorded data, of data compilation, presentation, and interpretation.*

7. Development and Employment of Data Collection and Analysis Systems

How

■ *Discussion*

■ *Observation of System Development for the Student. Exercise: Development and use of data collection system (skill and behavior) for student in the model class; development of data collection system for the student in the trainee's class*

■ *Follow-up and in-class consultation should involve application, review, and feedback in this area*

8. Overall/Standardized Assessments (as appropriate)

    A. Purposes

    B. Intelligence and Achievement

    C. Adaptive Living

    D. Developmental

    E. Psychological

    F. Speech

    G. Other Specific Areas of Functioning

        1. Play/Leisure/Recreation

        2. Social Skills

        3. Behavior

        4. School Functioning/Success/Inclusion Readiness

How

■ *Introduction to this area and typical testing devices, through readings, discussion, and presentation of materials should occur as relevant and as appropriate*

PART VIII
THE CLASSROOM TEAM, PROFESSIONALISM, AND LIAISONING

1. **Overarching Considerations**

   A. Importance of Intra and Inter-Classroom Team Professional Relationships

   B. Importance of Development and Maintenance

   C. Importance of Strong yet Collaborative Leadership

   D. Can preclude operation and implementation of program/instructional elements

   E. Complications of multiple constituencies

   F. Need for underlying orientation

   G. Need for ongoing, systematic mechanisms and efforts

2. **Professionalism**

   A. Legal and Ethical Guidelines

      1. Familiarity

      2. Resources for questions

   B. Appearance and Clothing

      1. Safety

      2. Fit position

      3. Fit activities

      4. Tastefulness

   C. Conduct

      1. Responsibility and role fulfillment

      2. Reliability

      3. Follow through Timeliness

      4. Respectful/Dignifying Manner

      5. Positive Approach

      6. Caring and Empathic Style

      7. Openness, Availability, and Responsivity

      8. General Attitude

     9.   Constructivity in Problem Solving

  D. Professional Boundaries

     1.   Staying within role

     2.   Disclosures

     3.   Separating the personal from the professional

     4.   Dual Relationships

     5.   Effectiveness/Achievements/Accomplishments

How

- *Presentations/Discussions*

- *Resource materials (e.g. legal and ethical guidelines, district policies)*

- *Scenario worksheets; Vignette role plays*

3. Classroom Team Building and Maintenance

  A. Different, equally valid styles

  B. Importance of Team/Classroom Culture

  C. Importance of Respect, Contribution, and Role Significance

  D. Balance of Team Leadership and Collaboration

  E. Balance of Structure/Mechanisms with Adaptability

  F. Need for ongoing monitoring, assessment and modification as necessary

  G. Critical importance of regular team meetings

     1.   For Training

     2.   For Review and De-Briefing

     3.   For Proactivity and Planning

     4.   For Consistency and Continuity

     5.   For other Elements of Good Teams and Teamwork below

  H. Elements of Good Teams and Teamwork

     1.   Communication Mechanisms

     2.   Problem Solving Mechanisms

     3.   Training

     4.   Leadership Style

     5.   Supervision and Oversight

6. Support and Resource

7. Collaboration

8. Recognition/Acknowledgment

9. Continuity/Consistency

10. Defined areas of Responsibility/Authority

11. Established and coordinated program/classroom structure

12. Established purpose and objectives

13. Common Ground/Team Identification/Classroom Culture

How

- *Presentation/Discussion*

- *Observation*

- *Worksheets*

- *Exercise: "How would you maintain good team relationships and operation?"*

- *Follow-up and in-class consultation should involve application, review, and feedback in this area*

4. Classroom Team Performance and Skills

A. Initial Orientation

B. Initial Training

C. Ongoing Assistance

D. Ongoing Training, Feedback, and Supervision

    1. Proactive

        a. Individual

        b. Class wide

    2. Reactive

        a. Immediate, incident based

        b. Delayed, theme-based assignments

        c. Individual

        d. Class wide

E. Supportive Co-Training as appropriate

F. Performance Evaluation as appropriate

G. Establishment of Training and Supervision Protocol

H. Areas of Attention

    1. Monitoring of students

    2. Spending time with students

        a. Not just with adults or otherwise occupied

        b. In proximity of students

        c. Interacting with students

        d. Teaching, working with, and running programs with students

    3. Cooperation with requests

    4. Policy, procedure, and Guideline compliance

    5. Initiative/Independence/Innovation as appropriate

    6. Openness/Responsiveness/Attitude

    7. Teamwork

    8. Professionalism (see above)

    9. Integrating Multiple Inputs

    10. Sense of Big Picture and Details

    11. Instructional and Programmatic Skills

        a. ABA and other Teaching Techniques

        b. ABA Behavior Management and Instruction Technique

        c. Other ABA interventional capabilities

        d. Other role relevant abilities (e.g., set up, documentation, etc)

        e. Stylistic Elements

        f. Sense of Rationales and Objectives

How

■ *Discussion with Modeling*

■ *Hands on experience providing assistance, training, feedback and supervision to Demonstration site staff*

■ *Exercises: Conducting practice Performance Evaluation (as appropriate); "How would you adapt Training Protocol for Demonstration Class"; Set up of Training and Supervision Protocol for own class*

■ *Follow-up and in-class consultation should involve application, review, and feedback in this area*

5. **Working with Other Professionals, Agencies, and Services**

    A. Challenges

    B. Includes Professionals within and without School

        1.   Administrators

        2.   Other Teachers

        3.   Speech Pathologists

        4.   Occupational Therapists and Physical Therapists

        5.   APE Teachers

        6.   Psychologists

        7.   Psychiatrists

        8.   Behavior Specialists

        9.   Physicians

        10. Others

    C. Trans disciplinary Teaming

        1.   Possible Trans disciplinary Assessment: Team Product

        2.   Interchangeability and imbedded emphasis: Push in vs. Pull out

    D. Regular contacts/communication

        1.   Not just crisis/problem oriented

        2.   Inputs and outputs

    E. Problem Solving Mechanisms

    F. Cross Site Visits as appropriate

    G. Coordination of Efforts

    H. Clarity in Role Differentiation

    I. Professionalism (see above)

    J. Establishment of Professional Liaisoning Policy/Protocol

        1.   Provided on initial contact

        2.   What

        3.   Who

How

   ■ *Presentation/Discussion*

■ *Observation as appropriate and available*

■ *Example of Liaison Policy*

■ *Exercise: "Create a Liaisoning Policy for your classroom"*

■ *Follow-up and in-class consultation should involve application, review, and feedback in this area*

6. Working with Parents/Families

A. Collaboration

    1. Rationale

    2. Challenges

    3. Operating from a position of empathy

B. Ongoing Contacts/Communication

    1. Communication Mechanisms

        a. Ongoing, not just crisis/problem oriented

        b. Log books, home notes, and data

        c. Regular Phone Meetings

        d. Periodic, proactive in person conferences and/or clinics

        e. General Information Dissemination (e.g. newsletter, web site)

    2. Parent Visits

        a. Observations

        b. Visit Policy

C. Parent/Family Involvement and Input

    1. Parent Forum or Parent Advisory (or similar) Committees

    2. Parent event or classroom assistance

D. Parent Training as appropriate

E. Problem Solving Mechanisms

F. Professionalism (see above)

G. Establishment of Collaboration with Families Policy/Procedures

    1. Provided on student's placement

    2. Who

    3. What (including communication mechanisms and protocol)

How

- *Presentation/Discussion*

- *Modeling with Discussion*

- *Typical scenario worksheets*

- *Role playing of typical vignettes*

- *Exercises: Provide a scenario regarding a school family issue written from a school personnel perspective. Ask the trainee to re-write the same scenario from a family perspective. Have the trainee generate: a communication form to be used with parents, a visitation policy, a system for problem solving, a proposed agenda for a Parents' Forum meeting. "Create a Collaboration with Families policy for your classroom"*

- *Follow-up and in-class consultation should involve application, review, and feedback in this area*

7. Resistance/Dissatisfactions

A. Can be issues within and without the team

B. It's a process (often long term)

C. Communication and problem solving mechanisms as well as proactivity is crucial

D. Collaboration promotes ownership, investment, and buy in

E. Attempt to address and remediate subtle as well as overt aspects

   1. Attempt to identify forms and manifestations of resistance/dissatisfaction

   2. Attempt to identify range of potential causes for resistance/dissatisfactions

   3. Attempt to collaboratively and constructively derive positive solutions

   4. Have system and schedule for review, assessment (and possible modification) of remediative plan

F. Derive and employ supportive resources, individuals, and entities to address challenges when internal remediative efforts have been less then effective

G. Have compensatory, circumventing, discontinuation, or other plans for intractable circumstances

How

- *Discussion*

- *Examples: Exposure to simulated situations with resolutions*

- *Scenario worksheets and role plays*

- *Exercises: Video tapes of varied (e.g., with staff, professionals, parents) circumstances of resistance/dissatisfaction–trainees identify manifestations, potential causes, and possible solutions. Development of a list of potential external, supportive resources and mechanisms for more challenging situations. Develop communication and problem solving mechanisms for own class (see above)*

- *Follow-up and in-class consultation should involve application, review, and feedback in this area*

Appendix B

CLASSROOM CHECKLISTS

In Appendix B:

1. Classroom Assistance Checklist

The briefer Classroom Assistance Checklist is designed to assist consultation, supervision, and oversight efforts. It is intended to facilitate the provision of feedback. It is derived from the Classroom Checklist but is abbreviated and utilizes a unique rating scale.

2. Classroom Checklist

The longer Classroom Checklist is intended to aid periodic classroom evaluation efforts. It is tied to the Training Curriculum and is designed to assist in fidelity and quality control assessments, as well as evaluations of the impact of training and consultation.

School _____ Class/Grade _____ Instructor _____

Date _____ # of Instructional Staff _____ # of Students _____

CLASSROOM ASSISTANCE CHECKLIST

Rate the quality of all items according to following scale:

1 *Needs Substantial Training*   **2** *Early Stage of Development*

3 *Middle Stage*   **4** *Later Stage*   **5** *Mastered*

PREPAREDNESS/STRUCTURE/ORGANIZATION

1. Level of Preparedness   1 2 3 4 5 N/A

2. Organization of Data/Documentation   1 2 3 4 5 N/A

3. Instructional Themes/Lesson Plans   1 2 3 4 5 N/A

4. Rotation of Students   1 2 3 4 5 N/A

5. Rotation and Assignment of Staff   1 2 3 4 5 N/A

SETUP AND CLASSROOM ENVIRONMENT

1. Functionality of Design and Setup of Class   1 2 3 4 5 N/A

2. Age Appropriateness of Classroom Environment   1 2 3 4 5 N/A

3. Thematic Nature of Classroom Environment   1 2 3 4 5 N/A

STIMULUS/CURRICULUM MATERIALS

1. Organization of Materials	1 2 3 4 5 N/A
2. Cleanliness/Condition of Materials	1 2 3 4 5 N/A
3. Age Appropriateness of Materials	1 2 3 4 5 N/A
4. Functionality/Utility of Materials	1 2 3 4 5 N/A
5. Attractiveness of Materials	1 2 3 4 5 N/A
6. Employment of Materials	1 2 3 4 5 N/A

REINFORCERS

1. Organization of Reinforcers	1 2 3 4 5 N/A
2. Condition of Reinforcers	1 2 3 4 5 N/A
3. Age Appropriateness of Reinforcers	1 2 3 4 5 N/A
4. Variety of Reinforcers	1 2 3 4 5 N/A
5. Quality of Reinforcers	1 2 3 4 5 N/A
6. Utilization of Reinforcers	1 2 3 4 5 N/A

SCHEDULE

1. Schedule Established	1 2 3 4 5 N/A
2. Fit/Functionality of Schedule	1 2 3 4 5 N/A
3. Individualization within Schedule	1 2 3 4 5 N/A
4. Quality of Activities	1 2 3 4 5 N/A
5. Balance of Activities	1 2 3 4 5 N/A
6. Sufficiency of Breaks	1 2 3 4 5 N/A
7. Implementation of Schedule	1 2 3 4 5 N/A

INSTRUCTIONAL CURRICULUM

1. Curriculum Established   1 2 3 4 5 N/A

2. Fit/Functionality of Curricula   1 2 3 4 5 N/A

3. Individualization of Curricula   1 2 3 4 5 N/A

4. Comprehensiveness of Curricula   1 2 3 4 5 N/A

5. Implementation of Curricula   1 2 3 4 5 N/A

BEHAVIOR PROGRAMS

1. Behavior Programs Established   1 2 3 4 5 N/A

2. Fit/Functionality of Behavior Programs   1 2 3 4 5 N/A

3. Individualization of Behavior Programs   1 2 3 4 5 N/A

4. Soundness/Sufficiency of Reactive Elements   1 2 3 4 5 N/A

5. Soundness/Sufficiency of Proactive Elements   1 2 3 4 5 N/A

6. Application of Behavior Programs   1 2 3 4 5 N/A

DATA COLLECTION

1. Instructional Data Collection Protocol Established   1 2 3 4 5 N/A

2. Behavior Data Collection Protocol Established   1 2 3 4 5 N/A

3. Curriculum Assessments   1 2 3 4 5 N/A

4. Behavior/Functional Assessments   1 2 3 4 5 N/A

5. Functionality of Data Collection Systems   1 2 3 4 5 N/A

6. Practicality of Data Collection Systems   1 2 3 4 5 N/A

7. Utilization of Data Collection Systems   1 2 3 4 5 N/A

8. Compilation/Analysis/Use of Data   1 2 3 4 5 N/A

INSTRUCTION/PROGRAM IMPLEMENTATION

1. Capture of Teachable Moments   1 2 3 4 5 N/A

2. Capture of Program Implementation Opportunities   1 2 3 4 5 N/A

3. Systematic Nature of Instruction/Implementation   1 2 3 4 5 N/A

4. Balance of Activity Related Assistance and Actual Teaching   1 2 3 4 5 N/A

5. Balance of Imbedded and Isolated Instruction/
    Implementation   1 2 3 4 5 N/A

6. Balance of Individual and Group Instruction/
    Implementation   1 2 3 4 5 N/A

7. Balance/Pacing of Intensity of Instruction   1 2 3 4 5 N/A

INTEGRATION/INTERRELATEDNESS/INTERACTION

1. Students with Each Other   1 2 3 4 5 N/A

2. Students with Typically Developing Students   1 2 3 4 5 N/A

3. Students' Individualized Curricula with Other Layers of
    Curricula   1 2 3 4 5 N/A

4. Students' Curricula and Programs with Each Other's   1 2 3 4 5 N/A

5. Students' Curricula and Programs with Classroom as a Whole 1 2 3 4 5 N/A

6. Classroom Elements in Aggregation   1 2 3 4 5 N/A

STYLE OF INTERACTION W/STUDENTS

1. Rapport/Relationship Building   1 2 3 4 5 N/A

2. Rapport/Relationship Maintenance   1 2 3 4 5 N/A

3. Fun/Positive Style as Appropriate   1 2 3 4 5 N/A

4. Age Appropriate Manner   1 2 3 4 5 N/A

5. Respectful/Dignifying Manner   1 2 3 4 5 N/A

STAFF

1. Degree of Staff Attending to Students   1 2 3 4 5 N/A

2. Degree of Staff Proximity to Students   1 2 3 4 5 N/A

3. Degree of Teaching by Staff   1 2 3 4 5 N/A

4. Degree of Program Implementation by Staff   1 2 3 4 5 N/A

5. Degree of Initiation by Staff   1 2 3 4 5 N/A

6. Degree of Staff Openness/Responsiveness to Feedback/
Training   1 2 3 4 5 N/A

7. Staff Skill and ABA Guideline Adherence   1 2 3 4 5 N/A

8. Staff Sense of Objectives   1 2 3 4 5 N/A

9. Staff Stylistic Quality   1 2 3 4 5 N/A

10. Staff Attitude   1 2 3 4 5 N/A

TEAM

1. Cohesiveness   1   2   3   4   5   N/A

2. Coordination   1   2   3   4   5   N/A

3. Consistency   1   2   3   4   5   N/A

4. Distribution of Responsibility   1   2   3   4   5   N/A

5. Leadership   1   2   3   4   5   N/A

6. Meetings   1   2   3   4   5   N/A

7. Training   1   2   3   4   5   N/A

8. Supervision/Support   1   2   3   4   5   N/A

NOTES AND COMMENTS

_____

_____

_____

_____

_____

_____

_____

_____

_____

_____

_____

_____

_____

_____

_____

_____

School _____ Class/Grade _____ Instructor _____

Date _____ # of Instructional Staff _____ # of Students _____

CLASSROOM CHECKLIST

Rate the quality of all items according to following scale:

1 *Needs Substantial Training*   **2** *Below Average*

3 *Average*   **4** *Above Average*   **5** *Superior*

PREPAREDNESS/STRUCTURE/ORGANIZATION

1. Level of Preparedness   **1 2 3 4 5 N/A**

2. Overall/Underlying Philosophy/Orientation   **1 2 3 4 5 N/A**

3. Organization of Data/Documentation   **1 2 3 4 5 N/A**

4. Instructional Themes/Lesson Plans   **1 2 3 4 5 N/A**

5. Stations/Centers/Subjects/Periods   **1 2 3 4 5 N/A**

6. Rotation of Students   **1 2 3 4 5 N/A**

7. Rotation and Assignment of Staff   **1 2 3 4 5 N/A**

8. Pulling In of Ancillary Staff as Appropriate   **1 2 3 4 5 N/A**

SETUP AND CLASSROOM ENVIRONMENT

1. Functionality of Design and Setup of Class   1 2 3 4 5 N/A

2. Attractiveness of Design, Setup, and Environment of Class   1 2 3 4 5 N/A

3. Age Appropriateness of Classroom Environment   1 2 3 4 5 N/A

4. Thematic Nature of Classroom Environment   1 2 3 4 5 N/A

5. Display of Students' Work   1 2 3 4 5 N/A

STIMULUS/CURRICULUM MATERIALS

1. Organization of Materials   1 2 3 4 5 N/A

2. Cleanliness/Condition of Materials   1 2 3 4 5 N/A

3. Age Appropriateness of Materials   1 2 3 4 5 N/A

4. Functionality/Utility of Materials   1 2 3 4 5 N/A

5. Attractiveness of Materials   1 2 3 4 5 N/A

6. Employment of Materials   1 2 3 4 5 N/A

REINFORCERS

1. Organization of Reinforcers   1 2 3 4 5 N/A

2. Condition of Reinforcers   1 2 3 4 5 N/A

3. Age Appropriateness of Reinforcers   1 2 3 4 5 N/A

4. Variety of Reinforcers   1 2 3 4 5 N/A

5. Quality of Reinforcers   1 2 3 4 5 N/A

6. Utilization of Reinforcers   1 2 3 4 5 N/A

SCHEDULE

1. Schedule Established	1 2 3 4 5 N/A
2. Fit/Functionality of Schedule	1 2 3 4 5 N/A
3. Individualization within Schedule	1 2 3 4 5 N/A
4. Quality of Activities	1 2 3 4 5 N/A
5. Balance of Activities	1 2 3 4 5 N/A
6. Sufficiency of Breaks	1 2 3 4 5 N/A
7. Implementation of Schedule	1 2 3 4 5 N/A

INSTRUCTIONAL CURRICULUM

1. Curriculum Established	1 2 3 4 5 N/A
2. Fit/Functionality of Curricula	1 2 3 4 5 N/A
3. Individualization of Curricula	1 2 3 4 5 N/A
4. Comprehensiveness of Curricula	1 2 3 4 5 N/A
5. Implementation of Curricula	1 2 3 4 5 N/A

BEHAVIOR PROGRAMS

1. Behavior Programs Established	1 2 3 4 5 N/A
2. Fit/Functionality of Behavior Programs	1 2 3 4 5 N/A
3. Individualization of Behavior Programs	1 2 3 4 5 N/A
4. Soundness/Sufficiency of Reactive Elements	1 2 3 4 5 N/A
5. Soundness/Sufficiency of Proactive Elements	1 2 3 4 5 N/A
6. Application of Behavior Programs	1 2 3 4 5 N/A

IEPs

1. Clarity	1 2 3 4 5 N/A
2. Functionality	1 2 3 4 5 N/A
3. Useability	1 2 3 4 5 N/A
4. Relationship to Curricula and Programs	1 2 3 4 5 N/A
5. Implementation of IEPs	1 2 3 4 5 N/A

DATA COLLECTION

1. Instructional Data Collection Protocol Established	1 2 3 4 5 N/A
2. Behavior Data Collection Protocol Established	1 2 3 4 5 N/A
3. Curriculum Assessments	1 2 3 4 5 N/A
4. Behavior/Functional Assessments	1 2 3 4 5 N/A
5. Use of Video	1 2 3 4 5 N/A
6. Functionality of Data Collection Systems	1 2 3 4 5 N/A
7. Practicality of Data Collection Systems	1 2 3 4 5 N/A
8. Application of Data Collection Systems	1 2 3 4 5 N/A
9. Compilation/Analysis/Use of Data	1 2 3 4 5 N/A

INSTRUCTION/ PROGRAM IMPLEMENTATION

1. Capture of Teachable Moments   1 2 3 4 5 N/A

2. Capture of Program Implementation Opportunities   1 2 3 4 5 N/A

3. Systematic Nature of Instruction/Implementation   1 2 3 4 5 N/A

4. Balance of Activity Related Assistance and Actual Teaching   1 2 3 4 5 N/A

5. Balance of Imbedded and Isolated Instruction/
Implementation   1 2 3 4 5 N/A

6. Balance of Individual and Group Instruction/
Implementation   1 2 3 4 5 N/A

7. Balance of Guided Natural Occurrences and Direct
Intervention   1 2 3 4 5 N/A

8. Balance/Pacing of Intensity of Instruction   1 2 3 4 5 N/A

INTEGRATION/INTERRELATEDNESS/INTERACTION

1. Students with Each Other   1 2 3 4 5 N/A

2. Students with Typically Developing Students   1 2 3 4 5 N/A

3. Students' Individualized Curricula with Other Layers of
Curricula   1 2 3 4 5 N/A

4. Students' Curricula and Programs with Each Other's   1 2 3 4 5 N/A

5. Students' Curricula and Programs with Classroom as a
Whole   1 2 3 4 5 N/A

6. Students' Curricula and Programs with Home Program   1 2 3 4 5 N/A

7. Students' Curricula and Programs with Other Services   1 2 3 4 5 N/A

8. Classroom Elements in Aggregation   1 2 3 4 5 N/A

9. Classroom with Entire School   1 2 3 4 5 N/A

STYLE OF INTERACTION W/ STUDENTS

1. Rapport/Relationship Building   1 2 3 4 5 N/A

2. Rapport/Relationship Maintenance   1 2 3 4 5 N/A

3. Fun/Positive Style as Appropriate   1 2 3 4 5 N/A

4. Age Appropriate Manner   1 2 3 4 5 N/A

5. Respectful/Dignifying Manner   1 2 3 4 5 N/A

STAFF

1. Degree of Staff Attending to Students   1 2 3 4 5 N/A

2. Degree of Staff Proximity to Students   1 2 3 4 5 N/A

3. Degree of Teaching by Staff   1 2 3 4 5 N/A

4. Degree of Program Implementation by Staff   1 2 3 4 5 N/A

5. Degree of Initiation by Staff   1 2 3 4 5 N/A

6. Degree of Staff Openness/Responsiveness to Feedback/
   Training   1 2 3 4 5 N/A

7. Staff Skill and ABA Guideline Adherence   1 2 3 4 5 N/A

8. Staff Sense of Objectives   1 2 3 4 5 N/A

9. Staff Stylistic Quality   1 2 3 4 5 N/A

10. Staff Attitude   1 2 3 4 5 N/A

11. Staff Ethics   1 2 3 4 5 N/A

12. Staff Professionalism   1 2 3 4 5 N/A

TEAM

1. Cohesiveness	1 2 3 4 5 N/A
2. Coordination	1 2 3 4 5 N/A
3. Consistency	1 2 3 4 5 N/A
4. Distribution of Responsibility	1 2 3 4 5 N/A
5. Leadership	1 2 3 4 5 N/A
6. Meetings	1 2 3 4 5 N/A
7. Training	1 2 3 4 5 N/A
8. Supervision/Support	1 2 3 4 5 N/A

PARENTS/PROFESSIONALS

1. Liaisoning with Other Professionals/Services	1 2 3 4 5 N/A
2. Parent Meetings	1 2 3 4 5 N/A
3. Parent Training	1 2 3 4 5 N/A
4. Parent Visits	1 2 3 4 5 N/A
5. Parent Input	1 2 3 4 5 N/A
6. Parent Involvement	1 2 3 4 5 N/A
7. Information Dissemination Mechanisms	1 2 3 4 5 N/A
8. Problem Solving Mechanisms	1 2 3 4 5 N/A
9. Quality of Relationships with Other Professionals/Services	1 2 3 4 5 N/A
10. Quality of Relationships with Parents	1 2 3 4 5 N/A

NOTES AND COMMENTS

Appendix C

DISCRETE TRIAL TEACHING

INTRODUCTION

Discrete trial teaching is a specific methodology used to maximize learning. It is a teaching process used to develop most skills, including cognitive, communication, play, social and self-help skills. Additionally, it is a strategy that can be used for all ages, levels of functioning and populations.

The technique involves:

1) breaking a skill into smaller parts;

2) teaching one sub-skill at a time until mastery;

3) providing concentrated teaching;

4) providing prompting and prompt fading as necessary;

5) using reinforcement procedures.

A teaching session involves many trials, with each trial having a distinct beginning and end, hence the name "discrete." Each part of the skill is mastered before more information is presented.

In discrete trial teaching, a very small unit of information is presented and the student's response is immediately sought. This contrasts with continuous trial or more traditional teaching methods which present large amounts of information with no clearly defined target response on the student's part.

Discrete trial teaching ensures that learning is an **active** process. We cannot rely on children with ASD to simply absorb information through passive exposure.

EXAMPLE: Teaching a receptive label

ANTECEDENT ("A")	BEHAVIOR ("B")	CONSEQUENCE ("C")
"touch juice"	touches juice; good attention	"great"
"touch cookie"	touches cookie; good attention	"terrific"
"touch juice"	touches juice; poor attention	"OK"
"touch cookie"	touches juice; good attention	"uh-uh"
"touch cookie"	no response; poor attention	no reinforcement (student must understand what this consequence means)
"touch cookie"	no response; poor attention	"You're not looking"; "too slow"; etc.

COMPONENTS OF A DISCRETE TRIAL

INSTRUCTION/ANTECEDENTS/DISCRIMINATIVE STIMULUS (SD)

■ The trial must have a distinct beginning. Often it is a verbal instruction, but it may also be another discrete event or a visual stimulus. The event that occurs at the start of the trial should signal to the student that the correct response will result in positive reinforcement. Such a signal is known technically as a Discriminative Stimulus (SD).

■ In the beginning stage of teaching or if the student is having difficulty with a certain skill, instructions should be simple and concise (e.g., "cookie" vs. "juice" instead of "touch the cookie please" or "can you show me which one the juice is?").

- Reduces confusion

- Highlights the relevant stimuli

AS THE STUDENT PROGRESSES, INSTRUCTIONS SHOULD BECOME MORE COMPLEX AND MAY BE MORE WORDY

■ Using more natural language promotes generalization

■ Prepares the student better to learn from incidental situations

■ Makes the session more interesting

■ Models more natural language

■ Make sure the instruction is appropriate to the task. Think carefully about what it is that you want the student to do and then select a verbal instruction or other cue that is appropriate to link to the response.

■ For example, if you want the student to count, "One, two, three, four," the instruction should be "Count." If you want the student to tell you how many objects there are, the instruction should be, "How many?" and the student's response should be "Four."

- Give the student **approximately** three to five seconds to respond. This provides an opportunity to process the information.

- However, the teacher must be sensitive to the pace of instruction that is optimal for the student.

  - Too fast may result in confusion and chaos

  - Too fast is artificial accommodation to facilitate attention

  - Too slow may result in inattention

  - Gradually the pace should approach what occurs in the natural environment (often teachers use a rapid pace to maintain attention, therefore it is critical to eventually slow the pace)

- The best learning occurs when the student is paying good attention. If the student exhibits poor attending, it is essential to focus on developing better attending skills. This is discussed in a later section.

STUDENT RESPONSE

- Know in advance precisely what response and what level of quality you expect in order for the student to earn reinforcement. Use consistent criteria. For example, how close does the student need to come to touching the object if the instruction was "Touch ball"? It should be obvious to any observer (and to the student!) what criterion is being used.

  - Promotes consistency among staff

  - Increases the likelihood of correct responding

  - Increases the objectivity of the teacher

  However, readjust criteria based upon the student's changing performance.

- Beware of extraneous undesired behavior. If you reinforce when such behavior accompanies a correct response, undesired behavior may also be strengthened.

> Example 1: The student gives you a good answer but is looking away. If you praise at that moment, you are likely to get more responses in the future with looking away.

> Example 2: You praise the student for touching the ball but by the time the toy reinforcer is received, he has fallen out of the chair. He may think the reinforcer is a result of falling on the floor.

- Be sure to reinforce spontaneous desirable behavior such as good attention, good sitting, or spontaneous speech!

- If there is no response within the time limit (three to five seconds), treat inaction as a failed trial.

- **SHAPE BEHAVIOR**: The goal is for the overall quality of responses to improve over time. This is done by gradually adjusting the requirement for earning reinforcement. (Differential reinforcement will be discussed further in the section on consequences.)

  - Use differential consequences to simultaneously shape correct responding and appropriate attending behavior

  - Example: Let the student take a break when fussing is decreasing rather than increasing.

  - Use differential consequences to reinforce better approximations to desired target behavior.

- Do not allow the student to anticipate the response. If the student starts responding before you finish the instruction, then one of these things may be happening:

  - You are being predictable. Vary the order of presentation so that the student cannot read the pattern.

  - The student may be guessing. Do not allow guesses to occur, because the student may get lucky and make the correct response. Giving reinforcement at this time would only promote further guessing.

  - The student may not be paying attention. Do not allow responses to occur when the student is not paying attention.

■ Sometimes self-correction is an acceptable response and even highly valued. For example, if the student is attentive and corrects the mistake without any cues from the teacher you may want to provide reinforcement. The process the student is displaying (e.g., problem solving) is actually a very important skill.

However, it is important to repeat the trial at some point to make sure the response occurs without self-correction.

FEEDBACK/CONSEQUENCE

■ The response should be followed immediately with feedback. Reinforcement provides feedback that the response was correct and increases the likelihood that the response will be repeated. Corrective feedback and the absence of reinforcement provide information that the response was incorrect and decreases the likelihood of the response being repeated.

- **CORRECT**: Praise plus constantly rotating selection of backup rewards.

    Correct + good attention = best reinforcement

    Correct + poor attention = mild reinforcement

- **INCORRECT**: Informational feedback that the response was incorrect.

- Incorrect + good attention = supportive feedback (e.g., "good try")

- Incorrect + poor attention = stronger corrective feedback (e.g., "no"; "pay attention"; "you need to look"; "try harder"; "you can do it better"; etc.)

- **NO RESPONSE**: After five seconds with no response, give feedback and end the trial. If attending and seat behavior is correct and no off-task behavior occurs, the consequence may simply be non-reinforcement. Be sure to insert an intertrial interval (see below). It may be necessary to clear the materials briefly to emphasize that the trial has ended.

- **OFF-TASK BEHAVIOR**: If the student exhibits inappropriate behavior (e.g., getting out of the chair, grabbing, self-stimulatory behaviors, etc.), immediately give feedback, correct the behavior, and end the trial. Do not wait to see what response the student gives.

- Feedback should be unambiguous in meaning. For example, do not smile while you are saying "no" or frown and say "good".

- Consequences should be planned in advance and the criterion consistently applied.

However, use spontaneous reinforcement for unexpected outstanding behavior and performance.

- Reinforcement must be selected based on each individual student's preferences (e.g., not all students like lavish praise or food).

Effectiveness must be monitored continuously and adjustments made as necessary.

- The reinforcer must be faded as quickly as possible to natural levels of frequency, delays and intensity. At the beginning, the reinforcer may follow 100% of correct responses (continuous reinforcement schedule). As learning progresses, the rate should be decreased to intermittent levels.

  - Reduces dependency

  - Reduces external control thereby facilitating internal control

  - Approximates what student will encounter in natural environments thereby promoting generalization

  - Avoids possible chaos (lavish reinforcers can often escalate the student's disruptive behaviors or may simply be overwhelming)

- Use differential consequences. This provides more information regarding the desired response:

  - Excellent response results in the best reinforcer

  - Response which requires more prompting or is of lower quality gets a moderate level of reinforcement

  - Incorrect response, but good attention, gets a mild informational "no" or "try again"

  - Aggression or blatant off-task behaviors receive strong corrective feedback

- Use feedback that is informational if the student can process this level of feedback.

Examples are "keep your hands down," "you're not looking," "too slow," "say it better," etc.

- Provides more information

- More natural feedback

- Models language

INTERTRIAL INTERVAL

- Allow a few seconds to separate each trial.

  - Allows the student time to process the information (i.e., that the response made was correct or that the response needs to change)

  - Allows staff time to process what just occurred (e.g., think about what reinforcement to use on the next trial, when to prompt, what step of the prompting hierarchy to use, how to word the instruction for the next trial, etc.)

  - Teaches the student to wait, which will commonly occur in more natural settings

  - Allows collection of data

  - Makes the onset of the next trial more discrete

- You may need to remove or reposition stimuli to make the trials more discrete. Leaving the stimuli visible on the table between trials provides the student the opportunity to rehearse the correct response or may promote switching responses without paying attention to the instructions.

Although removing stimuli or looking away for a moment accentuates the discreteness of trials, it also provides a cue to the student to get ready. Over time, you will need to make sure that the student does not become dependent on these attentional cues by deliberately making the trials less discrete.

> ### THE INTERTRIAL INTERVAL SHOULD BE ADJUSTED
> ### TO MAINTAIN AN OPTIMAL WORKING PACE
>
> ■ Too rapid a pace may be chaotic and therefore result in poor performance and increase agitation
>
> ■ Too slow a pace may create inattention
>
> ■ Make sure the teacher is directing the pace, not the student

PROMPT

■ Prompts are assistance given by the teacher to promote correct responding.

- Speeds up learning process

- Reduces frustration

■ A prompt should accompany or immediately follow the instruction (SD), thus associating the response with the instruction.

■ Consider the full range of prompt levels, including visual, positional, pointing, full physical, partial physical, verbal, demonstration, matching for receptive, receptive for expressive, within-stimulus, recency/time delay, etc. These prompts can be organized into a hierarchy from least intrusive to most intrusive. Teachers should select a prompt that provides just enough assistance to ensure success, but never more than needed.

- Easier to fade the prompt

- Reduces prompt dependency

Try to maintain successful responding (approximately 80% correct responding is optimal for many students).

■ If the first prompt does not work, then move up the prompting hierarchy (i.e., increase the level of assistance). For example, move from a positional prompt to a pointing prompt.

■ Prompts should be used to avoid prolonged failure by providing necessary assistance.

A frequently invoked "rule" is when two consecutive incorrect responses occur, then a prompt should occur during the next trial. This rule was developed for situations involving a two-part discrimination and where students already had a basic understanding of the concept being taught.

- Corrective feedback follows the first incorrect response and allows the student to learn from the feedback. Therefore, the second trial would provide the student an opportunity to make the correct response.

- More than two incorrect responses indicate that the student is not learning from corrective feedback. It may also exceed the student's tolerance for failure and the lack of reinforcement may lead to an escalation of negative behaviors.

**IT IS ESSENTIAL TO BE FLEXIBLE WHEN
DECIDING WHETHER TO PROMPT**

- If the student has no understanding of the correct answer, then you may prompt after one incorrect response OR even on the first trial

- If the student appears to understand the task after the second incorrect trial, then you may give another unprompted opportunity

- If you have followed the "Wrong-Wrong-Prompt-Test" sequence and the test results in another error, then you should move up to a Wrong-Prompt-Prompt-Test sequence. If the test still results in an error, then go to a Prompt-Prompt-Prompt-Test sequence, etc.

- Prompt whenever you need to help the student maintain a higher level of success

---

■ If it was necessary to use a prompt, move quickly to the next trial and repeat the instruction with reduced or no prompts.

- Reduces prompt dependency

- Provides the student an opportunity to demonstrate learning from the previous trial

However, if the student is just learning the task or has had tremendous difficulty with the concept, it may be beneficial to continue providing the same level of prompting for several more trials

■ If the student has made an error due to inattention or off-task behavior, then it is preferable to provide a consequence for the inappropriate behavior rather than give a prompt. Prompting at that point may only serve to reinforce the student for off-task behavior, since prompts make it easier to get the response correct. You should give corrective feedback regarding the off-task behavior and repeat the trial, but do not prompt.

■ Unprompted correct trials should receive the strongest reinforcement (e.g., praise accompanied by tangible backup reinforcer).

■ Prompted trials should result in a lower level of reinforcement (e.g., mild praise such as "okay," "that's right," "yup," etc.). However, it is essential that at least some reinforcement occur on prompted trials in order to:

- Provide feedback that response was correct

- Strengthen the correct response

- Avoid pattern of failure

However, if the student requires an extended period of prompting, you should occasionally provide tangible reinforcers for prompted trials in order to:

a. Increase the student's motivation

b. Reduce the student's withdrawal and frustration

c. Provide an opportunity for the student to experience the more desirable reinforcer

■ Be hypersensitive to inadvertent prompts. Extraneous prompts result in the student not mastering the concept because of:

  ▪ Prompts not getting faded

  ▪ Inconsistent responding (e.g., performance will seem to be better with trainers who provide inadvertent prompts)

  ▪ Heightened student vigilance to irrelevant cues

INADVERTENT PROMPTS			
Non-Verbal	**Patterns**	**Feedback**	**Other**
- Glances - Posturing - Positional	- Massed Trials - Alternating - What was Not Asked	- Expressions - Fast when Correct - Slow when Incorrect	- Mouthing Answer - New Object - Voice Inflection

■ Make a strong commitment to fading prompts. By using progressively less intrusive prompts you will promote greater independence and mastery of concepts.

■ One way of fading a prompt is to systematically increase the delay between the instruction and the prompt. This allows the student the opportunity to initiate the response before a prompt occurs. However, beware that if more than two or three seconds elapse before the prompt is given, any verbal instruction may not be retained in memory.

■ Whenever possible, use within-stimulus prompts (e.g., position, size, color, etc.). Within-stimulus prompts are easier to fade and direct the student's attention to the stimulus itself rather than some extraneous cue such as pointing.

ESTABLISHING ATTENTION

■ It is important to reinforce good attention when it occurs. Be sure your praise specifies what behavior has earned reinforcement (e.g., "That was GREAT looking!!!," "I love how you are paying attention," etc.).

■ For many students, the best way to teach appropriate attending is to start the trial regardless of attending behavior. Let your student experience the natural consequence of not attending.

   This requires the use of highly motivating reinforcers.

■ The student will learn faster to attend to natural cues if the tasks being presented require close visual attention (e.g., finer nonverbal imitation responses, matching on finer details, chaining, etc.).

■ Another way to teach attending skills is to time instruction onset to coincide with spontaneous looking and/or pauses in off-task behavior. You can prompt by waiting up to five seconds before beginning a trial to see if the student spontaneously orients.

   Since the instruction represents an opportunity to earn reinforcement, the presentation of the instruction is itself a secondary reinforcer. For this to be effective, it is essential that the task be motivating; otherwise the student will be happy to delay the onset of the trial. Additionally, waiting longer than about five seconds merely provides additional opportunity for the student to engage in undesired behavior.

■ If the inattention is extreme, interferes with learning, and the above steps do not work, it may be necessary to give a specific cue (e.g., "look at me"). If the student does not understand the language, you can do a "look at me" program. Remember that this is a prompt which must be faded as quickly as possible.

AVOID EXCESSIVE CUING TO SECURE ATTENTION

Instructions such as "look at me," "hands quiet," "sit still," or calling the student's name, can easily become a habit that is very difficult to break. You should rely primarily on strong differential reinforcement for good performance and attending skills. This will reduce reliance on external cueing and help develop internal control.

For example, when the student spontaneously looks at the teacher, say "Hey, that was great looking!!!"

GUIDELINES FOR MAXIMIZING PROGRESS

- Conduct enough trials so that learning can take place.

    - Session length should be gradually increased in duration to increase learning opportunities.

    - Do not exceed developmental age expectations for the duration of attention span and length of session.

    - Do not conduct so many trials that the student becomes bored or frustrated.

PROBLEMS WITH SHORT SESSIONS

- Reduces learning opportunities

- Breaks momentum

- Not natural, thereby reduces generalization and integration into school

- Short breaks may not be sufficiently reinforcing

■ If the student is having difficulty on certain tasks, arrange the task order so that difficult tasks occur between easier tasks (e.g., "sandwiching the more difficult task—the "meat"—between the easier tasks)

- Easier tasks may increase the student's motivation

- Easier tasks may reinforce completion of more difficult tasks

- Builds momentum

■ End the session on a pattern of successes. This increases the likelihood that the student will want to return.

However, if the student is extremely frustrated,it may be advisable to end the session anyway.

YOU DO NOT HAVE TO WIN EVERY BATTLE!!!

■ Create behavioral momentum. Response patterns established over a series of trials can facilitate desired responding over subsequent trials. To establish momentum, decrease the intertrial interval, prompt heavily, and spend only a very short period of time on the delivery of reinforcement/feedback. Then give a bigger reinforcement at the end of a series of trials.

Another way to establish momentum is to create a pattern of successes through "sandwiching."

- To increase compliance, switch to several trials of a high probability response. Higher probability responses include easier tasks, fully-mastered material, and ones that are inherently reinforcing.

- If there is a problem with echolalia or closure, embed the target response in a series of verbal trials that are not associated with the problem.

If a response is about to happen that you cannot control, insert an appropriate instruction so that the student is actually being compliant (e.g., when the student is in the process of moving a block off the table, say "put the block on the floor").

■ When teaching a discrimination, do not promote "mindless" responding or mere perseveration on a response. If the student can get the next response correct without listening to the instruction, then you are not really teaching anything. Massed trials can create this problem.

> Use expanded trials to force the student to concentrate on what you are saying. Insert a progressively longer series of distractor trials between trials on the target item.

■ Incorporate a good balance of play into the overall program. Play is critical in order for the student to have productive (i.e., non **self stimulatory**) free time. Play is also essential to help develop social skills. Most importantly, language is often facilitated through play skills.

**BE FLEXIBLE & PATIENT; YOU CANNOT SOLVE EVERY PROBLEM TODAY!!!
LEARNING IS A PROCESS. LANGUAGE, SOCIAL AND PLAY TYPICALLY
DEVELOP THROUGH MONTHS AND YEARS OF INTERVENTION.**

However, it is not good enough for the student to respond only on his own terms. The adult must be willing to set limits and enforce contingencies.

■ Maximize contrast between positive and corrective feedback.

- Do not confuse respondent behavior (frustration) with operant behavior (manipulation). If behavior is respondent, our approach will be much more supportive and accommodating, whereas with operant behavior we may need to be quite firm.

■ **Adjust training based upon the student's behaviors and performance!!!** Progression is based upon the student's responses to the trials. From observing the therapist (e.g., complexity of instructions, level of prompting, schedule of reinforcement, etc.) one should be able to predict the student's current level of performance.

■ Keep long term goals in view. Everything you work on should be designed to move the student toward the long term goals. A program is not an end, but a means to the end.

■ **Make teaching natural and fun!!!** While teaching needs to be systematic and some students may need a higher level of structure, it is not necessary to be overly regimented. Teaching should be as natural as possible to increase the student's motivation and participation and facilitate generalization.

MAKING THERAPY NATURAL, FUN & GENERALIZABLE

■ Use enthusiastic tones

■ Vary settings

■ Vary instructions (e.g., "What is it?," "What do you see?," "Tell me about this?")

■ Use interesting, preferred and functional materials

■ Do not bore the student by continuing a program that is already mastered

■ Do not punish the student for good attending and performance by dragging out tasks when the student is cooperative. Similarly, be careful about shortening programs when the student is fussing

---

■ Maintain a high success rate

- Use the student's preferences (even self-stimulatory objects can be used as reinforcers)

- Intersperse tasks

- Use varied and natural reinforcers

- Use language that is as natural as possible

- Use curriculum that is wide ranging in scope (e.g., language, play, social, self-help)

- Reduce structure as much as possible (e.g., sometimes work on the floor) instead of in the chair)

- Model natural language as much as possible without distracting the student.

    - More like what the student will encounter naturally

    - Models more appropriate language

    - Promotes better articulation

    - Exposes the student to new learning

Develop spontaneity

- Reinforce spontaneous variations

- Fade prompts and cues

- Train expressiveness of communication

- Link behavior to naturally occurring antecedents

- In labeling programs, stress commenting instead of question answering

- Use Communication Temptations; model desired language instead of asking "What do you want?"

- Use observational learning, modeling and group instructions whenever possible

    ONE-ON-ONE instruction should be considered as a prompt that needs to be faded!!!

- Do not create over-dependence by hovering unnecessarily

- Use probes to test whether the student already knows the material. If the student seems to know it, review quickly and move on to new material.

- When repeating instructions, voice inflection reduces boredom as well as signals to the student that the teacher is aware that the question is being repeated.

- Use a non-directive approach as much as possible. Set the stage for desired behaviors and then provide reinforcement when they occur. B.F. Skinner called this "reinforcement control" as opposed to utilizing "instructional control."